Twentieth-Century Critical Studies
of Women and Literature, 1660-1800

Garland Reference Library of the Humanities (Vol. 64)

An Annotated Bibliography
of Twentieth-Century Critical Studies
# of Women and Literature,
1660-1800

Paula Backscheider
University of Rochester

Felicity Nussbaum
Syracuse University

Philip B. Anderson
Lafayette College

Garland Publishing, Inc., New York & London

1977

333377

Library of Congress Cataloging in Publication Data

Backscheider, Paula.
  An annotated bibliography of twentieth-century
critical studies of women and literature, 1660-1800.

  (Garland reference library of the humanities ;
v. 64)
  Includes indexes.
  1. Women in literature--Bibliography. 2. Eng-
lish literature--18th century--History and criticism
--Bibliography. 3. English literature--Early
modern, 1500-1700--History and criticism--
Bibliography. 4. Women's studies--Bibliography.
I. Nussbaum, Felicity, joint author. II. Ander-
son, Philip B., joint author. III. Title.
Z2012.B13   [PR449.W65]   016.809'89287
ISBN 0-8240-9934-6   76-24746

Printed in the United States of America

for
Andrea

Contents

Preface

This bibliography includes critical and scholarly books and articles published between 1900 and 1975. Woman, not just literary woman, is the subject. Intended for scholars and students of the Restoration and eighteenth century, of social history, and of women's studies, the book is arranged as we imagine it being used. Annotations are descriptive rather than critical.

The first part of the bibliography contains general studies. Such books as Myra Reynolds' *The Learned Lady in England*, Josephine Kamm's *Hope Deferred*, and John R. Brown's "A Chronology of Major Events in Obstetrics and Gynaecology" introduce the reader to the position of women in many aspects of English society.

The second section is organized according to genres. Because of the amount of work on issues pertinent to social history and women in fiction, the genre fiction is sub-divided into general works and works associated with major male authors. The criteria for inclusion in the major author divisions were contributions to an understanding of the position of women, of contemporary discussion of the nature of women, or of the history of the interpretation of female behavior. Rather than being comprehensive, these sub-sections are representative of the types of work being done and the opinions held. The selections, admittedly, reflect our opinions.

The final section focuses on particular women. Women for whom a considerable corpus of work exists are treated separately, and the final sub-section contains works on women for whom only a few items were found.

Items pertinent to more than one division are cross-referenced by item number. The general index of women's names and the sections on general studies and genres should be consulted for works in which scant mention, insufficient to merit full cross-referencing, of particular women is made. There is also an index of modern critics.

Books and articles are listed under their authors' or editors' names; where the author is unknown, the item is listed under "Anonymous." In listing editions, the author of the introduction rather than the author of the substance of the work is cited.

No attempt is made to include every work about men associated with these women. Specialists will naturally find mention of Hester Piozzi in Johnson works, Aphra Behn in Jacob Tonson, Dorothy Osborne in William Temple. General works about women and male authors are included in the section on the genre with which they are associated. For example, works on Congreve's women are in "Drama" and Addison's opinions on witchcraft in "Periodicals."

Editions and collections are included only if the introduction provides new information. Dissertations appear only when they contribute to neglected areas. Finally, although many foreign-language items, bibliographies, and popular biographies appear, the bibliography is not intended to be inclusive in these areas.

The bibliography was compiled and annotated primarily at the libraries of the University of Rochester, Syracuse University, and Princeton University. The University of Rochester's inter-library loan office obtained many items from various American and British libraries. Our debt to them, and especially to Ann Schertz, is very great.

Douglas Howard of the University of Rochester's English Department checked every item, annotated several, and proofread the typescript. His dependability, resourcefulness, and good humor are much appreciated. Sarah Varhus helped in the final stages. Stephanie Frontz contributed a number of items in the fine arts, and Patricia Ford translated the Russian entries. The University of Rochester supported the project with clerical and computer assistance. Finally, we thank the English Departments and colleagues at our three institutions who gave practical advice and friendly encouragement.

To the numerous people who contributed an item or two, we are grateful. We know, however, that for every item we found in *The Bath Weekly Chronicle* or the Wales *Western Mail*, we may have overlooked another in *PMLA*. Such is the bibliographer's nightmare.

Twentieth-Century Critical Studies
of Women and Literature, 1660-1800

GENERAL STUDIES

GENERAL STUDIES

1 Abbott, John L. "Dr. Johnson and the Amazons." PQ, 44
   (1965), 484-495. Johnson's Dissertation on the Amazons
   is translated from Histoire des Amazones Anciennes et
   Modernes.

2 Adburgham, Alison. Women in Print: Writing Women and
   Women's Magazines from the Restoration to the Accession of
   Victoria. London: George Allen & Unwin, 1972. Chapters
   include discussion of dramatists, educational reformers,
   essayists and novelists during the period as well as a
   chronological list of periodicals and a bibliography.

3 Aldridge, Alfred Owen. "Polygamy and Deism." JEGP, 48
   (1949), 343-360. The critic summarizes the major arguments for and against polygamy, relates them to discussions
   of the law of nature and deism, and mentions influences on
   novels.

4 Aldridge, Alfred Owen. "Population and Polygamy in Eighteenth Century Thought." Journal of the History of Medicine and Allied Sciences, 4 (1949), 129-148. The 1675
   Commons Bill to repeal the Act of King James ("Felony to
   marry a second husband, or wife, the former being living")
   began a century long discussion of polygamy as a means to
   increase population.

5 Alleman, Gellert Spencer. Matrimonial Law and the Materials of Restoration Comedy. Wallingford, Pennsylvania:
   no pub., 1942. Restoration comedy drew situations, characters, and satiric material from contemporary matrimonial
   laws and customs. Knowledge of contracts, types and fre-
   quency of irregular marriages, and of separation and divorce practices illuminates plays and allows us to judge
   the extent to which they mirror their society.

6 Altick, Richard D. "The Emergence of Popular Reading and
   Scholarly Activity in the Eighteenth and Nineteenth Centuries." Forum (Houston), 7 (1969), 9-14. This is a history of the changing reading habits in two centuries.

7 Anderson, Howard, Irvin Ehrenpreis, and Philip B. Dahglian.
   The Familiar Letter in the Eighteenth Century. Lawrence:
   University of Kansas Press, 1966. This collection contains
   two essays of especial interest: Robert Halsband's "Lady
   Mary Wortley Montagu as Letter-Writer" and Anderson and

Ehrenpreis's "The Familiar Letter in the Eighteenth-Century: Some Generalizations." The latter describes the development of the postal system, changes in prose style, published collections of letters, and the social quality of the age leading to the letter's becoming a pre-eminent literary form. Good letters were to be informal, substantive, candid, and revealing of the character of the writer.

8   Avery, Emmett L. "The Shakespearean Ladies Club." Shakespeare Quarterly, 7 (1956), 154-158. The Club was organized in 1736 to end neglect of Shakespeare. Though the names of the ladies remain unknown, the Club apparently sparked considerable growth in the number of performances of Shakespeare in 1737 and 1741, culminating in Garrick's revivals of Shakespeare.

9   Baker, C. H. Collins. Lely and the Stuart Portrait Painters; A Study of English Portraiture before and after Van Dyke. London: P. L. Warner, 1912. This survey of portrait painters includes a chapter on Mary Beale. She was "a painter of industry, scant training, and slight feeling." Her non-Lelyesque paintings are original and "feminine." The diaries and her work record changes in her technique and fortune.

10   Bay, J. Christian. "Women Not Considered Human Beings." Library Quarterly, 4 (1934), 156-164.

11   Bayne-Powell, Rosamond. Eighteenth Century London Life. London: Murray, 1937; New York: Dutton, 1938. A standard social history has considerable attention, in passing, to the lives and roles of women.

12   Bayne-Powell, Rosamond. The English Child in the Eighteenth Century. London: Murray, 1939. A description of the rearing of children.

13   Bayne-Powell, Rosamond. Housekeeping in the Eighteenth Century. London: Murray, and Hollywood-by-the-Sea: Transatlantic Arts, 1956. A description of houses, furnishings, servants, and household duties including money management, entertaining, and cleaning.

14   Beard, Mary R. Woman as A Force in History. New York: MacMillan, 1946. An effort to reconstruct the history of women from prehistoric to modern times and to end the "myth

4

of the subjection of women."

15   Black, George. "A Calendar of Cases of Witchcraft in
      Scotland, 1510-1727." BNYPL, 41 (1937), 811-847, 917-
      936; 42 (1938), 34-74. A brief history of witchcraft
      in Scotland including a listing of trials throughout
      Scotland and methods of torture until the repeal of
      statutes against witchcraft in 1736.

16   Blanchard, Rae. "Richard Steele and the Status of Women."
      SP, 26 (1929), 325-355. A study of Steele's views in
      his essays, periodicals, and plays places him as largely
      in agreement with other writers on the subject, 1650-
      1725.

17   Blease, Walter L. The Emancipation of English Women.
      London: Constable, 1910; revised, London: Nutt, 1913;
      reprinted, New York: Blom, 1971. A history of the
      increasing social and legal rights of women.

18   Blumenthal, Walter H. Brides from Bridewell: Female
      Felons sent to Colonial America. Rutland, Vermont:
      Tuttle, 1962. England transported large numbers of
      female felons in the eighteenth century. Between fif-
      teen and thirty percent of them died en route and another
      thirty-five percent died during their indenture. Other
      women were convoyed to Louisiana and married indiscrim-
      inantly. Statistics and documents record the circum-
      stances, extent, and results of this policy.

19   Bogardus, Janet. Some Bibliographical Notes about Women
      in Printing. New York: Parkway, 1937. A preliminary
      bibliography of female printers.

20   Bouchot, Henri F. X. M. La femme anglaise et ses peintres.
      Paris: Librarie de l'art ancien et moderne, 1903. A his-
      tory of women painters.

21   Bradley, Rose M. The English Housewife in the Seventeenth
      and Eighteenth Centuries.London: Edward Arnold, 1912. A
      domestic history with special attention to women's activ-
      ities and duties, undocumented and written in a somewhat
      fictional mode.

22   Brailsford, Dennis. Sport and Society. Elizabeth to Anne.
      (London: Routledge & Kegan Paul; Toronto: U. of Toronto
      Press, 1969. A portion of one chapter is devoted to the

"Sports of the Gentlewoman." In spite of increased attention to women's education, women's sport was limited to dancing.

23   Brissenden, R. F., ed. Virtue in Distress: Studies in the Novel of Sentiment from Richardson to Sade. New York: Barnes and Noble, 1974. A study of sentimentalism relates virtue to distress with particular attention to Clarissa and Jane Austen's early works.

24   Brooke, Iris. Dress and Undress: The Restoration and Eighteenth Century. London: Methuen, 1958; rpt. Westport, Connecticut: Greenwood Press, 1973. This is a history of fashion and clothing.

25   Brooke, Iris, and James Laver. English Costume of the Eighteenth Century. London: A. C. Black, 1931. Descriptions of clothing of the upper classes including hats, trimmings, and riding habits catalog changes in fashion through the century.

26   Brooke, Iris. English Costume of the Seventeenth Century. London: A. C. Black, 1934. Short illustrated descriptions of male and female clothing trace some of the influences on fashion and make-up.

27   Brown, John R. "A Chronology of Major Events in Obstetrics and Gynaecology." Journal of Obstetrics and Gynaecology, 71 (1964), 302-309. Major advances in obstetrics and gynaecology are listed.

28   Brustein, Robert. "The Monstrous Regiment of Women: Sources for the Satiric View of the Court Lady in English Drama." Renaissance and Modern Essays, G. R. Hibbard, ed. New York: Barnes and Noble, 1966. Satire entered drama in 1599 when the Bishops' Edict banned it elsewhere. The essay discusses the kinds of attacks directed at court ladies.

29   Bye, A. E. "Women and the World of Art." Arts and Decoration, 10 (1918), 86-87. Lists some women in the arts.

30   Camden, Charles. The Elizabethan Woman: A Panorama of English Womanhood, 1540-1640. Houston: Elsevier Press, 1952. A useful book for comparative study, The Elizabethan Woman discusses education, marriage, domestic and leisure activities, dress, and opinions about the nature of women.

31   Clark, Alice. The Working Life of Women in the Seven-
      teenth Century. New York: Dutton, 1919. A survey of
      the conditions, wages, and occupations of women.

32   Clinton, Katherine. "Femme et Philosophe: Enlighten-
      ment Origins of Feminism." ECS, 3 (1975), 283-299. The
      debate on the "woman question" at the end of the eigh-
      teenth century in Europe centered on an assault on tra-
      ditional institutions and accepted social beliefs. The
      article examines the attitudes of the philosophes and
      suggests they provided the intellectual foundation for
      the political theory underlying legal equality.

33   Cohen, Selma Jean. "Theory and Practice of Theatrical
      Dancing in England in the Restoration and Early Eigh-
      teenth Century as Seen in the Lives and Works of Josias
      Priest, John Weaver, and Hester Santlow." BNYPL, 63 (1959),
      541-554; 64 (1960), 41-54 and 95-104. Choreographers and
      dancers contributed to the cultural brilliance of the Res-
      toration and eighteenth century. Hester Santlow, a much
      praised dancer and actress, played a number of famous
      dramatic parts in the early eighteenth century.

34   Cole, Francis J. Early Theories of Sexual Generation.
      Oxford: Clarendon, 1930. A survey of theories of sex-
      ual generation with some attention to their origin.

35   Cumming, Alan. "Pauline Christianity and Greek Philoso-
      phy: A Study of the Status of Women." JHI, 34 (1973),
      517-528. Any study of the rights, duties, and capaci-
      ties which have determined Western women's role and
      status must begin with an understanding of Hebrew and
      Greek thought as transmitted through Paul.

36   Cummings, Dorothea. "Prostitution as Shown in Eigh-
      teenth-Century Periodicals." Ball State University Fo-
      rum, 12 (1971), 44-49. The number of references to
      prostitution reflects its frequency and attitudes toward
      it.

37   Cunnington, Cecil W. and Phillis Cunnington. Handbook
      of English Costume in the Eighteenth Century. London:
      Faber, 1957. Brief descriptions and illustrations of
      details of clothing include the changing styles.

38   Dark, Sidney. Twelve More Ladies: Good, Bad and In-
      different. Freeport, New York: Books for Libraries,

1969. Popular biographies including one of Nell Gwynne.

39   Darquenne, Roger. "L'Obstétrique aux xviiie et xix^e
      siècles: Pratique, Enseignement, Législation" in Ecoles
      et livres d'école en Hainaut du xvie au xixe siècle.
      Mons: Université de Mons, 1971. During the seventeenth
      and eighteenth centuries, the practice of medicine as we
      know it, medical education and significant legislature
      which dictated the technical and moral norms of medicine
      evolved.

40   Davis, Elizabeth Gould. The First Sex. New York: G. P.
      Putnam's Sons, 1971. A superficial chapter on the age
      of reason cites selections from Mary Astell and Mary
      Wollstonecraft.

41   Davis, Gaius. "The Puritan Teaching on Marriage and the
      Family." Evangelical Quarterly, 27 (1955), 15-30. Puri-
      tan writings defined and praised marriage, guided the
      choice of spouse and the manner of courtship, and laid
      down rules for a successful marriage. The relationship
      between man and woman was one of mutual sharing, but the
      authority was the man's. Manuals about family life em-
      phasized religion, order, love, and education.

42   Dayot, Armand Pierre Marie. Famous Beauties in Art, 1700-
      Present Day. Boston: L. C. Page, 1907.

43   Delaney, Paul. British Autobiography in the Seventeenth
      Century. London: Routledge & Kegan Paul; New York:
      Columbia University Press, 1969. A section on female
      authors treats the Duchess of Newcastle, Ann Lady Fan-
      shawe, Ann Lady Halkett, Mary Countess of Warwick, Lucy
      Hutchinson, and Mary Pennington.

44   de Vries, Leonard and Peter Fryer. Venus Unmask'd or, An
      Inquiry into the Nature and Origin of the Passion of Love.
      New York: Stein and Day, 1967. An introduction discusses
      the collection of contemporary manuals, pamphlets, and
      broadsides.

45   Dobrée, Bonamy, ed. From Anne to Victoria: Essays by
      Various Hands. New York: Scribner's, 1937. The book
      includes essays on Sarah, Duchess of Marlborough, Eliza-
      beth Montagu, and Mary Wollstonecraft.

46 Dobrée, Bonamy. Introduction to <u>The</u> <u>Lady's</u> <u>New-Year's-</u><u>Gift</u>; <u>or</u>, <u>Advice</u> <u>to</u> <u>a</u> <u>daughter</u>. London: Cayme Press, 1927. <u>Advice</u> <u>to</u> <u>a</u> <u>Daughter</u> was tremendously popular in its own time and has lasting appeal because of its bitter sweet opinion of the world and its fatherly tenderness.

47 Douglas, Emily Taft. <u>Remember</u> <u>the</u> <u>Ladies</u>. New York: Putnam, 1966. A tribute to feminine achievement.

48 Doyle, Charles C. "Nature's Fair Defect: Milton and William Cartwright on the Paradox of Woman." <u>ELN</u>, 11 (1973), 107-110. The author analyzes Milton's phrase "this fair defect/Of Nature" (<u>Paradise</u> <u>Lost</u>, X, 888-892), and cites sources in Aristotle, Bartholomew Keckermann, and Anglican divine William Cartwright to show the paradoxical language indicates Adam's confusion in his fallen state. Milton thus condemns Adam's anti-feminism.

49 Drew, Elizabeth. <u>The</u> <u>Literature</u> <u>of</u> <u>Gossip</u>: <u>Nine</u> <u>English</u> <u>Letter</u> <u>Writers</u>. New York: Norton, 1964. Chapters on Dorothy Osborne and Lady Mary Wortley Montagu are largely biographical.

50 Duncan, Carol. "Happy Mothers and other New Ideas in French Art." <u>Art</u> <u>Bulletin</u>, 55 (1973), 570-583. Paintings by moralists such as Greuze and Fragonard challenged long accepted attitudes about marriage and family. By portraying married life as blissful, motherhood as sexually gratifying, and childcare as emotionally satisfying, the artists helped popularize the rising "cult of motherhood."

51 Earengey, Florence. <u>A</u> <u>Milk-White</u> <u>Lamb</u>, <u>The</u> <u>Legal</u> <u>and</u> <u>Economic</u> <u>Status</u> <u>of</u> <u>Women</u>. London: National Council of Women of Great Britain, 1953. A survey of the gains made by English women.

52 Edgerton, Giles. "Is there a sex distinction in art? The attitude of the critic toward women's exhibits." <u>Craftsman</u>, 14 (1908), 238-251. Discusses critics' opinions of exhibits.

53 Edwards, Irene L. "The Women Friends of London." <u>Journal</u> <u>of</u> <u>the</u> <u>Friends'</u> <u>Historical</u> <u>Society</u>, 47 (1955), 3-21. Traces the membership and activities of the organization.

54 Ehrenpreis, Irvin and Robert Halsband. <u>The</u> <u>Lady</u> <u>of</u> <u>Letters</u> <u>in</u> <u>the</u> <u>Eighteenth</u> <u>Century</u>: <u>Papers</u> <u>Read</u> <u>at</u> <u>a</u> <u>Clark</u> <u>Library</u> <u>Seminar</u>. Los Angeles: Clark Library, 1969.

55   Ehrenpreis' "Letters of Advice to Young Spinsters" dis-
      cusses Swift's attitudes on the education of women and
      the status of spinsters. Halsband's "Ladies of Letters"
      places Lady Mary Wortley Montagu in the context of the
      age.

56   Esmond, Rosalee E. "Body, Soul, and the Marriage Re-
      lationship: The History of an Analogy." JHI, 34 (1973),
      283-290. Few analogies in early seventeenth century
      writings are more common than that between body, soul
      and husband,wife. Sources for and influences on the
      analogy include the Biblical account of the fall, Aris-
      totle's explanations of generation, and Medieval debates
      about the origin of temptation and sin. The analogy of
      man-soul is opposed to the common visual representations
      of the soul but reflects the combined influences and the
      need to make the woman subservient.

57   Figes, Eva. Patriarchal Attitudes. New York: Stein and
      Day, 1970. An exploration of the world created by men
      in which the images of women, God, and spheres of in-
      fluence are defined by men.

58   Fletcher, Ifan K. "The History of Ballet in England,
      1660-1740." BNYPL, 63 (1959), 275-291. After the Res-
      toration, dancing as entertainment regained its popu-
      larity. Records of dancing lessons, performances of
      ballets, the flowering of ballroom dancing, and devel-
      opment of opera ballets show the changes in dance. A
      brief summary of Marie Salle's life and reforms conclude
      the discussion of great dancers, early masters, and
      choreographers.

59   Forbes, Thomas. The Midwife and the Witch. New Haven:
      Yale University Press, 1966. The church and society
      feared midwives' opportunities to acquire the materials
      for and to practice witchcraft. Midwifery and witchcraft
      shared common associations and this opinion influenced
      the way midwifery was practiced.

60   Forbes, Thomas. "The Regulation of English Midwives in
      the Sixteenth and Seventeenth Centuries." Medical His-
      tory, 8 (1964), 235-244. The author traces the estab-
      lishment of regulations regarding midwives. The infor-
      mation is derived from A Book of Oaths (1649), church
      records, and Guild Hall licenses and shows the develop-
      ment of professional standards. A bibliography is in-
      cluded.

61 Foxon, David. <u>Libertine Literature in England</u>, <u>1660-</u>
    <u>1745</u>. New York: University Books, 1965. A detailed
    study of the origins of pornography with notes on the
    major texts, including the libel trials which resulted
    from literary sexual license.

62 Franks, A. H. <u>Social Dance</u>: <u>A Short History</u>. London:
    Routledge & Kegan Paul, 1963. This history includes a
    chapter on the eighteenth century, discussing the rise
    of theatrical dancing and the influence of dress and
    middle class manners on social dancing.

63 Fries, Maureen, and Anne Daunis. <u>A Bibliography of</u>
    <u>Writings by and about British Women Authors</u>, <u>1957-1969</u>.
    Charleston, Illinois: Women's Caucus for the Modern
    Languages, 1971. Includes women writers from 1660-
    1800 but is very incomplete.

64 Fry, Roger, J. B. Manson, W. W. Watts, <u>et</u>. <u>al</u>. <u>Georgian</u>
    <u>Art</u> (<u>1760-1820</u>). London: Batsford, 1929. Including
    sections on sculpture, ceramics, metalwork, textiles
    and furniture, the book mentions a number of women es-
    pecially in the chapter "The Minor Arts."

65 Fussell, G. E. and K. R. Fussell. <u>The English Country-</u>
    <u>woman</u>: <u>A Farmhouse Social History</u>, <u>1500-1900</u>. London:
    Andrew Melrose, 1953. A semi-popular account of the
    daily activities of countrywomen, without documentation.
    Four chapters deal with women from 1660-1800.

66 Fyvie, John. <u>Some Famous Women of Wit and Beauty</u>. <u>A</u>
    <u>Georgian Galaxy</u>. London: Constable, 1905. Biographies
    of Mrs. Fitzherbert, Lady Hamilton, Mrs. Montagu, Lady
    Blessington, Mrs. Lennox, Mrs. Grote, Mrs. Norton, and
    Lady Eastlake explain the fascination they held for
    their contemporaries.

67 Gagen, Jean E. <u>The New Woman</u>: <u>Her Emergence in English</u>
    <u>Drama</u>, <u>1660-1730</u>. New York: Twayne, 1954. Focuses on
    women of learning, science, and fashion with plot sum-
    maries and uncritical catalogues of their appearances in
    plays.

68 Gardiner, Dorothy. <u>English Girlhood at School</u>: <u>A Study</u>
    <u>of Education through Twelve Centuries</u>. London: Oxford
    University Press, 1929. Chapters twelve through eighteen
    treat the seventeenth and eighteenth centuries. Women

11

were criticized for their lack of learning, but education for women should be different than for men. The book identifies the milestones in female education.

69   George, M. Dorothy. _England in Johnson's Day_. New York: Harcourt, Brace and Co., 1928. Excerpts from eighteenth century essays, including women's education, housewives, and modern women, by various literati.

70   George, M. Dorothy. _England in Transition: Life and Work in the Eighteenth Century_. London: Routledge, 1931. Mention of the employment of women.

71   George, M. Dorothy. _London Life in the Eighteenth Century_. London: Kegan Paul; New York: Knopf, 1925. Mention of women in the labor force and conditions of their employment.

72   Gilboy, Elizabeth W. _Wages in Eighteenth Century England_. Cambridge: Harvard, 1934. Some mention of the payment of women.

73   Greenberg, Janelle. "The Legal Status of the English Woman in Early Eighteenth Century Common Law and Equity." _Studies in Eighteenth Century Culture_, Harold E. Pagliaro, ed. Cleveland: Case Western Reserve, 1975; iv, 171-182. A thorough study of the legal rights of single and married women.

74   Greven, Philip J., Jr. _Child-Rearing Concepts, 1628-1861: Historical Sources_. Primary Sources in American History. Itasca, Illinois: Peacock, 1973.

75   Gule, Janet Z. "Centuries of Womanhood: An Evolutionary Perspective on the Feminine Role." _WS_, 1 (1972), 97-110.

76   Haller, William and Malleville. "The Puritan Art of Love." _HLQ_, 5 (1942), 235-272. Milton's conception of woman and marriage was that of most men and women, and certainly most Puritans, of his time. The Puritan clergy emphasized conjugal relations in sermons and tracts, developing precepts for an orderly marriage and for the conduct of women.

77   Halsband, Robert. "Editing the Letters of Letter-Writers." _SB_, 11 (1958), 25-37. Recent editions of letters are excessively annotated. Halsband includes his editorial decisions on Lady Mary Wortley Montagu's letters.

78 Hamill, Frances. "Some Unconventional Women Before
    1800: Printers, Booksellers, and Collectors." PBSA,
    49 (1955), 300-314. A brief history of women in pub-
    lishing from the Empress Shiyau-toku of Japan to Mary
    Catherine Goddard. Though the Company of Stationers
    made it difficult for a widow to continue her husband's
    printing business, in the seventeenth century sixty
    women are listed as printers and booksellers.

79 Hamilton, Adrian, ed. The Infamous Essay on Woman; or,
    John Wilkes Seated between Vice and Virtue. London:
    Deutsch, 1972. A lavishly illustrated biography of
    John Wilkes with facsimiles of his work including An
    Essay on Woman.

80 Hardie, Martin, Water-colour Painting in Britain. New
    York: Barnes and Noble, 1966. Volume I covers the
    eighteenth century.

81 Hargreaves-Mawdsley, W. N. The English Della Cruscans
    and their Time, 1783-1828. Hague: Martinus Nijhoff,
    1967. The Anglo-Florentines who claimed affiliation with
    the Accademia della Crusca occasionally allowed mixed
    gatherings. The Florence Miscellany (1785) brought the
    group public recognition and reproach. Among the women
    associated with them was Hester Thrale Piozzi.

82 Harth, Phillip, ed. New Approaches to Eighteenth Century
    Literature: Selected Papers from the English Institute.
    New York: Columbia, 1974. Several essays of interest
    including Leo Braudy's "Penetration and Impenetrability
    in Clarissa."

83 Haviland, Thomas P. "The Serpent in Milady's Library."
    University of Pennsylvania Library Chronicle, 4 (1936),
    57-61. The Ladies Calling (1677), among other texts,
    warned young ladies against reading romances. The Mock
    Clelia (1678), an heroic romance, is a source for Char-
    lotte Lennox's Female Quixote.

84 Hayden, Mary. "Charity Children in Eighteenth-Century
    Dublin." Dublin Historical Record, 5 (1943), 92-107.
    Charity schools, orphanages, Charter Schools, and work
    houses cared for poor children. Parish "lifters" (women
    employed by church wardens to carry foundlings to the
    next county) were phased out in 1730, but the conditions
    in which the children lived continued to be a disgrace in

spite of the efforts of dedicated people such as Lady
Arabella Denny, John Howard, and Nano Nagle.

85 Hayward, Arthur L., ed. A Complete History of the Lives
and Robberies of the Most Notorious Highwaymen, Footpads,
Shoplifts and Cheats of Both Sexes. London: Routledge,
1926. Criminal biographies including some of women.

86 Hecht, J. Jean. The Domestic Servant Class in Eighteenth-
Century England. London: Routledge & Kegan Paul, 1956.
A detailed study of the economic and social situation of
servants has scattered sections on women.

87 Highfill, Philip H., Jr., Kalman Burnim and Edward A.
Langhans. A Biographical Dictionary of Actors, Actresses,
Musicians, Dancers, Managers, and Other Stage Personnel
in London, 1660-1800 (12 volumes projected). Carbondale:
Southern Illinois University Press, 1973. Biographical
notices including a large number of women connected with
the theatre.

88 Hill, Georgiana. Women in English Life. 2 vols. London:
Richard Bentley & Son, 1896. A somewhat superficial social history dealing with women from the lower classes
to the queens.

89 Hill, Vicki L. Female Artists Past and Present. Berkeley: Woman's History Research Center, Inc., 1974. An
alphabetical list by media of women in the visual arts
gives the dates of their lives with bibliographies.

90 Hine, Ellen M. "Madame de Lambert, Her Sources and Her
Circle: On the Threshold of a New Age." SVEC, 102
(1973), 173-191. Her salon influenced opinion for nearly twenty-five years. An independent and outspoken woman,
she championed women's rights and brought together many
of the new ideas she heard discussed.

91 Holdsworth, William. A History of English Law. London:
Methuen, 1903-1921; rptd, 1966. A continuous history of
English law to 1700 with some topics such as the relationship between common law, parliamentary law, and equity
pursued into modern times. Volumes ten, eleven, and
twelve are concerned with the eighteenth century.

92 Hole, Christina. The English Housewife in the Seventeenth
Century. London: Chatto & Windus, 1953. Domestic life

14

The domestic life of the seventeenth century woman is arranged around kitchen, nursery, and sickroom. The book includes a description of fashions and recreation.

93   Hole, Christina. English Sports and Pastimes. New York: Batsford, 1949. Some mention of recreation for women.

94   Howard, George E. A History of Matrimonial Institutions. 3 vols. Chicago: University of Chicago Press; London: Unwin, 1904. This history examines theories about the development of marriage as an institution and traces legal codification.

95   Humphreys, A. R. "The 'Rights of Woman' in the Age of Reason." MLR, 41 (1946), 256-269. This is an important survey of the battle between "conservatives" who argued for subordination of women and "progressives" who defended women's equality. Provides a context for Mary Wollstonecraft's Vindication.

96   Ireland, Norma O. Index to Women of the World from Ancient to Modern Times: Biographies and Portraits. Westwood, Massachusetts: F. W. Faxon, 1970. Reference guides to 13,000 women with a brief introduction on women and literature.

97   Jackson, Robert W. Swift and His Circle: A Book of Essays. Dublin: Talbot Press, Ltd., 1945. Esther Johnson married Swift; Vanessa Vanhomrigh surprised Swift by falling in love with him; Rebecca Dingley has been unjustly neglected. In addition to these personal relationships, Swift encouraged a "poetical triumfeminate" (Barber, Grierson, Sican) of Dublin businessmen's wives as well as encouraging Laetitia Pilkington.

98   Jarrett, Derek. England in the Age of Hogarth. London: Hart-Davis, MacGibbon, 1974. A social history with some mention of women.

99   Jerrold, Walter, and Clare. Five Queer Women. New York: Brentano's, 1929. Brief biographies of women classified as eccentric including Pilkington.

100   Johnson, J. The Laws Respecting Women. Dobbs Ferry: Oceana Publications, 1974. Essays on legal rights of women.

101   Johnson, R. Brimley. Blue Stocking Letters. London:
      John Lane, 1926. Selections from a representative group
      of Bluestockings with an introduction.

102   Kamm, Josephine. Hope Deferred: Girls' Education in
      English History. London: Methuen, 1965. A survey of
      education for women from Old English times with brief
      introductions to important personalities.

103   Kaufman, Michael W. "Spare Ribs: The Conception of
      Woman in the Middle Ages and the Renaissance." Sound-
      ings, 56 (1973), 139-163. Contrasts "literary images"
      of women to sociological data to provide an historical
      survey of attitudes toward women in Europe. The shift
      from a primary economy to a money economy brought more
      restrictions for women.

104   Kelso, Ruth. Doctrine for the Lady of the Renaissance.
      Urbana: University of Illinois Press, 1956. The posi-
      tion of women.

105   Kerman, Sandra Lee. Introduction to The Newgate Calen-
      dar; or, Malefactors' Bloody Register. New York: Capri-
      corn, 1962. The Newgate ordinaries "edited" criminal
      biographies for didactic purposes. Includes some women
      felons and crimes against women.

106   Lieberman, Marcia R. "Sexism and the Double Standard
      in Literature" in Images of Women in Fiction: Feminist
      Perspectives. Bowling Green, Ohio: Bowling Green U.
      Press, Popular Press, 1972.

107   Lochhead, Marion. The Scots Household in the Eighteenth
      Century: A Century of Scottish Domestic and Social Life.
      Edinburgh: Moray Press, 1948. A description of the
      daily life of Scottish people centered around the home.

108   Lorence, Bogna W. "Parents and Children in Eighteenth
      Century Europe." History of Childhood Quarterly, 2 (1974),
      1-30. Two attitudes toward children prevailed: indiffer-
      ent and neglectful upper class parents and intrusive and
      sometimes cruel middle class parents. Innovative parents
      sought to minister to their children's needs.

109   Loschky, David J., and Donald F. Krier. "Income and
      Family Size in Three Eighteenth-Century Lancashire Pa-
      rishes: A Reconstruction Study." Journal of Economic

<u>History</u>, 29 (1969), 429-448. Without drawing broader inferences, the author provides statistics on income and family size in three parishes.

110   Mackaness, George. "Female Convicts: A Hell-Voyage to Botany Bay." <u>American Book Collector</u>, 13 (1962), 6-9. Description of behavior of female felons.

111   Malcolmson, Robert W. <u>Popular Recreations in English Society, 1700-1850</u>. Cambridge: University Press, 1973. Describes holidays and women's part in their celebration and lists sports at which women were spectators.

112   Margetson, Stella. <u>Leisure and Pleasure in the Eighteenth Century</u>. London: Cassell, 1970. The pleasures of the fashionable set, the court, the country people, and the lower classes are described and classified into such categories as "intellectual," "refined," and "romantic." No notes, but selected bibliography.

113   Marshall, Dorothy. "The Domestic Servants of the Eighteenth Century." <u>Economica</u>, 9 (1929), 15-40. Charges directed at domestic servants that they lacked sobriety and were disrespectful were probably true since servants were gamers and drinkers in the first half of the century. Some attention to women.

114   Marshall, Dorothy. <u>English People in the Eighteenth Century</u>. London: Longmans, Green, 1956. Very short section on women in industry.

115   Marshall, Dorothy. <u>Industrial England, 1776-1851</u>. New York: Scribner's, 1973. Briefly treats women in industry.

116   McAllester, Susan, ed. "Women in the Colleges: Status, Teaching, Feminist Criticism." <u>College English</u>, 32 (1971). Essayists include Florence Howe, Elaine Showalter, Annis Pratt, and Lillian Robinson. None of the essays deals only with issues relating to eighteenth century British women.

117   McCoy, Raymond F. "Hygienic Recommendations of <u>The Ladies Library</u>." <u>Bulletin of the Institute of the History of Medicine</u>, 4 (1936), 367-372. Extraction from <u>The Ladies Library</u> of advice relating to child and infant care and nutrition.

17

118   McDowell, M. M. "A Cursory View of Cheating at Whist
       in the Eighteenth Century." HLB, 22 (1974), 162-175.
       Discusses the stereotypes of gaming women.

119   Mathey, Jacques. Portraits and Studies of Women: Old
       Masters' Drawings from the Fifteenth to the Nineteenth
       Century. London: Faber & Faber, 1937.

120   Mead, Kate C. H. A History of Women in Medicine From
       the Earliest Times to the Beginning of the Nineteenth
       Century. Haddam, Connecticut: Haddam Press, 1938.
       Chapters nine and ten describe women in medicine in
       England, America, and on the continent in the seven-
       teenth and eighteenth centuries with sections devoted
       to such topics as midwifery, epidemics, and quacks.

121   Melville, Lewis (pseud. Lewis Saul Benjamin). More
       Stage Favorites of the Eighteenth Century. London:
       Hutchinson, 1929. Biographical sketches aimed at
       describing personality and defining formative influ-
       ences. Quotes letters and memoirs for such notables
       as Frances Abington, Sarah Siddons, Mary Robinson, and
       Dorothy Jordan.

122   Melville, Lewis (pseud. Lewis Saul Benjamin). Stage
       Favorites of the Eighteenth Century.Garden City: Double-
       day, 1929. Biographical sketches of Anne Oldfield,
       Charlotte Charke, Peg Woffington, George Anne Bellamy,
       Susannah Cibber, and others.

123   Meyer, Gerald D. The Scientific Lady in England 1650-
       1760: an account of her rise, with emphasis on the
       major roles of the telescope and microscope. Berkeley:
       University of California Press, 1955. A history of
       women in science, their efforts and reception, litera-
       ture for, and a brief discussion of the satires of
       the female virtuoso.

124   Miller, Henry K., Eric Rothstein, and G. S. Rousseau.
       The Augustan Milieu. Oxford: Clarendon Press, 1970.
       The collection contains two essays of interest: James
       Sutherland's "Anne Greene and the Oxford Poets" and
       Robert Halsband's "'Lady's Dressing Room' Explicated
       by a Contemporary."

125   Minogue, Valerie. "'Les Liaisons Dayereuses': A Prac-
       tical Lesson in the Art of Seduction." MLR, 67 (1972),

775-786. Of some comparative interest.

126 Moore, C. A. "The First of the Militants in English Literature." The Nation, 17 February 1916, pp. 194-196. Argues that the Sophia pamphlets (1739-1740) adapted from Poulain de la Barre, are more feminist than Wollstonecraft.

127 Morrow, Thomas W. Early Methodist Women. London: Epworth Press, 1967. A history of women in the Methodist movement with more detailed information about such major figures as Selina, Countess of Huntingdon.

128 Mourey, Gabriel. Les Peintres de la femme du xviii^e siecle. Ecole Anglaise. Paris: Art et les Artistes, 1909, Tome 9, pp. 77-98.

129 Munsterberg, Hugo. A History of Women Artists. New York: Clarkson, 1975. A history of women's contribution to art; the eighteenth century section demonstrates the proliferation of painters without male artist-relatives and puzzles over Angelica Kauffmann's fame.

130 Murray, Adrian. "English women Silversmiths." Antique Dealer and Collectors' Guide, London, March 1952, pp. 21-23. Lists some silversmiths and how to recognize their work.

131 Myers, Sylvia H. "The Ironies of Education." Aphra, 4 (1973), 61-72. Women's education was full of inconsistencies and contradictions.

132 Neuburg, Victor E. Popular Education in Eighteenth Century England. London: Woburn Press, 1971. Some attention to the education of women.

133 Nicolson, Marjorie Hope. The Microscope and English Imagination. Northampton: Smith College Studies in Modern Languages, 1935. The author reconstructs the discovery, development, and influence of the microscope in science and literature. She finds the first record of popular interest in Pepys' diary entry for 13 February 1664 and a rapid proliferation of references after that. Section IV describes the interest of the "Philosophical Girl" in microscopical science.

134 Notestein, Wallace. A History of Witchcraft in England
     from 1558 to 1718. New York: Russell and Russell, 1965.
     Carefully documented study of witchcraft which uses po-
     litical, literary, and social perspectives. The account
     is structured around records and literature about major
     trials; uses pamphlets, court records, memoirs, news-
     papers, local historians and theologians, and state pa-
     pers.

135 Noyes, Gertrude E. "John Dunton's Ladies Dictionary,
     1694." PQ, 21 (1942), 129-145. The Ladies Dictionary
     provides a broad scope and content. The article cites
     the principal sources of the Dictionary with printing
     of parallel columns.

136 Oake, Roger B. "Polygamy in the Lettres Persanes."
     Romanic Review, 32 (1941), 56-62. Literature discussing
     polygamy proliferated after Johann Leyser's Discursus
     Politicus de Polygamia (1674). Lettres persanes shows
     Montesquieu's familiarity with the controversy, drama-
     tizes his objections to the practice, and contains the
     ideas to be developed in L'Esprit des lois including
     many on the relationship between the sexes.

137 O'Dowd, M. C. "Writing and Injustice." Contrast:
     South African Quarterly, 23 (1970), 48-61. Although
     writers such as Austen did not mention social injus-
     tice, it did exist in their times.

138 O'Faolain, Julia and Laura Martines, eds. Not in God's
     Image: Women in History from the Greeks to the Vic-
     torians. New York: Harper and Row, 1973. A section
     on the early modern period includes a short discussion
     of diaries and letters as a social history.

139 Ormsbee, Thomas H. "The Women Silversmiths of England."
     American Collector, May 1938, pp. 8-9.

140 Percival, Alicia C. The English Miss to-day and Yester-
     day; Ideals, methods, and personalities in the education
     and upbringing of girls during the last hundred years.
     London: Harrap, 1939. A history of education.

141 Petherick, Maurice. Restoration Rogues. London: Hollis
     & Carter, 1951. Biographical sketches including Barbara
     Palmer.

142 Phillips, Margaret, and W. S. Tomkinson. English Women
     in Life and Letters. London: Oxford, 1927; rpt. New
     York: B. Blom, 1971. Includes chapters on two centuries
     of English women covering housekeeping, fashionable women,
     education, women criminals, and women in the professions.

143 Pierce, Robert. "Moral Education in the Novel of the
     1750's." PQ, 44 (1965), 73-87. Traces conventions of
     movement from novels of morality to novels of sentimen-
     tality with discussion of novels by Charlotte Lennox
     and Eliza Haywood.

144 Pinchbeck, Ivy, and Margaret Hewitt. Children in English
     Society. 2 vols. London: Routledge & Kegan Paul, 1973.
     Volume I includes Tudor times to the eighteenth century
     and Volume II discusses the eighteenth century.

145 Pinchbeck, Ivy. Women Workers and the Industrial Revo-
     lution, 1750-1850. London: Routledge & Sons, 1930.
     The entry of women into work, conditions and legisla-
     ture affecting them.

146 Plant, Marjorie. The Domestic Life of Scotland in the
     Eighteenth Century. Edinburgh: University Press, 1952.
     The author describes Scottish households including fur-
     nishings, gardens, food, housekeeping practices, cloth
     ing and leisure pasttimes, with such specific information
     as the average family size and clothing expenditure per
     year. Some comparisons to England.

147 Plant, Marjorie. The English Book Trade: An Economic
     History of the Making and Sale of Books. London: no
     pub., 1939. Scant mention of the women who worked as
     book-binders, compositors, paper makers and printers.

148 Posner, Donald. Watteau: "A Lady at Her Toilet." Lon-
     don: Allen Lane; New York: Viking, 1973. The paint-
     ing is a revelation of voluptuous beauty and sensual
     grace. An analysis of the content explicates the mean-
     ing and sets it in the context of early eighteenth cen-
     tury art.

149 Radzinowicz, Mary A. N. "Eve and Dalila: Renovation
     and the Hardening of the Heart." Reason and the Imagin-
     ation, J. A. Mazzeo, ed. New York, 1962.

150   Rawson, C. J. "The phrase 'legal prostitution' in
       Fielding, Defoe and others." N&Q, 209 (1964), 298.
       "Legal prostitution" is a cant phrase in the eigh-
       teenth century.

151   Redman, Ben Ray. "Sex and Literary Art." American
       Mercury, 63 (1946), 412-417 and 760-761.

152   Rees, Christine. "Gay, Swift and the Nymphs of Drury-
       Lane." Essays in Criticism, 23 (1973), 1-21. Contrasts
       the pastoral ideal (nature) and the artificial city
       nymph (art). Gay exaggerates the fiction while com-
       paring it to reality; Swift subverts the fiction of
       pastoral convention in the name of truth.

153   Reich, Emil. Women Through the Ages. 2 vols. London:
       Methuen, 1908. Volume II includes a chapter on English
       women in the eighteenth century with emphasis on Lady
       Mary Wortley Montagu and Fanny Burney.

154   Revard, Stella P. "Eve and the Doctrine of Responsi-
       bility in Paradise Lost." PMLA, 88 (1973), 69-78. Eve
       alone is responsible for the fall. Nowhere is it as-
       sumed that Adam should control his wife and it is not
       intellectual prowess but love of God which enables a
       person to resist sin.

155   Reynolds, Myra. The Learned Lady in England, 1650-1760.
       New York: Houghton Mifflin, 1920. A pioneering and
       comprehensive study of learned ladies, the education of
       women, and satiric attacks on women in drama. Includes
       a bibliography of works by women.

156   Rodgers, Betsy. Cloak of Charity. Studies in Eighteenth
       Century Philanthropy. London: Methuen, 1949. Studies
       of the treatment of the poor, orphans, prostitutes, and
       prisoners, with chapters on Mrs. Trimmer and Hannah More.

157   Rogal, Samuel J. "The Selling of Sex: Mandeville's
       Modest Defence of Publick Stews." Studies in Eighteenth
       Century Culture, Ronald C. Rosbottom, ed. Madison: Uni-
       versity of Wisconsin Press, 1976, pp. 141-150. Mande-
       ville reasoned that lawful prostitution was necessary
       because of the appetites of men and the "unconscious ac-
       tions of virtuous women." Public Stews is a satiric sally
       in his defense of transforming private vices into benefi-
       cial social institutions.

158   Rosbottom, Ronald C. "Parody and Truth in Mme. Riccobo-
       ni's Continuation of La Vie de Marianne." Studies in
       Voltaire and the Eighteenth Century, 81 (1971), 163-
       175. Her parody of Marivaux's La Vie de Marianne shows
       that Mme. Riccoboni understood Marivaux's technique
       and reasons for leaving Marianne "unfinished." Her
       parody also provides contemporary comment and evalua-
       tion of an influential work.

159   Rosen, Marvin S. "Authors and Publishers, 1750-1830."
       Science and Society, 32 (1968), 218-232. Relationships
       between them.

160   Rowbotham, W. B. "Soldiers' and Seamen's Wives and
       Children in H. M. Ships." Mariner's Mirror, 47 (1961),
       42-48. Wives and children of mariners accompanied their
       husbands and fathers on ships in the war against France,
       1793, and some were apparently present during battles to
       attend to the wounded.

161   Sachse, William L., comp. Restoration England 1660-1689.
       Cambridge: Cambridge University Press, 1971. A series
       of bibliographies.

162   Schleiner, Winfried. "Rank and Marriage: A Study of
       the Motif of 'Woman Willfully Tested.'" CLS, 9 (1972),
       365-375. Although no eighteenth century books are men-
       tioned the theme is important. Testing female patience
       reflects societal attitudes.

163   Schulz, Dieter. "The Coquette's Progress from Satire to
       Sentimental Novel." Literatur in Wisschschaft und Unter-
       richt (Kiel), 6 (1973), 77-89. Character changes in the
       coquette show that sentimentality and the feminine novel
       were closely related phenomena.

164   Scott, Walter S. The Bluestocking Ladies. London: John
       Green, 1947. Chapters on Mary Delany, Elizabeth Carter,
       Elizabeth Montagu, Hester Chapone, Hester Lynch Thrale,
       Hannah More, Fanny Burney, and Elizabeth Vesey.

165   Senior, Francesca Dorothy P. The King's Ladies: Charles
       II and His Ladies of Pleasure. London: Hale, 1936. A
       biography of the king organized around the succession of
       his mistresses. Barbara Villiers, Hortense Mancini, Nell
       Gwynn, Anne Hyde, Mary of Modena, and the Duchess of Ports-
       mouth are included.

166 Sergeant, Philip W. Witches and Warlocks. London:
     Hutchinson, 1936. A survey of what witches were accused of.

167 Sewell, Ernestine P. "Name Calling in English Litera-
     ture." Love and Wrestling, Butch and O. K., Fred Tarp-
     ley, ed. Commerce, Texas: Names Institute Press, 1973,
     pp. 58-64. By the twelfth century, name calling was
     well established in English literature. Political writing,
     satire, and the roman à clef expanded the uses and types
     of name calling.

168 Singleton, Robert R. "English Criminal Biography, 1651-
     1722." HLB, 18 (1970), 63-83. Discusses the Mary Carle-
     ton narratives, Moll Cutpurse's The Life and Death of
     Mrs. Mary Frith, and sources of Moll Flanders. Has a
     bibliography of criminal biographies.

169 Smith, Eric. Some Versions of the Fall: The Myth of
     the Fall of Man in English Literature. Pittsburgh: U.
     of Pittsburgh Press, 1973.

170 Smith, Warren H. Originals Abroad: The Foreign Careers
     of Some Eighteenth Century Britons. New Haven: Yale
     University Press, 1952. Descriptions of the lives of
     Englishmen abroad including some women.

171 Soulbury, Viscount. "Women of Influence, 1750-1800."
     Quarterly Review, 297 (1959), 400-407. Briefly remarks
     on various women of political influence including Geor-
     giana, Duchess of Devonshire; Lady Hester Stanhope;
     Isabella Strange; Elizabeth Carter; Elizabeth Montagu;
     and Fanny Burney.

172 Spacks, Patricia Meyer. "Early Fiction and the Frightened
     Male." Novel: A Forum on Fiction, 8 (1974), 5-15. The
     eighteenth century novel reveals profound fear of women.

173 Spacks, Patricia M. "Ev'ry Woman is at Heart a Rake."
     Eighteenth Century Studies, 8 (1974), 27-46. A scholarly
     examination of woman's sexuality using a variety of gen-
     res.

174 Spacks, Patricia M. The Female Imagination. New York:
     Knopf, 1975. Themes in literature written by women with
     many Restoration and eighteenth century novelists and
     memoirists mentioned.

175   Spacks, Patricia M. "Free Women." Hudson Review, 24
       (1971), 559-573.

176   Spacks, Patricia M. "Reflecting Women." Yale Review,
       63 (1973), 26-42. Identifies aspects of women's auto-
       biographies peculiar to the sex with especial attention
       to Hester Thrale.

177   Sparrow, Walter S. Women Painters of the World, from
       the Time of Caterina Virgri (1413-1463) to Rosa Bonheur
       and the Present Day. London: Hodder & Stoughton, 1905.

178   Spencer, Anna. Women's Share in Social Culture. London:
       Kennerley, 1913. Women's contributions.

179   Stauffer, Donald A. "A Deep and Sad Passion" in The
       Parrott Presentation Volume, Hardin Craig, ed. Prince-
       ton: Princeton University Press, 1935, pp. 289-314.
       Elizabeth Folkland probably wrote The History of Edward
       II which shows considerable influence from poetic drama.

180   Stebbins, Lucy. London Ladies: True Tales of the Eigh-
       teenth Century. New York: Columbia University Press,
       1952. Sketches of the lives of Martha Ray, Elizabeth
       Inchbald, Amelia Opie, and Sally and Maria Siddons.

181   Stenton, Mary. The English Woman in History. London:
       George Allen and Unwin, 1957. The place and influence
       of women in English society with substantial treatment
       of the eighteenth century.

182   Stewart, J. Douglas. "Pin-ups or Virtues? The Concept
       of the 'Beauties' in Late Stuart Portraiture." English
       Portraits of the Seventeenth and Eighteenth Centuries.
       Los Angeles: Clark Library, 1974. Pictorial evidence
       in the series and in their other paintings, especially
       symbolism, shows that Peter Lely's "Windsor Beauties"
       and Godfrey Kneller's "Hampton Court Beauties" were based
       on Neo-Platonic doctrines of love and beauty. Opinions
       about the series have changed repeatedly.

183   Stokes, Sylvia. "Women as Artists." Decorators' Digest,
       6 (1936), 18-23.

184   Thompson, C. J. S. Love, Marriage and Romance in Old
       London. London: Heath Cranton, 1936. Social customs.

25

185   Tompkins, J. M. S. _Polite Marriage_. Cambridge: Cam-
       bridge University Press, 1938; Freeport, New York: Books
       for Libraries, 1969. A collection of essays on the mar-
       riage of Richard and Elizabeth Griffith, Ann Yearsley,
       Nell Macpherson, and Mary Hays.

186   Trevelyan, George M. _English Social History; A Survey
       of Six Centuries, Chaucer to Queen Victoria_. London:
       Longmans, 1942. A history of the daily life of English
       men and women including work and home conditions, the
       class system, and the cultural milieu.

187   Tufts, Eleanor. _Our Hidden Heritage. Five Centuries
       of Women Artists_. New York: Paddington Press, 1974.
       Women artists are unknown, not non-existent. Women have
       long been professionals, court painters, and respected
       by their contemporaries. The eighteenth century sec-
       tion describes Angelica Kauffmann and three continental
       painters.

188   Upham, A. H. "English _Femmes Savantes_ at the End of the
       Seventeenth Century." _JEGP_, 12 (1913), 262-276. Out-
       lines the late seventeenth century movement for equality
       of women in religious works, hack writing, and satires.

189   Ure, Peter. "The Widow of Ephesus: Some Reflections
       on an International Comic Theme." _Durham University
       Journal_, 49 (1956), 1-9. The tale has remained popular
       since Petronius's time. Modifications in the tale record
       each era's opinion of the widow's decision.

190   Utley, Francis L. _The Crooked Rib; An Analytical Index
       to the Argument about Women in English and Scots Litera-
       ture to the End of the Year 1568_. New York: Octagon
       Books, 1970. Useful background source.

191   Utter, Robert P. and Gwendolyn B. Needham. _Pamela's
       Daughters_. New York: Macmillan, 1936. A study of the
       influence of Pamela, especially on theme, character, and
       the concept of the ideal woman.

192   Wallas, Ada. _Before the Bluestockings_. London: Allen
       and Unwin, 1929. Six essays on Hannah Wooley, Lord
       Halifax and his daughter Elizabeth, Lady Masham, Mary
       Astell, Elizabeth Elstob, and Steele's attitudes toward
       women.

26

193   Wark, Robert R. Meet the Ladies, Personalities in the
       Huntington Portraits. San Marino, California: Hunting-
       ton Library, 1972. The art gallery's portrait collec-
       tion includes a number of friends and acquaintances
       painted by the same artists. By focusing on Penelope
       Pitt, Lady Ligonier; Georgiana,Duchess of Devonshire;
       and Emma, Lady Hamilton, Mr. Wark demonstrates the in-
       triguing discrepancies between the decorous images in
       the paintings and the vibrant personalities of the
       women themselves.

194   Waters, Clara E. C. Women in the Fine Arts, From the
       Seventh Century, B.C., to the Twentieth Century, A. D.
       New York: Houghton, Mifflin, 1904.

195   Watson, Melvin R. "Mrs. Grey's Family." Periodical
       Post Boy, 14 (1953), 2-5. The periodical fiction of
       "The Matron" is sentimental, didactic domestic drama.

196   Weinkauf, Mary S. "Eve and the Sense of Beauty." Tennes-
       see Studies in Literature, 14 (1969), 103-109 . Satan
       exploits Eve's "traditional feminine trait"--apprecia-
       tion of beauty. She is content to leave Eden because
       she will bear children to redeem mankind.

197   Weitenkampf, Frank. Catalogue of a Collection of En-
       gravings, Etchings, and Lithographs by Women. New York:
       DeVinne Press, 1901. A large number of professional
       women engravers produced meritorious work. Royal and
       noble women often did amateur work.

198   Wheeler, Ethel Rolt. Famous Blue Stockings. London:
       Methuen, 1910.

199   Whinney, Margaret, and Oliver Millar. English Art 1625-
       1714. Oxford: Clarendon, 1957. The history discusses
       taste and aesthetic principles and surveys such arts as
       tapestry weaving, architecture, and painting.

200   White, W. D. "Misogyny in Hebrew Wisdom?" Southern
       Humanities Review, 7 (1973), 143-153. Examines atti-
       tudes toward women.

201   Wiles, Roy M. "Crowd-Pleasing Spectacles in Eighteenth
       Century England." Journal of Popular Culture, 1 (1967),
       90-105. Women attended some of the many spectacles.

202 Williams, Neville. _Powder_ _and_ _Paint_: _A_ _History_ _of_ _the_
     Englishwoman's _Toilet_, _Elizabeth_ _I_ - _Elizabeth_ _II_. Lon-
     don: Longmans, Green, 1957. A history of cosmetics
     between the Elizabeths.

203 Williamson, George. "_The_ _Ephesian_ _Matron_ versus the
     Platonic _Lady_." _RES_, 12 (1936), 445-449. Two presen-
     tations of womanhood.

204 Williamson, George. "The Platonic Lady" in _Seventeenth_
     Century _Contexts_. Revised edition, Chicago: University
     of Chicago Press, 1969. Katherine Philips' "Society of
     Friendship" and Walter Charleton's satiric _The_ _Ephesian_
     Matron attacked the ideal of Platonic love.

205 Williford, Miriam. "Bentham on the Rights of Women."
     Journal _of_ _the_ _History_ _of_ _Ideas_, 36 (1975), 167-176.
     Jeremy Bentham defended full equality for women, in-
     cluding the right to vote, participation in government,
     and in marriage and divorce. He did not, however, act
     to realize his theories.

206 Wolff, Cynthia G. "A Mirror for Men: Stereotypes of
     women in Literature." _MR_, 13 (1972), 205-218. Although
     women figure prominantly in literature since the Ren-
     aissance, their problems dominate an insignificant per-
     centage of works and are often misrepresented. The
     stereotyped images of women in literature have become
     an image of reality perpetrated by women.

207 Woolf, Virginia. _The_ _Second_ _Common_ _Reader_. New York:
     Harcourt, Brace, 1932.

GENRE STUDIES

BIOGRAPHIES, LETTERS, AND MEMOIRS

208   Anderson, Howard, Irvin Ehrenpreis, and Philip B. Dahglian.
The Familiar Letter in the Eighteenth Century. Lawrence:
University of Kansas Press, 1966. See item #7.

209   Elwood, Anne K. Memoirs of the Literary Ladies of England, from the Commencement of the Last Century. 2 vols.
New York: AMS, 1973. This reprint of the 1843 edition
includes biographies of Elizabeth Carter, Hester Chapone,
Piozzi, Burney, More, and Sarah Trimmer.

210   Fothergill, Robert A. Private Chronicles: A Study of
English Diaries. London: Oxford University Press, 1974.
The study classifies conceptual perspectives, treats
diaries as a genre, and develops critical discussions
of a few major diarists. Fanny Burney and a few other
women are mentioned.

211   Hamilton, Catherine J. Women Writers: Their Works and
Ways. Freeport, New York: Books for Libraries Press,
1971. This reprint of the 1892 edition has biographies
of Burney, Inchbald, Barbauld, More, Baillie, Radcliffe,
Opie, and others.

212   Hornbeak, Katherine. The Complete Letter Writer in English, 1568-1800. Northampton, Massachusetts: Smith
College, 1934. Discusses French influence on English
letter writing, models for young ladies' correspondence,
Richardson's Familiar Letters, and provides a bibliography of the English letter-writer genre, 1568-1800.

213   Hufstader, Alice A. "Musical References in Bluestocking
Letters." Musical Quarterly, 47 (1961), 73-90. This
essay notes references to opera and theatrical music in
the letters of Lady Mary Wortley Montagu and the Bluestockings.

214   Humiliata, Sr. Mary. "Standards of Taste Advocated for
Feminine Letter Writing, 1640-1797." Huntington Library
Quarterly, 13 (1950), 261-277. The author traces the revolution in standards of letter writing from mid-seventeenth
century to the end of the eighteenth century, from "pseudo classical" form to more spontaneous and familiar forms
of correspondence.

215   Ingpen, Ida M. Women as Letter-Writers. New York:
       Baker and Taylor, 1910. A collection of "representa-
       tive" letters by women including some by Dorothy Os-
       borne, Lady Mary, Elizabeth Carter, and Kitty Clive.

216   Irving, William Henry. The Providence of Wit in the
       English Letter Writers. Durham: Duke University Press,
       1955. Chapters on Lady Mary, Lady Suffolk, and the
       Bluestockings.

217   Johnson, Edgar. One Mighty Torrent: The Drama of
       Biography. New York: Stackpole, 1937. Lady Mary,
       Margaret Cavendish, and Lucy Hutchinson are mentioned.

218   Johnson, R. Brimley. Bluestocking Letters, Selected
       with an Introduction. London: Lane, 1926. See item
       # 101.

219   Matthews, William. British Autobiographies: An Anno-
       tated Bibliography of British Autobiographies Published
       or Written before 1951. Los Angeles: University of
       California Press, 1955. Lists a large number of women's
       memoirs and autobiographies with brief notes.

220   Stauffer, Donald. The Art of Biography in Eighteenth
       Century England, with Bibliographical Supplement. 2
       vols. Princeton: Princeton University Press, 1941.
       The book gives attention to memoirs of numerous women
       including Bellamy, Sophia Baddeley, Manley, Pilkington,
       Robinson, Burney, and Thrale. The supplements list
       English biographies and autobiographies, 1700-1800,
       alphabetically and chronologically.

221   Stauffer, Donald. English Biography before 1700. Cam-
       bridge: Harvard University Press, 1930. Includes brief
       studies of Margaret Baxter, Margaret Godolphin, Margaret
       Cavendish, Lady Fanshawe, and Anne Halkett.

222   Tinker, Chauncey Brewster. The Salon and English Letters.
       New York: MacMillan, 1915. The author treats the ori-
       gin of French and English salons and mentions Mrs. Mon-
       tagu, the Bluestockings, and Fanny Burney.

223   Tucker, William J. "Great English Letter Writers."
       Catholic World, 143 (1936), 695-701. A survey with
       some mention of Lady Mary Wortley Montagu.

224   Backscheider, Paula R. "Defoe's Women: Snares and Prey."
      Studies in Eighteenth Century Culture. Ed. Ronald C. Ros-
      bottom. Madison: University of Wisconsin Press, 1976.
      V, 103-120. Although Defoe's women are victimized by a
      society inhospitable to unmarried women, they are not in-
      tended to be models for behavior. Defoe's conduct books
      provide a guide to judging characters in the novels.

225   Hemlow, Joyce. "The Courtesy Book Element in Fanny Bur-
      ney's Works." Radcliffe dissertation, 1948. Burney used
      courtesy book material extensively in her novels.

226   Hemlow, Joyce. "Fanny Burney and the Courtesy Books."
      PMLA, 65 (1950), 732-761. The "age of courtesy books for
      women' began with the publication of Lord Chesterfield's
      Letters to his Son. This article explains their rise,
      ranks the major conduct books by their popularity, and
      assesses their content and influence. The conduct books
      presented and defended a double standard of morals and
      manners. Burney accepts the code for women but demands
      more for men. Camilla should be understood and judged
      as a "courtesy novel," a sub-genre.

227   Hodges, James. "The Female Spectator, A Courtesy Periodi-
      cal." Studies in the Early English Periodical. Ed. Rich-
      mond P. Bond. Chapel Hill: University of North Carolina
      Press, 1957. 151-182. The Female Spectator's advice is
      strikingly similar to that of the conduct books. It is
      highly practical and recognizes the realities of problems
      as shown by examples from Eliza Haywood's discussion of
      love, marriage, education and social behavior.

228   Hornbeak, Katherine. Richardson's Familiar Letters and
      the Domestic Conduct Books. Northampton, Mass: Smith
      College Studies in Modern Languages, 1938. XIX. In "spirit
      and content" Richardson's Letters Written to and for Particu-
      lar Friends is closer to domestic conduct books than to
      other guides for letter writing. His novels consider and
      adapt conduct book material, and his last work Moral and
      Instructive Sentiments is a more conventional conduct book.

229   Larned, J. N. A Multitude of Counsellors. Being a Collec-
      tion of Codes, Precepts, and Rules of Life from the Wise
      of All Ages. New York: Houghton, Mifflin, 1901. This
      collection of admonitory documents displays the precepts

of a variety of social classes and societies throughout world history. Selections from such writers as Halifax, Fenelon, Chesterfield, and Chatham and a topical index are included.

230   Mason, John E. Gentlefolk in the Making: Studies in the History of English Courtesy Literature and Related Topics from 1531 to 1774. Philadelphia: University of Pennsylvania Press, 1935. Courtesy Books record the ethical and social norms for gentlemen and women. Although not even the best (Locke's, Chesterfield's) were original, certain types (parental advice, education) and a few examples (Braithwait's Gentleman, Gregory's Advice to his Daughters) had great influence and marked changes in social norms.

231   Noyes, Gertrude E. Bibliography of Courtesy and Conduct Books in Seventeenth Century England. New Haven: privately printed, 1937.

232   Quinlan, Maurice. Victorian Prelude: A History of English Manners, 1700-1830. Hamden, Connecticut: Archon Books, 1965. The chapter, "The Model Female," discusses Mary Wollstonecraft, Hannah More, and turn of the century conduct books.

233   Wilkinson, D. R. M. The Comedy of Habit: An Essay on the Use of Courtesy Literature in a Study of Restoration Comic Drama. Leiden: Universitaire Pers, 1964. Conduct books such as Osbourne's Advice to a Son provide normative standards of judgment applicable to characters, situations, and dialogue.

234   Alleman, Gillert S. <u>Matrimonial</u> <u>Law</u> <u>and</u> <u>the</u> <u>Material</u>
      <u>of</u> <u>Restoration</u> <u>Comedy</u>. Wallingford, Pennsylvania: no
      publisher, 1942. See item #5.

235   Anon. "Costumes a la Mode." <u>Theatre</u> <u>Arts</u> <u>Monthly</u>, 10
      (1926), 471. Portraits of actresses dressed for parts
      in Shakespeare productions.

236   Anon. "Lavinia Fenton." <u>Bookman</u>, 44 (1913), 217. Very
      short biography.

237   Avery, Emmett. "Two French Children on the English
      Stage, 1716-1719." <u>PQ</u>, 13 (1934), 78-82. Marie Sallé
      performed a number of popular dances and a burlesque
      on the London stage in 1716 and 1717. Her success tes-
      tifies to the popularity of "novelties" and types of
      dance interludes.

238   B., W. C. "Mrs. Booth, Actress." <u>N&Q</u>, 151 (1911), 146-
      147. The Rev. Joseph Benson announced the conversion
      and "happy death" of Mrs. Booth.

239   Bayley, A. R., and William Jaggard. "Helena in <u>All's</u>
      <u>Well</u> <u>That</u> <u>Ends</u> <u>Well</u>." <u>N&Q</u>, 181 (1941), 122. Helena
      became associated with superstition after a 1742 per-
      formance was followed by sickness and death. A number
      of actresses, however, played the part.

240   Bennett, Gilbert. "Conventions of the Stage Villain."
      <u>The</u> <u>Anglo-Welsh</u> <u>Review</u>, 14 (1964), 92-102. Increasingly
      the villain could be recognized by set speeches and
      conventional actions in early eighteenth century drama.
      Examples from the plays of Centlivre and Manley are in-
      cluded.

241   Berkeley, David S. <u>The</u> <u>Precieuse</u>, <u>or</u> <u>Distressed</u> <u>Heroine</u>,
      <u>in</u> <u>Restoration</u> <u>Comedy</u>. Stillwater: Oklahoma State U.
      Publications, 1959. Between 1660 and 1700, sentimental
      episodes were replaced by the tradition of sentimental
      comedy. The defining and counting of the type known as
      the "distressed heroine" help establish the growing
      sentimentalism.

242   Bode, Robert F. "A Study of the Development of the Theme
      of Love and Duty in English Comedy from Charles I to
      George I." University of South Carolina dissertation,

1970. Plays demonstrate changes in ideas about and in the treatment of love and duty.

243   Borkat, Roberta S. "The Cage of Custom." University of Dayton Review, 10 (1974), 47-57. The prescribed qualities of the ideal woman were obedience, chastity, and beauty.

244   Boswell, Eleanore. "Wycherley and the Countess of Drogheda." TLS, 28 November 1929, pp. 1001-1002. Investigation into the documents in the Public Record Office concerning Barnaby v. Wycherley suggests that Mrs. Barnaby's case was more sound than Hargest admits and that she probably got her money before Wycherley was sent to the Fleet in 1685.

245   Bowers, Fredson. "Underprinting in Mary Pix, The Spanish Wives (1696)." Library, 5th series, ix (1954), 248-254. Seventeenth century running-titles can be substituted for eighteenth century press figures as bibliographical evidence of reimpression especially in cases in which underprinting to speed publications was used.

246   Bradbrook, Frank. "Lydia Languish, Lydia Bennett, and Dr. Fordyce's Sermons." N&Q, 209 (1964), 421-423. Dr. Fordyce's Sermons for Young Women provoked a variety of responses from women writers.

247   Brooking, Cecil. "Actresses on the Tiles." N&Q, 179 (1940), 330-334. Brief biographies of Abington, Barry, Ward, Yates, Hartley, Kemble, Cibber, and Mattocks, the actresses who appear on Sadler's delft tiles, are given without notes.

248   Bruce, Donald. Topics of Restoration Comedy. New York: St. Martin's Press, 1974. Rather than laughing at or advocating licentiousness, Restoration comedy debates serious moral issues such as artificiality, the "new woman," and divorce. Aphra Behn's plays, for instance, depict a "dark moral comedy" like her own life. Her heroines are competitive and dominant, representative of the shift to the heroine-centered plays of the Restoration.

249   Brustein, Robert. "The Monstrous Regiment of Women: Sources for the Satiric View of the Court Lady in English

Drama." <u>Renaissance</u> and <u>Modern</u> <u>Essays</u>, G. R. Hibbard, ed. New York: Barnes and Noble, 1966. See item # 28.

250   Burnim, Kalman A. "'Here We Go Round the Mulberry Bush'--with Dr. Arne and Nancy Dawson." <u>RECTR</u>, 4 (1965), 39-48. In October 1759, Nancy Dawson replaced Miles as the hornpipe dancer in <u>The</u> <u>Beggar's</u> <u>Opera</u> and her fortune was made. A variety of versions of "The Ballad of Nancy Dawson" were written to the tune of "Here We Go Round the Mulberry Bush."

251   Burnim, Kalman A. "Nancy Dawson's Tombstone." <u>RECTR</u>, 5 (1966), 59. Her tombstone is the largest in St. George's Gardens. Stories that the legend "Nancy Dawson was a W---e" was carved on it are probably false.

252   Burwash, Ida. "English Play-Actresses from Anne to Victoria." <u>The</u> <u>Canadian</u> <u>Magazine</u>, 38 (1912), 261-271. Some actresses who worked with Garrick and Betterton achieved great success because of their help and influence.

253   Bushnell, George H. "The Original Lady Randolph." <u>The-</u> <u>atre</u> <u>Notebook</u>, 13 (1959), 119-123. Sarah Ward appeared in Edinburgh in 1756 in <u>Douglas</u>.

254   Carter, Herbert. "Three Women Dramatists of the Restoration." <u>Bookman's</u> <u>Journal</u>, 13 (1925), 91-97. In the context of a discussion of the position of women, the author outlines the careers of Manley, Pix, and Trotter.

255   Coleman, Antony. "'The Provok'd Wife' and 'The Ladies Defence.'" <u>N&Q</u>, 215 (1970), 88-91. Mary Chudleigh wrote <u>The</u> <u>Ladies</u> <u>Defence</u> to answer the criticisms about women made by the Rev. Sprint in a wedding sermon. She borrowed Sir John Brute from Vanbrugh's <u>Provok'd</u> <u>Wife</u> but changed the mode from the realistic to the sentimental.

256   Collins, Charles W. <u>Great</u> <u>Love</u> <u>Stories</u> <u>of</u> <u>the</u> <u>Theatre</u>: <u>A</u> <u>Record</u> <u>of</u> <u>Theatrical</u> <u>Romance</u>. London: Duffield, 1911. Popular account of notorious love affairs (Charles II and Nell Gwynn, for instance) involving actresses.

257   Crundell, H. W. "Actors and Actresses in xviii-c. Comedy." <u>N&Q</u>, 180 (1941), 44-45. The tradition of males taking minor female parts persisted throughout the century.

258 Dacier, Émile. Mlle. Sallé (1707-1756), une danseuse de l'Opéra sous Louis XV. Paris: Librairie Plon, 1909. A biography of Marie Sallé has chapters on her career on the London stage, her teachers and admirers, and her techniques.

259 Dammers, Richard H. "Female Characters and Feminine Morality in the Tragedies of Nicholas Rowe." University of Notre Dame dissertation, 1971. Rowe's plays portray married women and their importance in determining happiness and tranquility. The women characters are vehicles for the moral themes.

260 Dark, Sidney. Twelve More Ladies: Good, Bad, and Indifferent. Freeport, New York: Books for Libraries Press, 1969. Popular biographies including one of Nell Gwynn.

261 Doty, Gresdna. "Anne Brunton in Bath and London." Theatre Survey, 8 (1967), 53-65. A biographical survey of her life with special attention to her London debut and her career in America.

262 Eddison, Robert. "Topless in Jerusalem." Theatre Notebook, 22 (1967), 24-27. Susannah Cibber was a hit in Aaron Hill's Zara which ran fifteen consecutive nights in 1736. Her clothing and acting style are described.

263 Edmunds, J. M. "An Example of Early Sentimentalism." Modern Language Notes, 48 (1933), 94-97. Mary Griffith Pix's The Spanish Wives has sentimental touches.

264 Engel, Glorianne. "The Comic Actor in the Age of Garrick: His Style and Craftsmanship." University of Pittsburgh dissertation, 1967. Contemporary acting treatises and criticism provide background for the discussions of nine comic players including Kitty Clive, Peg Woffington, and Mrs. Abington.

265 Fothergill, Brian. Mrs. Jordan: Portrait of an Actress. London: Faber & Faber, 1965. A biography of Dorothy Jordan.

266 Fyvie, John. Comedy Queens of the Georgian Era. New York: Dutton, 1907. Brief biographies based on contemporary memoirs include Charke, Woffington, Bellamy, and others.

267 Fyvie, John. _Tragedy Queens of the Georgian Era_. New
York: Dutton; London: Methuen, 1909. Sketches of the
careers of actresses such as Bracegirdle, Oldfield,
Inchbald, and Siddons.

268 Gagen, Jean. "Congreve's Mirabell and the Ideal of the
Gentleman." _PMLA_, 79 (1964), 422-427. Mirabell embodies
the ideal of a gentleman. He has the "exterior accom-
plishments," ease in conversation, control of his passions,
and respect for a virtuous woman. His behavior toward
women was within the accepted norm of his time.

269 Gagen, Jean. _The New Woman: Her Emergence in English
Drama, 1660-1730_. New York: Twayne, 1954. Drama illustrates attitudes toward the "new woman" who insisted on
studying, learning, and making decisions. The dramatists
thoroughly examined, satirized, and established such type
characters as the learned lady, the Amazon, and the fashionable woman between 1600 and 1730.

270 Gale, Fred R. "Canning's Mother and the Stage." _N&Q_,
167 (1929), 183-185 and 201-204. Mary Ann Canning's
career (1773-1791).

271 Gilder, Rosamond. _Enter the Actress; the First Woman
in the Theatre_. London: Harrap, 1931. The reception
of actresses led to a number of revealing incidents.

272 Gilder, Rosamond. "Enter Ianthe, Veil'd." _Theatre
Arts Monthly_, 11 (1927), 49-58. The first serious heroic
part for a woman was Ianthe in Davenant's _The Siege of
Rhodes_. Discusses early parts played by women.

273 Gore-Brown, Robert. _Gay was the Pit: The Life and Times
of Anne Oldfield, Actress (1683-1730)_. London: Max
Reinhardt, 1957. This biography of Anne Oldfield, the
"most beautiful woman who ever trod the boards," describes
the theatre as Oldfield knew it, her acquaintances, and
contemporary reactions to her performances and appearance.

274 Gorowara, Krishna K. "The Treatment of Unmarried Women
in Comedy, 1584-1921." Glasgow University dissertation,
1962. Useful comparative study.

275 Gray, Charles H. _Theatrical Criticism in London to 1795_.
New York: Benjamin Blom, 1964. This is a chronological

collection of reactions to plays and performances, 1730-1795.

276   Greene, Godfrey. "Mrs. Sarah Gardner: A Further Note." _Theatre Notebook_, 8 (1953), 6-10. The press notices of Sarah Gardner's _The Advertisement_ and biographical data give insight into her behavior and personality.

277   Grice, F., and A. Clarke. "Mrs. Sarah Gardner." _Theatre Notebook_, 7 (1953), 76-81. A large manuscript book by Sarah Gardner contains provocative comments on the theatre as well as some of her literary works. Gardner's account of the single performance of _The Advertisement_ condemns Colman and describes an extraordinary interaction between audience, playwright, and actors.

278   Halsband, Robert. "The Noble Lady and the Player." _History Today_, 18 (1968), 464-472. Lady Henrietta Herbert scandalized her family by marrying the tenor and actor, John Beard. Their life was one of financial worry and loving regard.

279   Hargest, W. G. "Wycherley and the Countess of Drogheda." _TLS_, 21 November 1929, p. 960. Among the law costs and debts that finally sent Wycherley to debtor's prison were those he was ordered to pay after the death of his wife, the Countess, to her waiting-woman, Mrs. Sara Barnaby, who had won a lengthy chancery suit against the couple for non-payment of debts.

280   Hawkins, Harriet. _Likeness of Truth in Elizabethan and Restoration Drama_. Oxford: Clarendon, 1972. Elizabethan and Restoration plays explore the human experience. The plays present the ambiguities in situations and in motives and elicited varied responses from the audience.

281   Heltzel, Virgil B. _Fair Rosamond: A Study in the Development of a Literary Theme_. Evanston: Northwestern University Press, 1947. The book traces the treatment of the story in works such as Addison's opera.

282   Highfill, Philip, Jr., Kalman A. Burnim, and Edward A. Langhans. _A Biographical Dictionary of Actors, Actresses, Musicians, Dancers, Managers, and Other Stage Personnel in London, 1660-1800_. Carbondale: Southern Illinois University Press, 1973. See item #87.

283   Hodgson, Norma. "Sarah Baker 1736/7-1816: 'Gover-
      ness-general of the Kentish Drama.'" Studies in English
      Theatre History in Memory of Gabrielle Enthoven. Lon-
      don: Society for Theatre Research, 1952, pp. 65-83.
      Sarah Baker was one of the most successful circuit
      proprietors of her time. She established ten theatres,
      depended upon the support of ordinary townspeople, and
      provided plays, scenery, and costumes designed to please
      her audiences throughout her eventful life.

284   Hogan, Charles B. "A Note on Miss Nossiter." Shakes-
      peare Quarterly, 3 (1952), 284-285. Brief biography.

285   Hook, Lucyle. Introduction to The Female Wits, ARS #
      124. Los Angeles: Clark Library, 1967. The play sa-
      tirizes plays by women, especially Delariviere Manley's
      The Royal Mischief. Satires of Manley, Mary Pix, and
      Catharine Cockburn and of acting techniques allow in-
      sight into theatrical practices and personalities.

286   Hook, Lucyle. "Portraits of Elizabeth Barry and Anne
      Bracegirdle." Theatre Notebook, 15 (1961), 129-137.
      Kneller's emblematic portraits of the actresses in the
      equestrian picture of William III were painted from
      life. The author discusses a number of other portraits
      of the women.

287   Howarth, R. C. "Congreve and Anne Bracegirdle." English
      Studies in Africa, 4 (1961), 159-161. There is no evi-
      dence that Anne Bracegirdle was Congreve's mistress.

288   Hughes, Leo. The Drama's Patrons: A Study of the Eigh-
      teenth Century London Audience. Austin: University of
      Texas Press, 1970. The drama patrons were those who at-
      tended plays. The book examines the extent and means of
      their influence. Women's reactions contributed to chang-
      ing tastes.

289   Hunt, Hugh. "Restoration Acting" in Restoration Theatre,
      John Russell Brown and Bernard Harris, eds. London: Ed-
      ward Arnold and New York: St. Martin's Press, 1965, pp.
      179-192. Immediately after Charles II granted the patents
      making actresses the rule in the theatre, it was diffi-
      cult to acquire and train them. They were an immediate
      success, however, and provided the impetus for a number
      of changes in characterization, plot, and social behavior.
      The acting companies maintained "nurseries" in which young
      players were taught singing, dancing, stance, speech,

gesture, and the tragic and comic acting modes.

290   Izard, Forrest. Heroines of the Modern Stage. New
      York: Sturgis, 1915. Includes an essay on the first
      actresses.

291   Kaufman, Anthony. "'A Libertine Woman of Condition':
      Congreve's 'Doris.'" YES, 3 (1973), 120-123. Doris
      shares the dilemma of the "intelligent woman in a male-
      dominated society." Her solution protects her but
      leaves her heartless and sterile.

292   Kaufman, Anthony. "'This Hard Condition of a Woman's
      Fate': Southerne's The Wives Excuse." Modern Language
      Quarterly, 34 (1973), 36-47. Southerne uses precise
      language, noticeably lacking in wit, to present the
      position of the wife in the seventeenth century.

293   Klinger, George C. "English She-Tragedy, 1680-1715:
      Its Characteristics and Its Relationship to the Senti-
      mental Tradition." Columbia University dissertation,
      1970. The she-tragedies were a fairly well defined
      variation of sentimental tragedy by 1715. The author
      identifies four characteristics of these plays, identi-
      fies their antecedents, and the forces which brought
      them to prominence, and discusses a few of the most
      important examples.

294   Lanier, Henry W. The First English Actresses, from the
      Initial Appearance of Women on the Stage in 1660 till
      1700. New York: The Players, 1930. The first actresses
      came from varied backgrounds and represented various per-
      sonalities. Such women as Bracegirdle gave "dignity"
      to the profession.

295   Larson, Martin A. "The Influence of Milton's Divorce
      Tracts on Farquhar's Beaux' Stratagem." PMLA, 39 (1924),
      174-178. The material, ideas, and language of The
      Beaux' Stratagem concerning divorce was taken directly
      from Milton's Doctrine and Discipline of Divorce. The
      source attests to the seriousness of the theme.

296   Lightfoot, John E. "The Treatment of Women in Restora-
      tion Comedy of Manners." Texas Tech. dissertation, 1973.
      Etherege, Wycherley, and Congreve granted their women
      characters more social freedom and more intelligence

than did contemporary society. The first chapter describes the position of women.

297   Macqueen-Pope, W. Ladies First: The Story of Woman's
      Conquest of the British Stage. London: W. H. Allen,
      1952. The lives and personalities of the women who
      pioneered as actresses illuminate the contemporary
      theatre and the influence that women had on English
      drama. Such forgotten women as Margaret Hughes and
      Mrs. Long joined such immortals as Nell Gwynn in break-
      ing ground and establishing traditions.

298   Marinacci, Barbara. Leading Ladies, A Gallery of Fa-
      mous Actresses. New York: Dodd, Mead, 1961. The
      author traces the lives and careers of eleven repre-
      sentative actresses including Mary Betterton.

299   Martia, Dominic F. "The Restoration Love Ethos and
      the Representation of Love in the Plays of William
      Wycherley." Loyola University, Chicago, dissertation,
      1972. The "Restoration love ethos" was Hobbesian,
      skeptical, and based on court behavior during the
      reign of Charles II. Wycherley's plays show a grow-
      ing condemnation of this "love ethos."

300   McPharlin, Paul. "Boy-actors Playing Women's Parts."
      N&Q, 155 (1928), 304. Boys playing female roles seems
      to have been general practice in Portugal.

301   Melville, Lewis (pseud. Lewis Saul Benjamin). More
      Stage Favorites of the Eighteenth Century. London:
      Hutchinson, 1929. See item #121.

302   Melville, Lewis (pseud. Lewis Saul Benjamin). Stage
      Favorites of the Eighteenth Century. Garden City:
      Doubleday, 1929. See item #122.

303   Metcalf, Cranstown. Peeresses of the Stage. London:
      Melrose, 1913. Anastasia Robinson, Lavinia Fenton, and
      Elizabeth Farren were actresses who married nobility.

304   Mignon, Elizabeth. Crabbed Age and Youth: The Old
      Men and Women in the Restoration Comedy of Manners.
      Durham, North Carolina: Duke University Press, 1947.
      The most predictable characters in Restoration comedy
      are the aged. The analysis of these characters in the
      plays of the major Restoration playwrights through
      Farquhar shows few exceptions and an unremittingly

hostile attitude. The author suggests reasons and relates the treatment of the aged to the society.

305   Moore, J. R. "Lydia Languish's Library." N&Q, 202
      (1957), 76. The conflict over the young woman's choice
      of books in The Rivals was anticipated in Defoe's Re-
      ligious Courtship and The Family Instructor.

306   Morris, David B. "Language and Honor in The Country
      Wife." South Atlantic Bulletin, 37 (1972), 3-10. The
      Country Wife and much seventeenth century drama is
      about honor. Corruption of language symbolizes the
      corruption of honor; honor is no longer associated
      with virtue and words deceive.

307   Morrissey, LeRoy J. "The Erotic Pursuit: Changing
      Fashions in Eroticism in Early Eighteenth Century Eng-
      lish Comic Drama." University of Pennsylvania disser-
      tation, 1964. By mid-century, eroticism was sentimen-
      talized and suggested; the erotic conventions of the
      early eighteenth century had been modified or replaced.

308   Mukherjee, Sujit. "Marriage as Punishment in the Plays
      of Wycherley." Review of English Literature (Leeds),
      7 (1966), 61-64. Marriage frequently functions as the
      means of ending Wycherley's plays with poetic justice
      and is often punishment.

309   Nickles, Mary A. "The Women in Congreve's Comedies:
      Characters and Caricatures." New York University dis-
      sertation, 1973. The characters of Araminta, Angelica,
      and Millamant show that Congreve understood the "dilem-
      ma of the Restoration female." The social context, the
      supporting characters, and the changes in characteriza-
      tion of women as well as later treatment of Congreve's
      women provide evidence. Appendices include statistics
      on performances.

310   Novak, Maximillian E. "Love, Scandal, and the Moral
      Milieu of Congreve's Comedies" in Congreve Consider'd.
      Papers Read at a Clark Library Seminar, December 5,
      1970. Los Angeles: Clark Library, 1971. The "moral
      ideal for Congreve's comedies is a profound, private
      understanding and lasting love between two people of
      wit and sensibility." Congreve's presentation of the
      ideal had greater impact because it was set in a time

of scandal and adultery. Comparison with ordinary plays illustrates society's concern and Congreve's differences.

311   Noyes, Robert G., and Roy Lanson, Jr. "Broadside-ballad Versions of the Songs in Restoration Drama." <u>Harvard Studies and Notes in Philology and Literature</u>, 19 (1937), 199-218. The broadside ballad versions of songs from plays were expanded by hack writers by addition of concrete details, narrative elements, dialogue or by transforming them into question-answer form. The number of ballads based on the song gives an index to the popularity of such songs as Behn's "Ah Jenny gen your eyes do kill."

312   Parnell, Paul E. "<u>The Distrest Mother</u>, Ambrose Philips' Morality Play." <u>Comparative Literature</u>, 11 (1959), 111-123. Philips' adaptation of Andromaque simplified characterization, increased emotional impact, and emphasized the moral lessons. Hermione, for instance, becomes the conventional "ruined-girl" and Andromache is completely virtuous. What Philips did was consistent with his conception of art and with the English idea of the nature of the battle between the sexes.

313   Pearce, Charles E. <u>The Jolly Duchess: Harriot Mellon, Afterwards Mrs. Coults and the Duchess of St. Albans</u>. London: Stanley Paul, 1915. A description of her acting career is set in the milieu of the theatrical world.

314   Pitou, Von Spire. "Corneille, Racine, and Mlle. Barbier's <u>Le Faucon</u> (1719)." <u>Zeitschrift für französische Sprache und Literatur</u>, 80 (1970), 44-50. No other eighteenth century comedy by a woman achieved the acceptance of <u>Le Faucon</u>, an adaptation of the <u>Decameron</u>, v, 9, with elements of parody of well known tragedies by Racine and Corneille.

315   Raeburn, Eleanor. "Early Feminine Dramatists." <u>Theatre</u>, 18 (1913), 194-196. Short summaries of the careers of such women as Cavendish, Behn, and Trotter.

316   Robins, Edward. <u>Twelve Great Actresses</u>. New York: G. P. Putnam, 1900. Brief biographies of actresses including Anne Bracegirdle, Peg Woffington, and Mary Robinson.

317   Rodway, Allan. "Restoration Comedy Re-examined." <u>Renaissance and Modern Studies</u>, 16 (1972), 37-60. Restoration drama makes consistent attempts at evaluating

contemporary assumptions about courtships, marriage, and sexual morality.

318   Rogers, Francis. "Handel and the Five Prima Donnas." _Musical Quarterly_, 29 (1943), 214-224. Careers of actresses who appeared in Handel roles including Susannah Cibber for whom he wrote the role of Galatea.

319   Rogers, Francis. "Some Prima Donnas of the Latter Eighteenth Century." _Musical Quarterly_, 30 (1944), 147-162. Descriptions of Caterina Gabrielli, Lucresia Agujari, Elizabeth Bellington, Guiseppina Grassini, and Angelica Catalarie.

320   Rosenbalm, John O. "The Restoration Players: Their Performances and Personalities." North Texas State University dissertation, 1974. Restoration actors and actresses influenced playwrights considerably. Information on roles, ability, personality, and appearance when important for the actors and actresses in Part I of the _London Stage_ allows surmises about performances and the operation of the theatres.

321   Rosenfeld, Sybil. _Strolling Players and Drama in the Provinces, 1660-1765_. Cambridge: University Press, 1939. By 1765, playhouses were being built all through the provinces, and drama was respectable and well established. The strolling players of the previous one hundred years are an essential element in understanding the history of drama.

322   Rowan, D. F. "Shore's Wife." _SEL_, 6 (1966), 447-464. The author traces the popular and literary treatment of Jane Shore from her own time through 1714 (the year in which Rowe's _Tragedy of Jane Shore_ was produced).

323   Rubin, Barbara L. "'Anti-Husbandry' and Self-Creation: A Comparison of Restoration Rake and Baudelaire's Dandy." _Texas Studies in Language and Literature_, 14 (1972), 583-592. Restoration comedy "is a radical overturning of the comic norms," substituting a view of marriage as a sacrifice of self for a sign of adulthood and community stability. The rake is the logical creation of such a view.

324   Sawyer, Paul. "The Garrick-Mrs. Cibber Relationship." _N&Q_, 205 (1960), 303-305. David Garrick and Susannah Cibber were jealous of each others' popularity, and

Garrick was unwilling to produce a play in which his
role was not outstanding.

325   Schermerhorn, Karen R. "Women in Wycherley: Their
       Role in His Social Criticism." University of Minne-
       sota dissertation, 1974. Wycherley's women illustrate
       the changes in women's roles during the Restoration.
       Women are in active, problem solving, as well as exem-
       plary roles in the plays.

326   Schneider, Ben R. "The Coquette-Prude as an Actress's
       Line in Restoration Comedy during the Time of Mrs. Old-
       field." Theatre Notebook, 22 (1968), 143-156. A sur-
       vey of the actresses who played in eighty-three come-
       dies between 1660 and 1715 shows that eighteen out of
       one hundred seventy actresses monopolized the "coquette
       prude" line. The coquette-prude displayed a set of
       characteristics, yet there were several types of co-
       quette prudes within the overall profile. Knowledge
       of the dramatis personae may help interpret character.

327   Shafer, Yvonne B. "The Proviso Scene in Restoration
       Comedy." RECTR, 9 (1970), 1-10. The "proviso scene,"
       a witty duel to establish the conditions for marriage,
       has its roots in seventeenth century drama and possibly
       D'Urfey's L'Astree. It reveals a number of attitudes
       toward love and marriage. The four types of proviso
       scenes are those in which the heroine makes all the
       demands, those which invert conventions for comic ef-
       fect, those in which the lovers want personal freedom,
       and those which are a serious attempt to insure lasting
       love.

328   Simpson, Harold and Mrs. Charles Braun. A Century of
       Famous Actresses, 1750-1850. New York: Benjamin Blom,
       1971. A series of character studies of the greatest
       actresses selects dramatic events from their lives
       which epitomize their personalities, reputations, and
       life-styles.

329   Smith, John H. The Gay Couple in Restoration Comedy.
       Cambridge: Harvard University Press, 1948. The "gay
       couple," the hero and heroine whose courtship is an
       amusing game, exemplify the theory and practices of
       comedy and provide a barometer for society's moods. The
       changes in their characterization and behavior parallel
       changes in English drama and society.

330   Smith, John H. "Shadwell, the Ladies and Change in
       Comedy." MP, 46 (1948), 22-33. Comedy at the turn of
       the century replaced satire and realism with an empha-
       sis on reform and "standards as they ought to be, per-
       sonified in characters who should be examples for imi-
       tation." The new comic method was established by 1688-
       89 as the result of Shadwell's plays and the tastes of
       respectable female patrons of the theatre.

331   Speaight, George. The History of the English Puppet
       Theatre. London: Harrap, 1955. English puppet shows
       were popular with courtiers and servants. This history
       characterizes the audience, the shows, and the people
       who managed them including Charlotte Charke.

332   Stoll, Elmer E. "The'Real Society' in Restoration Come-
       dy: Hymeneal Pretenses." MLN, 58 (1943), 175-181. Dis-
       guise, impersonation, gullibility, blindness, slander,
       and forgery are the stuff of comedy. The "hymeneal
       pretenses" of Restoration comedy belong to dramatic
       convention, not to realistic portraits of society.

333   Stone, George Winchester, Jr. "The Authorship of A
       Letter to Miss Nossiter." Shakespeare Quarterly, 3 (1952),
       69-70. MacNamara Morgan wrote a pamphlet praising Maria
       Nossiter's stage debut in the role of Juliet (1753).

334   Suwannabha, Sumitra. "The Feminine Eye: Augustan So-
       ciety as Seen by Selected Women Dramatists of the Res-
       toration and Early Eighteenth Century." Indiana Univer-
       sity dissertation, 1973. Using the plays of Cavendish,
       Pix, Centlivre, Behn, and Haywood, the author describes
       a feminine perspective of the early eighteenth century.

335   Tasch, Peter A. "Garrick's Revisions of Bickerstaff's
       The Sultan." PQ, 50 (1971), 141-149. The changes in
       the play made between 1772 and 1775 are the result of
       compromises between Garrick and the actress Frances
       Abington who owned the play's copyright and played the
       lead. Public reaction dictated additional alterations.
       The article is a revealing example of the influence of
       player, manager, and audience.

336   Thaler, Alwin. "Strolling Players and Provincial Drama
       after Shakespeare." PMLA, 37 (1922), 243-280. Traveling
       companies brought great actors and new plays as well as
       rag-tag productions to the provinces. Mrs. Siddons and
       Mrs. Inchbald were among the women who earned their spurs

in country productions. Understanding provincial theatre
is essential for understanding drama in the period.

337   Tierney, James E. "Cibber's The Careless Husband." Ex-
      plicator, 32 (1973), 3. Lady Easy wins her husband back
      by exercising the expected virtues of the eighteenth-
      century woman. A fashionable piece of clothing, the
      steinkirk, had both dramatic and thematic significance
      for Cibber's audience.

338   Tisdall, E. E. P. Mrs. "Pimpernel" Atkyns: The Strange
      Story of a Drury Lane Actress Who Was the Only Heroine
      of the French Revolution. London: Jarrolds, 1965. This
      popular biography focuses on her revolutionary activities
      and her relationships to Sheridan and Garrick.

339   Troubridge, St. Vincent. "Helena in All's Well That Ends
      Well." N&Q, 181 (1941), 109-110. A number of famous
      actresses including Woffington and Jordan played the
      part of Helena.

340   Vernon, P. F. "Marriage of Convenience and the Moral
      Code of Restoration Comedy." Essays in Criticism, 12
      (1962), 370-387. Restoration comedy assumes a consistent
      moral framework.

341   Vieth, David M. "Wycherley's The Country Wife: An Anato-
      my of Masculinity." Papers on Language and Literature,
      2 (1966), 335-350. The Country Wife's central purpose
      is to define masculinity. The Sparkish plot represents
      the classical concept of virtue as the mean between the
      vices represented by the Pinchwife and Fidget plots. The
      relationship between word and object underscores theme.

342   Vince, Stanley W. E. "Camargo in London 1750-1754."
      Theatre Notebook, 12 (1958), 26-27. Marie-Anne Cupis
      de Camargo's younger sister danced in London from 1750-
      1754. Her reception was much cooler than that accorded
      Marie-Anne in the 1730's.

343   Vince, Stanley W. E. "Marie Sallé, 1707-1756." Theatre
      Notebook, 12 (1957), 7-14. Marie Sallé contributed sig-
      nificantly to the development of ballet, including cos-
      tuming and dramatic mime. She was well received in Lon-
      don. The essay summarizes her life.

344 Weil, Dorothy L. "Susanna Rowson, The Young Lady's Friend." University of Cincinnati dissertation, 1974. This is a biographical and critical study of Susanna Rowson.

345 Wheatley, Katherine E. "Andromacque as the 'Distrest Mother.'" _Romanic Review_, 39 (1948), 3-21. The Distrest Mother is not a faithful adaptation of _Andromache_. English poetic style and demand for "drama bourgeois" transform Racine's psychological drama into virtue rewarded.

346 Wiley, Autrey Nell. "Female Prologues and Epilogues in English Plays." _PMLA_, 48 (1933), 1060-1079. Over 200 plays before 1714 had "She-Prologues" or prologues and epilogues and, by 1711, "she-prologues" were so much the vogue that burlesques of them were common. The popularity of the form was explained by the actress's ability to use feminine pleas and coquettry to persuade. The pieces for women were usually on the following topics: adjuring or conjuring, occasional, begging, challenging, preaching, or merry. Actresses like Mrs. Bracegirdle had numerous pieces written for them and earned considerable acclaim.

347 Wilkinson, D. R. M. _The Comedy of Habit: An Essay on the Use of Courtesy Literature in a Study of Restoration Comic Drama_. Leiden: Universitaire Pers, 1964. See item #233.

348 Williams, Aubrey. "The 'Just Decrees of Heav'n' and Congreve's _Mourning Bride_" in _Congreve Consider'd. Papers Read at a Clark Library Seminar, December 5, 1970_. Los Angeles: Clark Library, 1971. The opinion that Congreve's plays were immoral and naturalistic is refuted by the plays themselves and by a number of Congreve's contemporaries. _The Mourning Bride_ displays the "patterns of piety" praised by Dryden and other critics.

349 Williams, Gordon. "The Sex-Death Motive in Otway's _Venice Preserv'd_." _Trivium_, 2 (1967), 59-70. Belvidera "woos a spurious martyrdom at the hands of her husband" and mingles murder with rape fantasies. Otway used the character and imagery to relate individual complexity and passion to the nature and overthrow of the state.

350 Wilson, John Harold. _All the King's Ladies: Actresses of the Restoration_. Chicago: University of Chicago

Press, 1958. The author characterizes the women who
became actresses between 1660 and 1689, discusses their
working conditions, their behavior, contemporary reaction to them, and their impact on English drama. An
appendix summarizes the actresses' careers.

351   Wilson, John Harold. "Biographical Notes on Some Res-
      toration Actresses." Theatre Notebook, 18 (1964), 43-
      47. Supplements biographical information in the appen-
      dix to his All the King's Ladies.

352   Wilson, John Harold. "Etherege's Julia." MLN, 62
      (1947), 40-42. There is no evidence that Etherege
      was involved with an actress named Julia. The single
      reference to "Julia" in his letters is an Ovidian al-
      lusion.

353   Wilson, John Harold. "Lord Oxford's 'Roxalana.'" The-
      atre Notebook, 12 (1957), 14-16. Hester Davenport,
      "Roxalana," left the stage in 1662 to marry Aubrey de
      Vere, twentieth Earl of Oxford. After a mock marriage,
      she demanded justice and was paid a pension. She con-
      tinued to insist that she was Countess of Oxford.

354   Wilson, John Harold. "The Marshall Sisters and Anne
      Quin." N&Q, 202 (1957), 104-106. The older Marshall
      sister used the name "Anne Quin" while the younger
      appeared as"Mrs. Marshall."

355   Wilson, John Harold. "Pepys and Peg Hughes." N&Q, 201
      (1956), 428-429. Pepys probably kissed Margaret Hughes
      backstage at the King's Theatre 7 May 1668.

356   Woods, Charles B. "The 'Miss Lucy' Plays of Fielding
      and Garrick." PQ, 41 (1962), 294-310. Garrick and
      Fielding's close friendship may have produced a collab-
      orative effort, Miss Lucy in Town, which took advantage
      of the popular aspects of The Virgin Unmask'd and Lethe.
      Kitty Clive and Dorothy Jordan acted the leading parts
      for years.

FICTION

357 Barnett, George L. (ed.) _Eighteenth Century British
     Novelists on the Novel_. New York: Appleton-Century
     Crofts, 1968. A collection of excerpts from the dis-
     cussions of the novel by eighteenth century novelists
     includes major and minor authors. Headnotes place the
     selections in context.

358 Bernard, Kenneth. "Charles Brockden Brown and the Sub-
     lime." _Personalist_, 45 (1964), 235-249. Brown owes a
     debt to Ann Radcliffe among others.

359 Boyce, Benjamin. "English Short Fiction in the Eigh-
     teenth Century: A Preliminary View." _Studies in Short
     Fiction_, 5 (1968), 95-112. The types of short fiction
     ("any kind of imaginative writing about people that con-
     tains or implies action and that does not exceed in
     length 12,000 words") in the eighteenth century, al-
     though often didactic, had both social and psychologi-
     cal realism and are distinctive for their elegant style.

360 Brissenden, R. F. _Virtue in Distress: Studies in the
     Novel of Sentiment from Richardson to Sade_. New York:
     Barnes & Noble, 1974. A study of sentimentalism relates
     virtue to distress with particular attention to _Clarissa_
     and Jane Austen's early works.

361 Brooks, Douglas. _Number and Pattern in the Eighteenth-
     Century Novel_. London: Routledge & Kegan Paul, 1973.
     "Patterns" in the novel are often ordered arrangements
     dependent on number symbolism. Chapter I summarizes
     the case of the viability of numerology in the century
     and asserts that the "Christianized Pythagorean-Platonic
     tradition" was the most pervasive. Sections of chapters
     deal with the active and passive roles of heroines, im-
     plications of sexual encounters, and how patterns in the
     novels are clues to the interpretation of female charac-
     ters' actions.

362 Day, Robert Adams. _Told in Letters: Epistolary Fiction
     before Richardson_. Ann Arbor: University of Michigan
     Press, 1966. Richardson's novels grew from the fertile
     soil of early fiction which was entirely epistolary, ex-
     tensively so, or ornamented with letters. The relation-
     ship between other roots of the novel such as familiar
     letter books and Behn, Haywood, and Manley is discussed.

363   Demarest, David. "Legal Language and Situation in the
      Eighteenth Century Novel." University of Wisconsin dis-
      sertation, 1964. The novels of Defoe, Richardson,
      Fielding, and Austen use legal language and situation
      both literally and metaphorically. For example, Moll
      Flanders expresses the Dissenter's distrust of all but
      pragmatic procedures and Clarissa applies legalistic
      codes to Lovelace as a reflection of her family's behavior
      toward her.

364   Epes, Sr. Alice Regina. "Her Fertile Fancy and Her Feel-
      ing Heart: The Anatomy of the Eighteenth-Century Woman
      Novelist." Fordham dissertation, 1964. The disserta-
      tion classifies the major themes and plot devices in a
      representative selection of novels by women. The edu-
      cation of the time and low self-esteem determined the
      unsatisfactory quality of the novels and the lack of
      literary theory.

365   Fauchery, Pierre. La Destinée Féminine dans le roman
      européen du dix-huitième siècle, 1713-1807: Essai de
      gynécomythie romanesque. Paris: Colin, 1972. This
      massive book explores the historical and moral demands
      on women which created and dictated such myths as the
      virgin victim, the prude, and the courtesan. Compara-
      tive studies of milieu (family, school), narrative
      patterns (entrance into world, test of virtue), and
      theme (space, time, the androgyne) are found in the
      novels of England, France, Italy, Spain, Holland, and
      Germany. Aubin, Brooke, Burney, Davys, Edgeworth, Sarah
      Fielding, Haywood, Inchbald, Manley, and Radcliffe are
      among the many women novelists included.

366   Friend, Beverly. "Virgin Territory: Women and Sex in
      Science Fiction." Extrapolation, 14 (1972), 49-58.
      Very little sex is to be found in science fiction.

367   Gregory, Allene. The French Revolution and the English
      Novel. New York: Putnam, 1915. Godwin, Inchbald, Opie,
      Hays, Smith, and Wollstonecraft dramatize "Revolutionary
      ethics" in their novels. Bibliography appended.

368   Horner, Joyce M. The English Women Novelists and their
      Connection with the Feminist Movement (1688-1797). Smith
      College Studies in Modern Languages, 11, #1, 2 and 3.
      Northampton, Massachusetts: Smith College, 1929-1930.
      This Smith College thesis explores the contemporary

opinion of women novelists and the types of novels they
wrote, then speculates about the existence of a feminine
"mind" which may be exhibited in the literature and
which allows women to make special contributions to
literature. The feminine mind gives their novels a
propensity toward psychological and situational realism
but limits their imagination and vision.

369   Howells, William Dean. Heroines of Fiction. 2 vols.
       New York: Harper & Brothers, 1901. Mr. Howells' sub-
       jective reflections on heroines and techniques are
       incisive and lively. "Some Nineteenth Century Heroines
       in the Eighteenth Century" argues that certain opinions
       of novelists such as Defoe and Richardson are charac-
       teristic of the later century. The chapter on Evelina
       typically finds her "the sweetest and dearest goose in
       all fiction." There are also chapters on Edgeworth and
       Radcliffe.

370   Hoyt, Charles A. Minor British Novelists. Carbondale:
       Southern Illinois Press, 1967. This collection of
       essays includes"Fanny Burney" by Eugene White and "An
       Early 'Irish' Novelist" (Edgeworth) by W. B. Coley. The
       essays include brief biographical sketches, references
       to contemporary opinion, and some critical discussion.

371   Ivker, Barry. "John Cleland and the Marquis d'Argens:
       Eroticism and Natural Morality in Mid-Eighteenth Century
       English and French Fiction." Mosaic, 8 (1975), 141-
       148. Erotic literature in France and England, although
       utilizing the same basic plot elements, comes to dif-
       ferent conclusions about what constitutes "natural" be-
       havior. Cleland rejects prudery and libertinism and af-
       firms the beneficial aspects of passion moderated by rea-
       son.

372   Johnson, R. Brimley. The Women Novelists. London: W.
       Collins, 1918. Between the publications of Evelina and
       Daniel Deronda, women wrote fiction clearly distinguish-
       able from fiction by men. Fanny Burney was the major
       influence.

373   Jost, François. "Le Roman épistolaire et la technique
       narrative au xviiie siècle." Comparative Literature
       Studies, 3 (1966), 397-427. The rise and decline of the
       popularity of the epistolary novel in the century parallel
       changes in literary values and in the society as a whole.

374 Leavis, Q. D. *Fiction and the Reading Public*. London:
Chatto & Windus, 1932. The development of the English
reading public revolutionized publishing; circulating
libraries, serial publication, and the division between
popular and cultured tastes radically affected the writing
of novels and expanded the reading public. Popular fiction catered to the tastes of the ordinary reader.

375 Lévy, Maurice. *Le Roman "Gothique" Anglais, 1764-1824*.
Toulouse: Publications de la Faculté de lettres et
sciences humaines de Toulouse, 1968. Chapters consider
major writers including Radcliffe and topics essential to
their understanding in the late eighteenth century. He
discusses readership, parodies, and the influence of
the French Revolution and architecture.

376 Loomis, Emerson R. "The Problem of the Gothic Novel in
Wales." *National Library of Wales Journal*, 13 (1963),
67-69. Isabella Kelly's *The Abbey of St. Asaph* seems to
be the only eighteenth century Gothic novel set in Wales.
Kelly uses names, dialect, legends and settings expertly.

377 Lott, John R. "The Vogue of the Betrayed-Woman Theme in
English Fiction, 1740-1755." Duke University dissertation, 1963. The betrayed-woman theme was at its height
in popularity in the eighteenth century because of social circumstances and literary trends. The myth took
different forms as the century passed.

378 McBurney, W. H. "Formative Influences on the English
Novel, 1700-1739." Harvard dissertation, 1948. Within
the context of social, economic, and literary influences,
the author examines fiction focusing on the work of Manley, Barker, Haywood, Davys, and Defoe. Lack of critical interest in the novel determined that any development in the form came from writers independent of book-
sellers (Swift, Defoe) or from "artistic compulsion."

379 MacCarthy, Bridget G. *The Later Women Novelists, 1744-
1818*. New York: Catholic University Press; Oxford:
Blackwell, 1948. This continuation of *Women Writers*
surveys the oriental, sentimental, domestic, gothic, and
didactic novels by women. Bibliography of works cited.

380 MacCarthy, Bridget G. *Women Writers: Their Contribution to the English Novel, 1621-1744*. Cork: Cork University Press, 1944. Woman's primary contribution to

literature was in the novel. Influences and types of writing are discussed beginning with the pastoral romances of Anne Weamys and the biographies of Margaret Cavendish through the epistolary novels of Behn and Manley.

381   MacCarthy, Bridget G. The Female Pen. 2 vols. New York: W. Salloch, 1948. Women Writers and The Later Women Novelists published as a set.

382   Mack, Edward C. "Pamela's Stepdaughters: the Heroines of Smollett and Fielding." College English, 8 (1947), 293-301. Pamela's Daughters sensibly draws from minor novelists in defining conventional beliefs about the heroine. This procedure, however, neglects the heroines created by the great novelists. In Smollett's hands the conventional heroine becomes a mockery, in Fielding's a reality, and in Richardson's an imaginative vehicle.

383   Masefield, Muriel. Women Novelists from Fanny Burney to George Eliot. London: Nicholson and Watson, 1934. Brief discussions of novelists including Edgeworth and Burney.

384   Mayo, Robert D. The English Novel in the Magazines 1740-1815 with a catalogue of 1375 Magazine Novels and Novelettes. London: Oxford U. Press, 1962. A survey of the tradition of prose fiction in periodicals from The Athenian Mercury through 1815 discusses types of fiction, development of trends, and the establishing of modern magazine fiction.

385   Mews, Hazel. Frail Vessels: Woman's Role in Women's Novels from Fanny Burney to George Eliot. London: Athlone Press, 1969. Women added a dimension to the novel because they were more sensitive to the human condition. Examination of women "awaiting marriage," of wives, of mothers, and of women alone shows the writers examining the status and roles of women with deep feeling and diverse conclusions.

386   Mise, Raymond W. "The Gothic Heroine and the Nature of the Gothic Novel." University of Washington dissertation, 1971. Six minor, three major novels, and three major satires of Gothic novels provide the material for the discussion of the literary and social functions of the Gothic heroine.

387 Moers, Ellen. _Literary Women_. New York: Doubleday, 1976. Women writers belong to a powerful literary undercurrent built and sustained upon the legacies of earlier women. Denied the social and educational opportunities of men, the best of them studied and improved upon aspects of "women's novels."

388 Morgan, Charlotte. _The Rise of the Novel of Manners_. New York: Columbia University Press, 1911. A survey of the types of fiction from 1600 to 1740 traces the transition from romances and rogue biographies to the "idealistic novel of manners." A chronological list of some 500 works of prose fiction printed during those years as well as major collections of fiction appear in an appendix.

389 Newell, A. G. "Early Evangelical Fiction." _Evangelical Quarterly_, 38 (1966), 3-21 and 81-98. Evangelical fiction flowered between 1789 and 1818 and influenced the course of the novel.

390 Park, William. "Fielding _and_ Richardson." _PMLA_, 81 (1966), 381-388. The novels of the mid-eighteenth century are a "distinct version of a general type of literature" with a set of well defined conventions. Fielding and Richardson are most original in the transformations they make in the formulae and their novels are the finest statements of these conventions.

391 Pierce, Robert. "Moral Education in the Novel of the 1750's." _PQ_, 44 (1965), 73-87. The author traces conventions of movement from novels of morality to novels of sentimentality with discussion of novels by Charlotte Lennox and Eliza Haywood.

392 Proper, C. B. A. _Social Elements in English Prose Fiction between 1700 and 1832_. Amsterdam: H. J. Paris, 1929. The emphasis is on politics and the novel. Burney, Inchbald, Opie, Smith, Robinson, Hays, and Edgeworth are among the authors considered.

393 Richetti, John. _Popular Fiction before Richardson_. Oxford, Clarendon, 1969. Early fiction provides the modern scholar with important information about the social, moral, religious, and psychological context of the English novel.

394 Rosbottom, Ronald C. "Parody and Truth in Mme. Riccoboni's Continuation of _La Vie de Marianne_." _Studies in_

Voltaire and Eighteenth Century, 81 (1971), 163-175.
Mme. Riccoboni's parody of Marivaux's work shows that
she understood the technique and the reasons for leaving Marianne "unfinished." Her parody also provides
contemporary comment and evaluation of an influential
work.

395   Rudolf, Jo-Ellen S. "The Novels that Taught the Ladies:
      A Study of Popular Fiction written by Women, 1702-1834."
      University of California, San Diego, dissertation, 1972.
      The novels of Haywood, Burney, Edgeworth and Austen
      are "tea-table novels" written to teach young ladies
      how to behave. The formulaic nature of the novels is
      determined by social reality and the conception of the
      feminine psyche and duty; considerable dissatisfaction
      with feminine roles is expressed in the novels.

396   Sabiston, Elizabeth. "The Provincial Heroine in Prose
      Fiction: A Study in Isolation and Creativity." Cornell
      dissertation, 1969. Although the focus is on four nine-
      teenth century novels, there is useful background infor-
      mation comparing the positive and negative connotations
      of being a provincial woman in English, French, and
      American fiction.

397   Sale, William M. "From Pamela to Clarissa." The Age of
      Johnson: Essays presented to Chauncey Brewster Tinker.
      New Haven: Yale University Press, 1949. Richardson's
      skill in handling class differences in character rela-
      tionships is improved in Clarissa. Both novels explain
      a great deal about the English class situation.

398   Sarchet, Helene C. "Women in English Fiction of the Mid-
      Eighteenth Century from 1740 to 1771." University of
      Minnesota dissertation, 1943. Women writers, readers,
      and characters occupied a central place in mid-century
      fiction.

399   Schulz, Dieter. "The Coquette's Progress from Satire to
      Sentimental Novel." Literatur in Wissenschaft und Un-
      terricht, 6 (1973), 77-89. Changes in the character
      type of the coquette show that sensibility and the "fem-
      inine novel" were closely related phenomena. Satire
      yields to psychological and didactic treatment of the
      coquette in the early eighteenth century. After the
      1720's, the coquette's behavior is associated with fem-
      inism and freedom. By the late eighteenth century, the

social implications and conflicts with traditional morality transform the coquette into a victim.

400   Schulz, Dieter. "'Novel,' 'Romance,' and Popular Fiction in the First Half of the Eighteenth Century." SP, 70 (1973), 77-91. The definitions of and attacks on "novels" and "romances" by male writers such as Defoe and Fielding indicate the building resistance toward the unrealistic plots and romanticized tales of such authors as Behn and Haywood.

401   Séjourné, Philippe. Aspects Généraux de Roman Feminin en Angleterre de 1740-1800. Aix-en-Provence: Editions Ophrys, 1966. The rise and development of the "feminine novel" after Richardson changed the course of literary history. Inseparably bound to the position of women in society and to women as readers, the novel introduced innovations in form, theme, and characterization.

402   Sharma, O. P. "Emergence of Feminist Impulse as Aesthetic Vision in the English Novel." Punjab University Research Bulletin (Arts), 2 (1971), 1-28. Women wrote fiction continually after the seventeenth century. Elements in their work were identifiably feminine. By 1840, feminist statements and longings were also present.

403   Sinclair, Upton. Another Pamela: Or, Virtue Still Rewarded, A Story. New York: Viking, 1950. A modern version of Pamela in which the heroine is secretary to a wealthy California socialite. Quotations from the original novel are used to express emotions.

404   Solomon, Stanley J. "Subverting Propriety as a Pattern of Irony in three Eighteenth-Century Novels: The Castle of Otranto, Vathek, and Fanny Hill." Erasmus Review, 1 (1971), 107-116. Unlike irony in most novels, irony in these three novels does not project a moral vision. Rather, it exposes the didacticism and facile acceptance of social and moral norms by their contemporaries.

405   Spacks, Patricia Meyer. "Early Fiction and the Frightened Male." Novel: A Forum on Fiction, 8 (1974), 5-15. There is evidence that men feared women and their sexuality.

406   Speakman, James S. "Wit, Humor and Sensibility in Evelina, Belinda, and Northanger Abbey." University of California, Davis, dissertation, 1973. These novels blend sensibility, wit and humor in ways already accepted in comic theory and in criticism about realism. The proportion of the blend of

sensibility and comedy at any given moment determines artistic success or failure.

407   Steeves, Edna L. "Pre-Feminism in Some Eighteenth Century Novels." _Texas Quarterly_, 16 (1973), 48-57. Fiction demonstrates a growing interest in improving the conditions of women. The emphasis on getting married as opposed to the portrayal of married or employed women allows the development of the heroine's independence of thought but prevents the exploration of basic rights for women.

408   Stevenson, Lionel. _The English Novel. A Panorama_. Boston: Houghton Mifflin, 1960. This survey of the development of the English novel describes influences, major authors (". . . the first professional authoress was Mrs. Aphra Behn, whose life seems to have been as eventful as any of her writings. . . ."), and representative works. Themes characteristic of each era are identified.

409   Taylor, Gordan R. _The Angel-Makers: A Study in the Psychological Origins of Historical Change, 1750-1850_. London: Heinemann, 1958. The eighteenth century was a "matrist period" (dominated by the mother image) and the immorality of the age was a sign of failure to develop conscience. Major political and social changes transformed society, and, by the nineteenth century, women were to be "veritable angels," as incorporeal as possible.

410   Taylor, John T. _Early Opposition to the English Novel_. New York: King's Crown Press, 1943. Between 1760 and 1830 moralists and literary critics mounted an attack on the popular novel. Ironically, circulating libraries, increased literacy, and increasing demands for didactic novels acted against literary experimentation.

411   Tieje, Arthur S. _The Theory of Characterization in Prose Fiction Prior to 1740. University of Minnesota Studies in Language and Literature_, 5 (1916). Minneapolis: U. of Minnesota Press, 1916. Compilation and examination of pre-Richardsonian theoretical discussions of characterization show that writers of the eighteenth century novel appreciated the necessity for emotional scenes, poetic justice, and consistent behavior but often produced caricatures or stereotypes.

412   Tompkins, J. M. S. _The Popular Novel in England 1770-1800_. London: Constable, 1932. This discussion of the

influences and demands upon the novel between Sterne and
Scott includes a number of women writers. The chapter,
"The Female Novelists," summarizes contemporary attitudes toward women writers, offers explanations for the
number of women who became novelists, and enumerates
the limitations under which they labored.

413   Towers, A. R. "Amelia and the State of Matrimony." RES,
       5 (1954), 144-157. The author compares Amelia and Booth's
       marriage to the contemporary ideal of a good marriage.
       It was Fielding's intention to show the inadequacies
       of the abstract rules.

414   Utter, Robert P. and Gwendolyn B. Needham. Pamela's
       Daughters. New York: Macmillan, 1936. Characters em-
       bodying the feminine virtues of Pamela in eighteenth and
       nineteenth century novels, plays, essays, and books
       changed but little with the years. Fragility, tears,
       and prudery are a few of Pamela's legacies.

415   Van Ghent, Dorothy. The English Novel: Form and Func-
       tion. New York: Harper and Row, 1961. This collection
       of essays discusses a number of female characters.

416   Vopat, James B. "The Denial of Innocence: The Theme of
       Social Responsibility in the Early British Novel." Uni-
       versity of Washington dissertation, 1973. "Passage from
       innocence to experience" provides thematic unity to the
       novels in the century. Five novels including Evelina
       allow the author to compare the ways the characters find
       a stable mental and physical place for themselves.

417   Watt, Ian. The Rise of the Novel. Berkeley: U. of
       California Press; London: Chatto & Windus, 1957. An
       exploration of the forces that affected the emergence
       and development of the novel has sections on formal
       realism and economic individualism as well as briefer
       studies of middle class women, the old maid, the Marriage
       Bill, and urbanization and the characterization of women.

418   Wiles, Roy M. "Prose Fiction in English Periodical Pub-
       lication before 1750." Harvard dissertation, 1936. Over
       two hundred of the twelve hundred serial publications
       before 1700 contain material pertinent to the understand-
       ing of prose fiction. These periodicals increased the
       popularity of prose fiction, called for changes in style,
       theme, and content, and contributed to the development
       of modern characterization and realism.

419   Williams, Ioan. _Novel_ and _Romance_ 1700-1800. A _Docu-_
       mentary _Record_. New York: Barnes & Noble, 1970. The
       introduction to a collection of prefaces, reviews,
       letters, and passages criticizing the novel summarizes
       the changing opinion of novels and novel writing and
       of women writers.

420   Woolf, Virginia. _Granite_ and _Rainbow_. London: Hogarth,
       1958. The collection of essays includes some of special
       interest, notably "Eliza and Sterne," "Fanny Burney's
       Half-Sister, "Phases of Fiction," and "Women and Fiction."
       "Women and Fiction" poses a number of questions such as
       why women wrote little before the eighteenth century and
       why fiction is the easiest thing for women to write.
       Changes in attitude and subject matter point to women's
       future entry in the fields of biography, history, and
       criticism.

421   Wurzback, Natascha. _The_ _Novel_ in _Letters_: _Epistolary_
       Fiction in _the_ _Early_ _English_ _Novel_. Miami: University
       of Miami Press, 1969. The introduction points out si-
       milarities in form and content between the nine epis-
       tolary novels in the book and such existing forms as
       autobiographies and manuals for letter writing. The
       novels illustrate changes in characterization and dialogue.

422   Yeazell, Ruth. "Fictional Heroines and Feminist Critics."
       Novel: A _Forum_ on _Fiction_, 8 (1974), 29-38. Feminist
       critics have been blinded by stereotype hunting. They
       have failed to acknowledge depth in certain female
       characters, to recognize the symbolic nature of marriage,
       and to propose new plots and metaphors.

423   Zinn, Zea. "Love and Marriage in the Novels of English
       Women, 1740-1840." University of Wisconsin dissertation,
       1937. The conclusion of most novels by women became a
       satisfactory marriage. Comparison of lovers and marriages
       provides a description of the social code and models for
       happiness.

424   Bradbury, Malcolm. "Fanny Hill and the Comic Novel."
       Critical Quarterly, 13 (1971), 263-275. Cleland, like
       many other novelists of his time, adds new material and
       new tones to conventional literary devices, producing
       Cartesian and Bergsonian comic dimensions.

425   Braudy, Leo. "Fanny Hill and Materialism." ECS, 4
       (1970), 21-40. Sexuality in the novel is related to
       the materialistic philosophy of human nature propounded
       by Helvétius, d'Holback, and especially La Mettrie.
       Cleland presents human beings as becoming a bête-machine
       in the sexual act, but ultimately sexuality becomes a
       means of gaining knowledge of the self.

426   Copeland, Edward W. "Clarissa and Fanny Hill: Sisters
       in Distress." SNNTS, 4 (1972), 343-352. The erotic
       effect of Clarissa can be explained by comparing style
       and conventions for presenting sexuality in Fanny Hill
       with those in Clarissa.

427   Ivker, Barry. "John Cleland and the Marquis d'Argens:
       Eroticism and Natural Morality in Mid-Eighteenth Century
       English and French Fiction." Mosaic, 8 (1975), 141-148.
       See item #371.

428   Morrissey, Slepian and L. J. "What is Fanny Hill?" Essays
       in Criticism, 14 (1964), 65-75. The novel has neither the
       structure nor the intent of pornography. Rather, its
       themes argue for the value of experience, reason, and
       love. Letter I shows the loss of sexual innocence and
       the second, loss of naivete. Comic euphemisms, meta-
       phors from business, the theatre, pictorial poetry, and
       riding, and puns argue the book's literary merit.

429   Mortier, Roland. "Libertinage littéraire et tensions
       sociales dans la littérature de l'Ancien Régime: De la
       'Picara' à la 'Fille de Joie.'" RLC, 46 (1972), 35-45.
       Libertine literature often examines serious social themes
       and scenes. A number of female characters embody liber-
       tine and social issues.

430   Sambrook, A. J. "John Cleland." TLS, 23 April 1971,
       p. 477. The Department of Oriental Books in the Bodleian
       owns a ms. volume containing evidence of correspondence
       between Cleland and Pope.

431   Shinagel, Michael. "_Memoirs of a Woman of Pleasure_:
      Pornography and the Mid-Eighteenth Century Novel."
      _Studies in Change and Revolution: Aspects of English
      Intellectual History, 1640-1800_, Paul J. Korshin, ed.
      Menston: Scolar Press, 1972, pp. 211-236. _Fanny Hill_
      is intended to be both entertaining and instructive.

432   Wilding, Michael. "_Paradise Lost_ and _Fanny Hill_."
      Milton Quarterly, 5 (1971), 14-15. Fanny Hill's ini-
      tiation into Mrs. Cole's employment begins with allu-
      sions from Adam's first postlapsarian intercourse with
      Eve (_PL_ ix, 1031-1045).

FICTION
DANIEL DEFOE

433 Baine, Rodney M. "Defoe and Mrs. Bargrave's Story."
     PQ, 33 (1954), 388-395. The Apparition of Mrs. Veal
     is the product of "the feverish imagination of a venge-
     ful woman." Mrs. Bargrave had both the ability and the
     motive to fabricate the story which Defoe and others
     described and discussed throughout the eighteenth cen-
     tury.

434 Blewett, David. "Roxana and the Masquerades." MLR,
     65 (1970), 499-502. Roxana evokes and takes advantage
     of the times of both Charles II and George. Defoe
     gains ambiguity of time and immediacy.

435 Brown, Lloyd W. "Defoe and the Feminine Mystique."
     Transactions of the Samuel Johnson Society of the North-
     west, Robert H. Carnie, ed. Calgary, U. of Calgary Press,
     1972, pp. 4-18. Defoe's ambivalence toward female eman-
     cipation results in female characters who are liberated
     but unequal. The Essay upon Projects as well as Roxana
     and Moll Flanders express his mixed feelings. The de-
     sire for independence is natural but the result may be
     an unnatural Amazon.

436 Foster, Joan C. "Daniel Defoe and the Position of
     Women in Eighteenth Century England: A Study of Moll
     Flanders and Roxana." University of New Mexico disser-
     tation, 1972. Defoe was always sympathetic to women.
     His treatment of them was influenced by his Puritan,
     rationalist background. As he grew older, he became
     increasingly disillusioned and "shrill."

437 Hartog, Curt. "Aggression, Feminity, and Irony in Moll
     Flanders." Literature and Psychology, 22 (1972), 121-
     138. The author develops Ian Watt's discussion of De-
     foe's identification with Moll Flanders to argue that
     by using the feminine point of view, Defoe could discuss
     his own aggressive drives and develop ideas he ordinarily
     would have been too inhibited to pursue.

438 Howson, Gerald. "Who was Moll Flanders?" TLS, 18 Jan-
     uary 1968, pp. 63-64. Defoe may have based many of
     Moll's criminal activities on the real life experiences
     of Moll King, alias Mary Godson, who was under sentence
     of death and remained in Newgate until January 1722. De-
     foe had many opportunities to talk to her.

439 Kestner, Joseph A. "Defoe and Madame de La Fayette: _Roxana_ and _La Princesse de Monpensier_." _Papers on Language and Literature_, 8 (1972), 297-301. The masked balls in the two novels are compared.

440 Kettle, Arnold. "In Defence of Moll Flanders." _Of Books and Humankind: Essays and Poems Presented to Bonamy Dobree_, John Butt, ed. London: Routledge and Kegan Paul, 1964, pp. 55-67. The social context of Moll's life explains her situation, some of her actions, and culminates in her realizing the _huis clos_ which is her true situation.

441 Krier, William J. "A Courtesy which Grants Integrity." _ELH_, 38 (1971), 397-410. Moll Flanders vacillates between feminine and masculine responses to situations. She rejects the feminine situation but ultimately is converted to it and her personality is integrated at that point.

442 Kropf, C. R. "Theme and Structure in Defoe's _Roxana_." _SEL_, 12 (1972), 467-480. The novel is unified by the Hagar-Rachel theme and the Puritan beliefs about destruction of the soul. At the end of the novel, Roxana "cannot see beyond immediate physical reality, a sure sign of spiritual damnation. . . ."

443 Legouis, Pierre. "Marion Flanders est-elle une victime de la Societe?" _Revue de l'Enseignement des Langues Vivantes_, 48 (1931), 284-299. Moll Flanders is not the victim of society. She is only intermittently sensual but always avaricious. She seldom dreams; her apologists have dreamed for her and blamed society for her misconduct.

444 McMaster, Juliet. "The Equation of Love and Money in _Moll Flanders_." _SNNTS_, 2 (1970), 131-144. Defoe indicts the bourgeois substitution of money for love and virtue. The judgment on Moll who knows that people see wealth as an index of goodness extends to her whole society.

445 Peterson, Spiro T. "The Matrimonial Theme of Defoe's _Roxana_." _PMLA_, 70 (1955), 155-191. Defoe explores domestic relations, matrimonial laws, wife-servant-husband relationships, and the defects in English marriage and divorce procedures. The characters speak "the language of the devil's agents" although Defoe shows great respect for

common law and modifies behavior only in the ways
approved by equity.

446   Shinagel, Michael. <u>Defoe</u> <u>and</u> <u>Middle</u> <u>Class</u> <u>Gentility</u>.
       Cambridge: Harvard, 1968. The centrality of the theme
       of middle class gentility is an outgrowth of Defoe's
       personal ambitions and the preoccupation of the age
       with gentility. Social stratification and the position
       of women are affected by the demands of gentility.

447   Shinagel, Michael. "The Maternal Theme in <u>Moll</u> <u>Flanders</u>."
       <u>Cornell</u> <u>Library</u> <u>Journal</u>, 7 (1969), 3-23. The maternal
       theme exposes Moll's character and helps the reader un-
       derstand Defoe's craftsmanship. Moll is an unnatural
       mother who rejects her moral and natural responsibilities
       for her children.

448   Starr, George·A. <u>Defoe</u> <u>and</u> <u>Casuistry</u>. Princeton: Prince-
       ton University Press, 1971. Casuistry furnished theme,
       plot, and subject matter for the early novel. Defoe,
       like the casuists, acknowledges legal and religious codes
       but recognizes that their obscure or contradictory na-
       ture may cast human beings in a "moral twilight."

449   Watson, Tommy G. "Defoe's Attitude toward Marriage and
       the Position of Women as Revealed in <u>Moll</u> <u>Flanders</u>."
       <u>Southern</u> <u>Quarterly</u>, 3 (1964), 1-8. Defoe's frequent
       use of this marriage theme testifies to his concern
       for unattached women and his awareness of injustices.
       Defoe's "manly voice" and opinions can be heard in many
       of the passages discussing marriage which reflect modern
       social protest and Puritan ethics.

450   Wilkinson, Andrew M. "Good Advice to the Ladies: A Note
       on Defoe." <u>N&Q</u>, 195 (1950), 273-275. This poem was
       written by someone not necessarily Defoe who disapproved
       of the Restoration conception of love and marriage. It
       is not proof that Defoe fathered a child by an "oyster
       wench."

451   Zimmerman, Everett. "Language and Character in Defoe's
       <u>Roxana</u>." <u>Essays</u> <u>in</u> <u>Criticism</u>, 21 (1971), 227-235. De-
       foe's language, more metaphorical in <u>Roxana</u> than in ear-
       lier novels, is an effective means of characterization.
       Amy is a surrogate for Roxana.

FICTION
HENRY FIELDING

452   Block, Tuvia. "The Prosecution of the Maidservant in
       Amelia." ELN, 6 (1969), 269-271. Betty was guilty of
       ingratitude and cruelty as well as theft, and Booth's
       anger was in character and expressed some of Fielding's
       opinions about human nature.

453   de Castro, J. Paul. "Ursula Fielding and _Tom Jones_."
       N&Q, 178 (1940), 164-167. The note quotes and explains
       passages in a letter from Ursula Fielding to Jane Barker.

454   Feil, J. P. "Fielding's Character of Mrs. Whitefield."
       PQ, 39 (1960), 508-510. A contemporary of Fielding's,
       Lewis Thomas, wrote to a friend that Fielding's praise
       of Mrs. Whitefield of the Bell in Gloucester in _Tom
       Jones_ was puzzling as he knew her as a vain and foolish
       coquette.

455   Johnson, Jeffrey L. "The Good-Natured Young Man and the
       Virtuous Young Woman in the Comedies of Henry Fielding."
       Florida State University dissertation, 1969. The char-
       acters in his novels develop directly from traditional
       dramatic types. For example, Sophia Western is the
       descendent of Wycherley's Hippolita and Farquhar's
       Sylvia and a representative of the ideal woman who ex-
       poses the shortcomings of other women in juxtaposed
       scenes.

456   Park, William. "Fielding _and_ Richardson." PMLA, 81 (1966)
       381-388. See item # 390.

457   Roberts, E. V. "Fielding's Lost Play _Deborah, or A Wife
       for You All_ (1733): Consisting Partly of Facts and Part-
       ly of Observations upon Them." BNYPL, 66 (1962), 576-588.
       Fielding's treatment of similar scenes and characters and
       the knowledge of the types of roles commonly played by
       the actors who performed Deborah allow us to reconstruct
       many of the play's significant details. For instance,
       Elizabeth Mullart and Kitty Clive played parts which allow
       us to make surmises about plot, about the courtroom epi-
       sode in the play, and about the music.

458   Thomas, Donald S. "Fortune and the Passions in Fielding's
       Amelia." MLR, 60 (1965), 176-187. The narrator and the

hero of <u>Amelia</u> hold different opinions about fortune. The narrator associates fortune and the passions, arguing for Christian stoicism, while Booth's belief in the psychological power of the passions causes much of his misery.

459   Towers, A. R.   "<u>Amelia</u> and the State of Matrimony."   <u>RES</u>, 5 (1954), 144-157. The marriage of Booth and Amelia reflects the mainline of English thought concerning the roles of husband and wife and the institution of marriage, yet there are significant variations in the characters and their behavior and in the functioning of their marriage.

460   Wendt, Allan.   "The Naked Virtue of Amelia."   <u>ELH</u>, 27 (1960), 131-148. Amelia is the "ethical center" of the novel, the subject of the study of the beautiful, virtuous Platonic love object which inspired men to virtue in Fielding's earlier novels, and a test and illumination of the benevolist philosophy.

461   Wolff, Cynthia G.   "Fielding's <u>Amelia</u>:   Private Virtue and Public Good."   <u>TSLL</u>, 10 (1968), 37-55. <u>Amelia</u> offers a solution to the problems of the good man in an evil society but is a flawed novel because Fielding's implicit assumptions about man's nature cannot be reconciled with his portrayal of man's behavior. Amelia represents innocent goodness, an influential force in the world, but she is too limited and too much a symbol of private goodness to be effective. Amelia and the novel fail because Fielding despairs of finding solutions in a corrupt world when law fails.

FICTION
SAMUEL RICHARDSON

462 Canby, Henry S. "Pamela Abroad." MLN, 18 (1903), 206-
213. Pamela is the familiar la belle âme with a start-
ling twist, Pamela marries her master. The revolutionary
aspect as well as the moral appealed to continental
readers; Pamela quickly became a central figure in the
comédie larmoyante.

463 Clancey, Richard W. "The Augustan Fair-Sex Debate and
the Novels of Samuel Richardson." University of Maryland dissertation, 1966. Richardson's novels take up
the most important philosophical, religious, legal, and
psychological issues in the "fair sex debate."

464 Cohen, Richard. "The Social-Christian and the Christian-
Social Doctrines of Samuel Richardson." Hartford Studies
in Literature, 4 (1972), 136-146. Pamela and Grandison
were written as social conduct books and the heroines
exemplify the development of a social-Christian. In
Clarissa, the pattern is reversed; Clarissa moves from
a social circle to an eternal condition, demonstrating
a "Christian-social" theme.

465 Copeland, Edward W. "Clarissa and Fanny Hill: Sisters
in Distress." SNNTS, 4 (1972), 343-352. See item #
426.

466 Duncan-Jones, E. E. "Proposals of Marriage in Pride and
Prejudice and Pamela." N&Q, 202 (1957), 76. Darcy quotes
the opening line of B.'s proposal to Pamela when he first
proposes to Elizabeth Bennett, emphasizing the implications of the wording.

467 Dussinger, John A. "Conscience and the Pattern of
Christian Perfection in Clarissa." PMLA, 81 (1966),
236-245. Clarissa was intended to invigorate the practice of religion. The novel dramatizes devotional manuals, sermons, and William Law's Serious Call and A
Practical Treatise upon Christian Perfection.

468 Dussinger, John A. "What Pamela Knew: An Interpretation."
JEGP, 69 (1970), 377-393. Pamela is neither paragon nor
reliable narrator. Her perceptions and judgments of the
world are subjective and indicative of her identity and
growth. She is a feminine archetype who triumphs in the
masculine world and embodies moral authority.

71

469   Folkenflik, Robert. "A Room of Pamela's Own." ELH, 39
      (1972), 585-596. Pamela is seeking her place and self-
      determination within the spatial constructs (social
      hierarchy, house, and her body) of the novel. B. grants
      her place and privacy in their marriage agreement.

470   Freeman, Carol M. C. "Richardson and the Uses of Romance:
      A Study of Art, Morality, and Ambiguity in Clarissa." Yale
      University dissertation, 1971. Richardson leads his
      readers into approaching Clarissa as a conventional ro-
      mance, then scrutinizes and transforms the conventions.

471   Golden, Morris. Richardson's Characters. Ann Arbor:
      University of Michigan Press, 1963. The most original
      aspect of Richardson's novels is characterization. His
      preoccupation with conflict between and within charac-
      ters and society animates his strong-willed characters,
      finally making his lessons in piety and propriety ir-
      relevant.

472   Hill, Christopher. "Clarissa Harlowe and Her Times."
      Essays in Criticism, 5 (1955), 315-340. By reconstructing
      the social environment with special attention to econ-
      omics, the author demonstrates that the moral issues of
      the novel are related to the tension between the society
      and the developing Puritan attitudes toward the indiv-
      idual. Demands on the heroine and on the institution of
      marriage dramatize the tension between the socio-economic
      demand and the religious and philosophical ones.

473   Hornbeak, Katherine. Richardson's Familiar Letters and
      the Domestic Conduct Books; Richardson's Aesop. North-
      ampton, Massachusetts: Smith College Studies in Modern
      Languages, 1938. See item #228.

474   Lynch, Kathleen M. "Pamela Nubile, L'Écossaise, and The
      English Merchant." MLN, 47 (1932), 94-96. Goldoni's
      Pamela Nubile is the best dramatic adaptation of Pamela
      and supplied plot elements for Voltaire's l'Écossaise.
      George Colman the Elder adapted Voltaire's play in The
      English Merchant.

475   McKillop, Alan D. "The Mock Marriage Devices in Pamela."
      PQ, 26 (1947), 285-288. The details of Lord B.'s plan to
      use a "broken Attorney in a Parson's Habit" to trick
      Pamela into a false marriage come from an alleged seduc-
      tion of Elizabeth Culling or Cullen by William, Earl of

Cowper and are familiar literary conventions. This minor
episode, like the main plot, takes advantage of romantic
devices and realistic possibilities.

476   McIntosh, Carey. "Pamela's Clothes." ELH, 35 (1968), 75-
      83. Allusions to clothing unify incidents and themes,
      serve as "emblems" of social standing, as sexual meta-
      phors, and testify to Richardson's "formal artistry."

477   McKillop, Alan D. Introduction to "Critical Remarks on
      Sir Charles Grandison, Clarissa, and Pamela." ARS #21,
      Los Angeles: Clark Library, 1950. The 1754 pamphlet
      represents the type occasionally written about very popu-
      lar novels. It comments on religion, ethics, taste in
      fiction, style, and, perhaps most significantly, on sex,
      duplication of characters, and Charlotte.

478   McKillop, Alan D. "Wedding Bells for Pamela." PQ, 28
      (1949), 323-325. Sir John Hershel told the story of
      villagers ringing the church bells when they heard of
      Pamela's marriage to B.

479   Mitrani, Charles. "Richardson and Mme. de Souza." West
      Virginia University Bulletin, 1 (1936), 28-35. Mme. de
      Souza published her first novel in England. She was in-
      fluenced by Richardson; both portray the "feminine heart"
      torn between passion and duty.

480   Moynihan, Robert D. "Clarissa and the Enlightened Woman
      as Literary Heroine." JHI, 36 (1975), 159-166. The
      "Thomistic" or "savilian" view of woman was opposed by Puri-
      tan defenses of feminine independence. The Puritan values
      and patterns, reflected in Defoe's Religious Courtship (a
      work Richardson printed) and other writings are essential
      to understanding structure and theme in Clarissa.

481   Napier, Elizabeth R. "'Tremble and Reform': The Inver-
      sion of Power in Richardson's Clarissa." ELH, 42 (1975),
      214-223. Power changes hands repeatedly in Clarissa.
      After the rape, Clarissa assumes control and dominates
      imagery, metaphor, point of view, narrative pace, struc-
      ture, and even "fate."

482   Rabkin, Norman. "Clarissa: A Study in the Nature of
      Convention." ELH, 23 (1956), 204-217. Richardson was

attempting to demonstrate a balance between "animal nature" and "external regulation." Because Lovelace represents animal nature and Clarissa social code, neither can be happy in the world. Anna Howe is the embodiment of the norm.

483   Rawson, C. J. "'Nice' and 'sentimental': A Parallel between _Northanger Abbey_ and Richardson's Correspondence." _N&Q_, 209 (1964), 180. Henry Tilney paraphrases comments by Lady Bradshaigh.

484   Roussel, Roy. "Reflections on the Letter: The Reconciliation of Distance and Presence in _Pamela_." _ELH_, 41 (1974), 375-399. The tension between withdrawal and communion in the act of letter writing parallels the tension in human nature which desires to reveal while it fears to expose the self. The letter represents the reconciling agent between distance (the social self) and presence (the loving self).

485   Sale, William M., Jr. "Samuel Richardson and _Sir William Harrington_. " _TLS_, 29 August 1935, p. 537. Richardson did share in the revising of Anne Meade's "History of Sir William Harrington."

486   Southam, B. C. "Jane Austen and _Clarissa_." _N&Q_, 208 (1963), 191-192. Mr. Collins is an echo of the clergyman Brand in _Clarissa_.

487   Ulmer, Gregory L. "_Clarissa_ and _La Nouvelle Heloise_." _Comparative Literature_, 24 (1972), 298-308. Mr. Ulmer compares sublimation and self-deception in the two novels, considering psychological techniques and Richardson's style.

488   Van Ghent, Dorothy. "Clarissa and Emma as Phedre." _Partisan Review_, 17 (1950), 820-833. Great love stories juxtapose instinct and society, and the lovers are sacrificed to their passion which is "elliptically" equalled with the passion for death. Richardson's _Clarissa_ is a paean to death with the same forces in conflict.

489   Wolff, Cynthia G. _Samuel Richardson and the Eighteenth Century Puritan Character_. Hamden: Archon, 1972. The book moves from a discussion of Richardson's psychology of character creation and his sources to a detailed

discussion of individual characters. Richardson wanted
to explore the threat of social change to the "coherence
of personal identity."

490   Zigerall, James. "The Patterns of Courtship and Mar-
        riage in the Novels of Samuel Richardson." University
        of Chicago dissertation, 1963.

FICTION
TOBIAS SMOLLETT

491   Buck, Howard S. _Study in Smollett_. New Haven: Yale University Press, 1925. Lady Vane wrote "The Memoirs of a Lady of Quality" which appear in _Peregrine Pickle_ with some help in revising them from Dr. Shebbeare.

492   Denizot, Paul. "Une mal Aimée: La Lady of Quality de Smollett." _Les Langues Modernes_, 65 (1971), 129-132. The Lady of Quality is immoral for the same reasons that Moll Flanders and Roxana are. She is a victime and the reflection of her society, however. Unlike Defoe's heroines, she does not acknowledge her immorality.

493   Kline, Judd. "Three Doctors and Smollett's Lady of Quality." _PQ_, 27 (1948), 219-228. Dr. Peter Shaw is probably the "Dr. S--" in "The Memoirs of a Lady of Quality." He possessed all of the qualifications of the fashionable woman's doctor.

494   Knapp, Lewis M. "Ann Smollett, Wife of Tobias Smollett." _PMLA_, 45 (1930), 1035-1049. The Smolletts were a devoted couple. Ann Smollett's letters, her will, her epitaph, and material from benefit nights survive.

495   Knapp, Lewis M. "Elizabeth Smollett, Daughter of Tobias Smollett." _RES_, 8 (1932), 312-315. Elizabeth Smollett, who died at age fifteen, was a child of unusual promise and especially beloved by her father.

496   Putney, Rufus D. "Smollett and Lady Vane's Memoirs." _PQ_, 25 (1946), 120-126. Lady Vane did not write the "Memoirs." The style is characteristic of Smollett, is masculine, and displays a vocabulary more diverse and learned than Lady Vane could have used.

497   Rousseau, G. S. "Pineapples, Pregnancy, Pica and _Peregrine Pickle_." _Tobias Smollett_, G. S. Rousseau and P. G. Bouce. New York: Oxford University Press, 1971. In explaining the medical allusions in the novel, the author provides considerable information about contemporary opinions and controversies about pregnancy, prenatal influence, pica, medical care, and the century's fascination with extraordinary births.

FICTION
LAURENCE STERNE

498   Faurot, Ruth M. "Mrs. Shandy Observed." SEL, 10 (1970),
       579-589. Rather than being a submissive wife, Mrs. Shan-
       dy practices "oneupmanship."

499   Hartley, Lodwick. "The Dying Soldier and the Love-Lorn
       Virgin: Notes on Sterne's Early Reception in America."
       Southern Humanities Review, 4 (1970), 69-80. Tristram
       Shandy was very popular in the United States. Politi-
       cians and common people read it, plays were based on it,
       and it influenced major writers like Irvine.

500   Houlahan, Michael O. "Sexual Comedy in Tristram Shandy."
       Northwestern University dissertation, 1971. The back-
       ground, incorporation, and reaction to sexual comedy
       in the novel explain the reader's, narrator's, and char-
       acters' impotence in understanding and ordering life.

501   Macafee, C. H. G. "The Obstetrical Aspects of Tristram
       Shandy." Ulster Medical Journal, 19 (1950), 12-22. Ob-
       stetrical details serve a variety of narrative functions
       (Tristram may have been premature or syphilitic), and
       Sterne has given a fairly accurate picture of opinions,
       controversies, and practices.

502   Putney, Rufus D. S. "Alas, Poor Eliza!" MLR, 41 (1946),
       411-413. The epitaph which Sterne wrote in the spring
       of 1767 was for Mrs. James, not Eliza Draper. Sterne's
       letters catalogue Mrs. James' admirable qualities.

503   Putney, Rufus D. S. "Sterne's Eliza." TLS, 9 March 1946,
       p. 115. Sterne stopped writing "Journal to Eliza" because
       he lost interest in her, not because his wife was coming
       home.

504   Woolf, Virginia. Granite and Rainbows. London: Hogarth,
       1958. See item #420.

77

PERIODICALS

505   Adburgham, Alison. Women in Print: Writing Women and
       Women's Magazines from the Restoration to the Accession
       of Victoria. London: Allen & Unwin, 1972. See item
       #2.

506   Anderson, Paul B. "The History and Authorship of Mrs.
       Crackenthorpe's Female Tatler." MP, 28 (1931), 354-
       360. Delariviere Manley was Mrs. Crackenthorpe. The
       author cites as evidence her arrest and the timing of
       the end of the Female Tatler, feminist elements, allu-
       sions to people, and references in the British Apollo.

507   Anderson, Paul B. "La Bruyère and Mrs. Crackenthorpe's
       Female Tatler." PMLA, 52 (1937), 100-103. La Bruyère's
       Caractères furnished the form of the Female Tatler as
       well as some copy. For example, #32 quotes Section 81
       from "Of Women."

508   Anderson, Paul B. "'Splendor out of Scandal.' The Lu-
       cinda-Artesia Papers in The Female Tatler." PQ, 15
       (1936), 286-300. Thirty-two of the last sixty-five is-
       sues of the Female Tatler were written by a single hand,
       probably Bernard Mandeville, under the pseudonyms of
       "Lucinda" or "Artesia." These numbers expose the com-
       parative shallowness of the Tatler and were attempts
       to elevate the moral sensibilities of the readers of
       the Female Tatler.

509   Baker, Donald D. "Witchcraft, Addison, and The Drummer."
       Studia Neophilologica, 31 (1959), 174-181. Addison's
       The Drummer is about the most famous seventeenth century
       incident of witchcraft and appeared when the debate over
       witchcraft was far from dead.

510   Bond, Richmond, P. (ed). New Letters to the "Tatler" and
       the "Spectator." Austin: University of Texas Press,
       1959. The unpublished letters to the two periodicals
       provide additional insight into eighteenth century Lon-
       don life, its "morals and manners." Some thirty letters
       are by or about women.

511   Ewald, W. B. Rogues, Royalty, and Reporters: The Age
       of Queen Anne through its Newspapers. Boston: Houghton
       Mifflin, 1956. This is an anthology of excerpts on a

79

variety of subjects including medicine, lotteries, religion, education, and crime from a representative sam-
ple of early eighteenth century periodicals. Selections
on elopement, marriage, domestic arts, "aids to beauty,"
and "amatory arts" indicate popular opinion about women.

512 Graham, Walter. The Beginnings of English Literary
     Periodicals. London: Oxford University Press, 1926.
     The English literary periodical sprang from such papers
     as The Athenian Mercury, Observator, Tatler, and London
     Spy.

513 Graham, Walter. English Literary Periodicals. New York:
     T. Nelson, 1930. A survey of English literary periodicals
     from the seventeenth century into the nineteenth, dis-
     cussing development, content, trends, and societal in-
     fluences including mention of Haywood, Manley, Montagu,
     and periodicals for women.

514 Graham, Walter. "Thomas Baker, Mrs. Manley, and the Fe-
     male Tatler." MP, 34 (1936/7), 267-272. The evidence
     for Baker's authorship of the Bragge-Baldwin Female
     Tatler is more persuasive than the evidence for Manley's
     of numbers 19-111.

515 Heinrich, Joachim. Die Frauenfrage bei Steele und Addi-
     son. Leipzig: Mayer and Muller, 1930. This is an ex-
     amination of the positions of Steele and Addison on
     women's rights, particularly with regard to the three
     most significant moral weekly papers from the years
     1709-1714. Background material is analyzed under three
     headings: general statements about the situation of
     women, marriage and education of women (werbliche Bildungs-
     frage). After examining Addison and Steele's position
     with regard to the reformation of manners, the author
     considers the place of women as participants in letters,
     in society, in love, and in marriage.

516 Hodges, James. "The Female Spectator: A Courtesy Peri-
     odical" in Studies in the Early English Periodical, Rich-
     mond P. Bond, ed. Chapel Hill: University of North Ca-
     rolina Press, 1957, pp. 151-182. The periodical is in
     the tradition of the earlier courtesy books. Themes,
     content, and tone reflect its roots.

517 Hodges, James. "A Study of the Female Spectator (1744-
     1746). University of North Carolina Record, 492 (1951),

129-131. This summary of his dissertation explains the nature of the periodical, calling it a "serialized courtesy book," and mentions the significance of research problems associated with it.

518   Kay, Donald. _Short Fiction in The Spectator._ University: University of Alabama Press, 1975. One hundred of the 555 issues of the _Spectator_ include prose fiction primarily in the tradition of the _Gesta Romanorum._ The author classifies them into characters, "dream vision cum-allegory," fable, "domestic apologue," satirical adventure, oriental tale, rogue literature, fabliaux, exemplum, and "mock-sentimental tale," giving some attention to their literary antecedents.

519   Margolis, John D. "Pekuah and the Theme of Imprisonment in Johnson's _Rasselas._" _English Studies,_ 53 (1972), 339-343. Pekuah's experiences contribute "to the moral sentence of the tale," specifically to the theme of imprisonment. She and the apologue exist to point out the differences between herself and Rasselas and Nekayah. Her resignation, belief in a spiritual reality, and positive faith remind the reader of St. Paul.

520   Mayo, Robert D. _The English Novel in the Magazines, 1740-1815 with a catalogue of 1375 Magazine Novels and Novelettes._ London: Oxford University Press, 1962. A survey of the tradition of prose fiction in periodicals from the _Athenian Mercury_ discusses types of fiction, development of trends, and the establishing of magazine fiction. Included are a catalogue of fiction, a chronological index, glossary, appendices on religious magazine fiction, magazines specializing in prose fiction, and fiction in translation.

521   Milford, R. T. "_The Female Tatler._" _MP,_ 29 (1932), 350-351. The Bodleian Library has a complete run of the periodical and all twenty-six numbers of the rival Baker edition.

522   Pollard, Graham. "The Early Poems of George Crabbe and _The Lady's Magazine._" _Bodleian Library Record,_ 5 (1955), 149-156. Two periodicals with the title _The Lady's Magazine_ were published next door to each other. Crabbe contributed to both and once won a prize for his poem on hope.

523   Smith, John H. "Thomas Baker and The Female Tatler."
       MP, 49 (1952), 182-188. The rival paper was written
       by Thomas Baker. The attribution is supported by
       the British Apollo, biographical data, and events sur-
       rounding Baker's Fine Lady's Airs.

524   Starr, George A. "From Casuistry to Fiction: The Im-
       portance of the Athenian Mercury." Journal of the His-
       tory of Ideas, 28 (1967), 17-32. Dunton's Athenian
       Mercury was the link between casuistry and the early
       eighteenth century novel. Many of the issues raised,
       methods of reasoning, and the view of life as a series
       of ethical crises are at the heart of the early novel.

525   Stearns, Bertha M. "Early English Periodicals for
       Ladies (1700-1760)." PMLA, 48 (1933), 38-60. Dunton's
       Athenian Mercury and Ladies' Mercury and especially John
       Tipper's Ladies' Diary determined the pattern for later
       periodicals for women and, by the end of the eighteenth
       century, the contents and magazine form were set. A
       survey of the periodicals for women attests to the growth
       and interests of the female reading public.

526   Stearns, Bertha M. "The First English Periodical for
       Women." MP, 27 (1930), 45-59. The Athenian Mercury
       came to depend heavily upon female readers and by its
       second year, became virtually a ladies' magazine. In
       the six years of its publication, Dunton experimented
       with and introduced a variety of material which would
       become the backbone of women's periodicals.

527   White, Cynthia L. Women's Magazines, 1693-1968. London:
       Michael Joseph, 1970. The section "Laying the Founda-
       tions" describes the development and origins of publi-
       cations for women. An appendix lists periodicals in-
       tended primarily for women between 1693 and 1968.

528   White, Robert B. "A Study of The Female Tatler (1709-
       1710)." University of North Carolina dissertation,
       1966. This is a survey of the background, development,
       and contents of the periodical.

POETRY

529 Adams, Percy (ed.). Tennessee Studies in Literature:
     Eighteenth Century Literature. Knoxville: University
     of Tennessee Press, 1974. Contains John Aden's "'Those
     Gaudy Tulips,' Swift's 'Unprintables'" and other studies
     of interest.

530 Brooks, Cleanth. "The Case of Miss Arabella Fermor."
     The Well-Wrought Urn: Studies in the Structure of
     Poetry. New York: Harcourt Brace, 1947. Belinda is
     both goddess and frivolous tease. Pope recognizes the
     complexity of the idea of woman as goddess and exploits
     it in a variety of ways.

531 Brooks, Elmer R. "An Unpublished Restoration Satire
     on the Court Ladies." English Language Notes, 10 (1973),
     201-208. Reprints the satire, perhaps by Rochester,
     with notes identifying the ladies.

532 Buxton, John. A Tradition of Poetry. London: Macmillan,
     1957. In this survey, there is a chapter on Anne Finch,
     Countess of Winchilsea, "the first Englishwoman to write
     poetry no man could have written."

533 Champion, Larry S. (ed.). Quick Springs of Sense: Stu-
     dies in the Eighteenth Century. Athens: University of
     Georgia Press, 1974. Contains James L. Tyne's "Swift
     and Stella: The Love Poems" and Wolfgang Rudat's "Be-
     linda's 'Painted Vessel:' Allusive Technique in The
     Rape of the Lock." The former argues that the poems to
     Esther Johnson are "love poems of distinction" and origin-
     ality. The latter traces the metaphor of a ship repre-
     senting a woman's body to Ovid and Ausonius.

534 Cohen, Ralph. "The Reversal of Gender in The Rape of
     the Lock." South Atlantic Bulletin, 37 (1972), 54-60.
     The women in the poem dominate the male characters and
     the poem itself. The men assume the role of the "weaker
     sex" as Pope systematically develops the role reversals.
     This "perversion of nature" is a major satirical device
     in the poem.

535 Crawford, Thomas. "Scottish Popular Ballads and Lyrics
     of the Eighteenth and Early Nineteenth Centuries, Some
     Preliminary Conclusions." Studies in Scottish Literature,
     1 (1963), 49-63. Includes manuscripts by Elizabeth Coch-
     rane and Agnes Thorburn Creighton.

536   Fairchild, Hoxie Neale. Religious Trends in English
       Poetry. Vols. I and II. New York: Columbia Univer-
       sity Press, 1929. These two volumes cover the eigh-
       teenth century and make passing references to women
       poets.

537   Ferguson, J. D. "Robert Burns and Maria Riddell."
       MP, 28 (1930), 169-184. Circumstances surrounding
       Burns quarrel with Riddell are explained. The author
       dissociates Burns from the lampoon Esopus to Maria.

538   Fullard, Joyce, and Rhoda W. Schueller. "Eighteenth
       Century Poets: A Bibliography of Women not Listed in
       the CBEL." Mary Wollstonecraft Journal, 2 (1974), 40-
       43. A bibliography of editions of their works.

539   Fullard, Joyce. "Some Remarks on the Representation of
       Eighteenth Century Women Poets in Anthologies." Mary
       Wollstonecraft Journal, 2 (1974), 44-46. Eighteenth
       and twentieth century editors include few women in their
       anthologies. Nineteenth century collections are more
       useful.

540   Gilbert, Dorothy L., and Russell Pope. "The Cowper
       Translation of Mme. Guyon's Poems." PMLA, 54 (1939),
       1077-1098. Posits various similarities between the
       French mystic Mme. Guyon to explain why he translated
       her spiritual songs.

541   Hagstrum, Jean H. "Kathleen Raine's Blake." MP, 68
       (1970), 76-82. Blake's view of the sexual body is sum-
       marized in a review of Raine's Blake and Tradition.

542   Harris, Brice. "'A Satyr on the Court Ladies.'" TLS,
       20 August 1931, p. 633. The publisher who attributed
       this Harvard Library poem to Wilmot was simply trying
       to market his wares. The poem was written by Goodwin
       Wharton.

543   Keogh, J. G. "Pope's 'Epistle to a Lady,' 1-4." Ex-
       plicator, 31 (1973), item 37. "Character" means a graven
       image on a coin.

544   Kulisheck, Clarence L. "Swift's Poems about Women."
       Johnsonian News Letter, 10 (1950), 11-12. The author
       finds precedents in Book IV of Lucretius' De Rerum
       Natura.

545 Mahaffey, Kathleen. "Pope's 'Artimisia' and 'Phryne' as Personal Satire." RES, 21 (1970), 466-471. Madame Kielmannsegge, Countess of Darlington, is Artimisia, and Ehrengard Melusina Schulenberg is Phryne.

546 Manch, Joseph. "Jonathan Swift and Women." University of Buffalo Studies, 16 (1941), 135-214.

547 Maud, R. N. "Pope and Miss Betty Marriot." Modern Language Notes, 72 (1957), 96-97. "To a Young Lady with the Works of Voiture" and "To the Same, On her Leaving the Town after the Coronation" were addressed to Miss Marriot as well as to Teresa Blount.

548 McManmon, John J. "Phalli non Erecti, Feminae non Fecundatae, et Entia Neutra." Antigonish Review, 2 (1971), 63-72. The portraits of Belinda, Clarissa, and Thalestris "belong in the rogues gallery of any respectable playboy." Each woman represents a different kind of sexual aggression. Pope is satirizing the male characters' lack of understanding "of the realities of female politics" and "of the female world" and the lack of sexual identity in his time.

549 Menon, K. P. K. Woman in English Poetry from Milton to Wordsworth. Kerala: University Institute of English, n.d. Studies of images of women in Milton, Swift, Pope, Thomson, and Crabbe.

550 Osborn, James M. "Pope, the 'Apollo of the Arts,' and His Countess" in England in the Restoration and Early Eighteenth Century: Essays on Culture and Society, H. T. Swedenberg, Jr., ed. Berkeley: University of California Press, 1972, pp. 101-143. Pope was a life long friend of Richard Boyle. His Countess was an amateur painter, an accomplished woman, and a friend and helper to Pope.

551 Paulson, Kristoffer. "'The Dog-Drawn Bitch' of Rochester's Ramble." Satire News Letter, 10 (1972), 28-29.

552 Peltz, Catharine W. "The Neo-Classic Lyric, 1660-1725." ELH, 11 (1944), 92-116. Traces four themes in love lyrics: the suing lover, carpe diem, compliment to the lady, and rebukes to her. Mention of Ann Finch.

553   Quaintance, Richard. "French Sources of the Restoration
       Enjoyment Poem." PQ, 42 (1963), 190-199. Five French
       and five Restoration poems repeat the commonplace of a
       rake lamenting the loss of sexual power to his mistress.

554   Renwick, W. S. "Notes on Some Lesser Poets of the
       Eighteenth Century." Essays on the Eighteenth Century
       Presented to David Nichol Smith in Honour of his Seven-
       tieth Birthday. Oxford: Clarendon, 1945, pp. 130-146.
       Includes Lady Mary Wortley Montagu.

555   Rodgers, Katherine M. "'My Female Friends:' The Misogyny
       of Jonathan Swift." TSLL, 1 (1959), 366-379. Swift
       attacks women's physical functions as well as the ro-
       mantic ideal in "a deep unconscious revulsion against
       Woman as Animal."

556   Rose, E. J. "'The Queenly Personality': Walpole, Melville,
       and Mother." Literature and Psychology, 15 (1965), 216-
       229. Incest themes in Walpole's verse drama The Mysteri-
       ous Mother influenced Melville.

557   Salomon, Louis B. The Devil Take Her. A Study of the
       Rebellious Lover in English Poetry. Philadelphia: Uni-
       versity of Pennsylvania Press, 1931. A study of poems
       hostile to the courtly love tradition in which the lover
       revolts against the woman's treatment. Chapters include
       discussions of attacks on women and on recurrent themes.

558   Simon, Irene. "Pope and the fragility of Beauty." Revue
       des Langues Vivants, 24 (1958), 377-394.

559   Stanford, Ann. Introduction to The Woman Poets in Eng-
       lish: An Anthology. New York: McGraw-Hill, 1972. The
       introduction sets each poet in the context of her time
       and comments on the reception of her work. Biographical
       sketches at the back; generous sampling of eighteenth
       century women.

560   Sutherland, James. "Anne Greene and the Oxford Poets."
       The Augustan Milieu: Essays Presented to Louis A. Landa,
       Henry K. Miller, et. al, eds. Oxford: Clarendon, 1970.
       A survey of the literature about Anne Greene who survived
       hanging.

561   Sutherland, John. "Blake: A Crisis of Love and Jealousy."
       PMLA, 87 (1972), 424-431. The relationship of the sexes
       in Milton, Jerusalem, and short poems.

562   Williams, Aubrey. "The 'Angel, Goddess, Montague' of
      Pope's Sober Advice from Horace." MP, 71 (1973), 56-
      58. The reference is perhaps to Elizabeth Montagu,
      but more likely to Lady Mary Churchill, Duchess of
      Montagu. It is not Lady Mary Wortley Montagu.

563   Wilson, John Harold. The Court Wits of the Restoration:
      An Introduction. London: Frank Cass, 1967. Attention
      is given to the wits' attitude toward their women and
      the poems addressed to them.

564   Wilson, John Harold. "Rochester's Marriage." RES, 19
      (1943), 399-403. The abduction of Elizabeth Malet re-
      sulted from her parents' disapproval of Rochester. The
      marriage was prompted by love.

565   Wright, H. Bunker. "Matthew Prior's Cloe and Lisetta."
      MP, 33 (1938), 9-23. Anne Durham was probably Cloe in
      "To Mr. Howard" and "Venus Mistaken." Later Elizabeth
      Cox, "Lisetta" of the poems, became a rival for Prior's
      affections.

INDIVIDUALS

566 Janes, Regina. "Mary, Mary Quite Contrary, Or, Mary Astell and Mary Wollstonecraft Compared." Studies in Eighteenth Century Culture. Ed. Ronald C. Rosbottom. Madison: University of Wisconsin Press, 1976. V, 121-139. The change in the ideal which provided shape and focus for Astell's and Wollstonecraft's aspirations marks the profound shift in thinking about women which occurred in the eighteenth century.

567 Norton, J. E. "Some Uncollected Authors XXVII: Mary Astell, 1666-1731." BC, 10 (1961), 58-65. A brief sketch of her life with contemporaries' reactions to her activities prefaces an annotated checklist of her works. The checklist comments on attributions and gives locations.

568 Smith, Florence M. Mary Astell. New York: Columbia University Press, 1916. The first and last chapters describe her life, personality, and influence. The middle chapters survey and discuss her writings on education, marriage, religion, and politics.

569 Smith, Florence M. "Mary Astell: A Seventeenth Century Advocate for Women." Westminster Review, 149 (1898), 440-449. A number of historical events had reduced the status of women, and Mary Astell joined the chorus of those arguing for the education of women. A Serious Proposal to the Ladies, A Defence of the Ladies, and Reflections on Marriage are pioneer works in the "Women's Rights movement."

570 Stephens, Kate. Workfellows in Social Progress. New York: Sturgis & Walton, Co., 1916. The section "Torch-bearers for Women" traces attitudes toward the education of women from antiquity through the seventeenth century very briefly with mention of several educated women. Mary Astell's proposal for a college for women met determined resistance but influenced the debate considerably.

PENELOPE AUBIN

571   Dooley, Roger B. "Penelope Aubin: Forgotten Catholic
      Novelist." Ren, 11 (1959), 65-71. Aubin wrote as a Catho-
      lic novelist in a time when "Catholic" had all of the nega-
      tive connotations of "Communist" to modern Americans. Her
      seven novels have good Catholic characters whose religion
      affects their lives in positive ways, have conversions, and
      the only miracle and the only martyr in eighteenth century
      fiction.

572   McBurney, William H. "Mrs. Penelope Aubin and the Early
      Eighteenth-Century English Novel." HLQ, 20 (1957), 245-
      267. Within a framework of biographical data, Mr. McBur-
      ney demonstrates that Aubin helped fuse the themes and
      techniques of Defoe with those of French fiction. He ex-
      plicates her novels, identifies French and English influ-
      ences, and weighs her contribution to the development of
      the novel.

573   Shugrue, Michael F. "The Sincerest Form of Flattery: Imi-
      tation in the Early Eighteenth-Century Novel." SAQ, 70
      (1971), 248-255. While the great works of fiction of the
      first half of the century were influenced by sub-literary
      genres, the great works, in turn, spawned a host of imita-
      tions. The influence of these major works has never been
      fully explored. Mr. Shugrue chooses four imitative works,
      including Aubin's The Strange Adventures of the Count de
      Vinevil and His Family, which imitates Robinson Crusoe in
      situation, details, and style to illustrate the kinds of
      influence and the implications of such modifications as the
      minor novelists made.

JOANNA BAILLIE

574 Badstuber, Alfred. <u>Joanna Baillie's Plays</u>. Vienna and
Leipzig: Braumuller, 1911. An analysis of her plays
with reference to influences on her dramatic theories.

575 Carhart, Margaret S. <u>The Life and Works of Joanna
Baillie</u>. New Haven: Yale University Press, 1921.
This survey of her life and works includes a generous
discussion of contemporary opinion and concludes that
she is the "greatest Scottish dramatist."

576 Colvin, Christina E. "Maria Edgeworth's Tours in Ireland, II. Killarney." <u>Studia Neophilologica</u>, 43 (1971),
252-256. Maria Edgeworth wrote a letter to Joanna
Baillie describing her tour.

577 Insch, A. G. "Joanna Baille's <u>De Monfort</u> in Relation
to her Theory of Tragedy." <u>Durham University Journal</u>,
54 (1962), 114-120. Her "Introductory Discourse" to <u>A
Series of Plays</u> (1798) explains her tragic theory and
examines contemporary tragedy. Her best tragedy, <u>De
Monfort</u>, however, succeeds in spite of this theory.

578 Lambertson, Chester L. "The Letters of Joanna Baillie
(1801-1832)." Harvard University dissertation, 1956.
The collection of 520 letters gives opinions of the
major and minor writers of the early Romantic period
and provides a picture of a warm and lively personality.
The dissertation reproduces the 340 letters written between 1801 and Scott's death (he ranked her with Shakespeare as a dramatist).

579 MacCunn, Florence A. <u>Sir Walter Scott's Friends</u>. London: Blackwood, 1909. Includes a chapter on her.

580 Meynell, Alice. "Joanna Baillie." <u>Second Person Singular and Other Essays</u>. 2nd impression. London: Milford, 1922, pp. 56-61. This discussion of her Plays
on the Passions emphasizes the comedies.

581 Pieszczek, Rudolf. <u>Joanna Baillie, ihr Leben, ihre
dramatischen Theorien, und ihre Leidenschaftsspiele</u>.
Berlin: Schade, 1910.

582 Plarr, Victor C. "Sir Walter Scott and Joanna Baillie."
<u>The Edinburgh Review</u>, 216 (1912), 355-371 and 217 (1913),
170-181. Prints letters to Baillie from Scott.

583   Anon. "A Forgotten Children's Book." Hibbert Journal,
       63 (1964), 27-34. Mrs. Barbauld's Hymns for Children
       was "endlessly reprinted" and appeared in every kind of
       edition. Her book demonstrates her principles of edu-
       cation, her belief that a child's religion is associated
       with the natural world, and her religious opinions. The
       texts of representative hymns accompany some of the 1840
       additions aimed at ending criticism of her "Unitarian
       principles."

584   Anon. "'Life, I know not.' Mrs. Barbauld: 1743-1825."
       TLS, 19 June 1943, 298. Besides these lines, for which
       Wordsworth envied her, Anna Laetitia Aikin Barbauld
       wrote other sound poems, firm, strong, and often con-
       taining a memorable phrase. Her life and contemporary
       reputation are summarized.

585   Moore, Catherine E. "The Literary Career of Anna Lae-
       titia Barbauld." North Carolina dissertation, 1970.
       The influences on her thought, writings, and position
       as representative of intellectual ideas and conflicts
       in her time are the subjects for the dissertation.

586   Rodgers, Betsy. Georgian Chronicle: Mrs. Barbauld and
       Her Family. London: Methuen, 1958. A biography of
       the Aikin family with a bibliography of their work and
       the texts of previously unpublished letters describes
       the family's contributions to literature, education,
       and science. Anna Laetitia was the most famous member
       of the well known family, a respected educator until she
       began participating in political controversies.

587   W., F. P. "Crabb Robinson, Mrs. Barbauld, Macauley, and
       Horace Walpole. N&Q, 185 (1943), 374. Walpole recorded
       the criticism of "1811."

JANE BARKER

588   Gibbons, G. S. "Mrs. Jane Barker." N&Q, 11 (1922), 278-
      279. Information about her life can be gleaned from the
      copy of her poems in the library at Magdalen College, Ox-
      ford.

589   McBurney, William H. "Edmund Curll, Mrs. Jane Barker and
      the English Novel." PQ, 37 (1958), 385-399. She was the
      first of many minor women novelists whose books were sold
      by Curll. Her works were typical of Curll's fictional of-
      ferings in that they were short, romantic tales which could
      be sold separately or in collections. Barker's works demon-
      strate an awareness of the new "histories" and the influences
      of the continental and English novelists of the late seven-
      teenth and early eighteenth centuries, especially of de
      Scudery, Behn, and Defoe. She was one of the first novel-
      ists to shun scandal and emphasize the edifying potential
      of novel reading.

590   Shugrue, Michael F. "The Sincerest Form of Flattery: Imi-
      tation in the Early Eighteenth Century Novel." SAQ, 70
      (1971), 248-255. See entry #573.

591   Stanglmaier, Karl. Mrs. Jane Barker. Ein Beitrag zur Eng-
      lischen Literaturge schichte. Berlin, 1906. Although the
      majority of the book summarizes the content of her works
      with special attention to her poetry, there is considerable
      discussion of the context of and influences on her work.

592   Ham, Roswell G. "Thomas Otway, Rochester, and Mrs.
       Barry." N&Q, 149 (1925), 165-167. Survey of her
       career.

593   Hook, Lucyle. "Mrs. Elizabeth Barry and Mrs. Anne
       Bracegirdle, Actresses, Their Careers from 1672 to
       1695, A Study in Influences." New York University
       dissertation, 1945. Biographies.

594   Hook, Lucyle. "Portraits of Elizabeth Barry and Anne
       Bracegirdle." Theatre Notebook, 15 (1961), 129-137.
       See item #286.

595   Shaaber, M. A. "A Letter from Mrs. Barry." Univer-
       sity of Pennsylvania Library Chronicle, 16 (1950),
       46-49. Publishes a letter to Lady Lisburne.

596   Summers, Montague. "Betterton and Mrs. Barry in Ham-
       let." TLS, 29 March 1934, p. 229. The Garrick Club
       paintings may depict Mrs. Barry.

597   Baker, Herschel. "Mrs. Behn Forgets." University of
      Texas Studies in English, 22 (1942), 121-123. She tried
      to disguise the fact that The Rover was written by a
      woman.

598   Barrett, Alberta G. "Plot, Characterization, and Theme
      in the Plays of Aphra Behn." University of Pennsylvania
      dissertation, 1965. Rather than mere exercises in en-
      tertainment, Behn's plays are serious comments on human
      nature, sin, and motivation.

599   Batten, Charles L., Jr. "The Source of Aphra Behn's The
      Widow Ranter." RECTR, 13 (1974), 12-18. The play is
      based on the King's Commission report of the Bacon "re-
      bellion" in Virginia (1677) rather than on the pamphlet
      Strange News from Virginia.

600   Bennett, R. E. "A Bibliographical Correction." RES, 3
      (1927), 450-451. Aphra Behn's title A Discourse of the
      World of the Moon refers to John Wilkins' The Discovery
      of a World in the Moone, not to Cyrano de Bergerac's
      Selenarchia.

601   Bernbaum, Ernest. The Drama of Sensibility. Cambridge:
      Harvard University Press, 1925. Aphra Behn's treatment
      of love and marriage in her plays foreshadows later
      drama of sensibility.

602   Bernbaum, Ernest. "Mrs. Behn's Biography a Fiction."
      PMLA, 23 (1913), 432-453. Autobiographical statements
      in Oroonoko and The Fair Jilt are either "lies" or "ab-
      solutely untrustworthy." The Life and Memoirs of Mrs.
      Behn (1696) is "a tissue of inaccuracies, improbabilities,
      and falsehoods" and was written by Gildon whose journal-
      istic practices were generally unscrupulous. The seven-
      teen letters written to or by Behn in the Calendar of
      State Papers of Charles II contradict Gildon and, there-
      fore, The Life should be seen as one of the many fictitious
      biographies popular at the time.

603   Bernbaum, Ernest. "Mrs. Behn's Oroonoko" in Anniversary
      Papers by Colleagues and Pupils of George Lyman Kittredge.
      Boston: Houghton Mifflin, 1913. Her novel is a romantic
      novel and, despite her claims, not realistic because of
      her special knowledge of Surinam. In fact, she never went

to Surinam. Mr. Bernbaum bases his argument on her lack of motive, chronological discrepancies, and the absence of any knowledge unavailable to the average Englishman.

604   Blashfield, Evangeline. Portraits and Backgrounds: Hrotsvitha, Aphra Behn, Aissé, Rosalba Carriera. Freeport, N. Y.: Books for Libraries Press, 1971 (rpt. of New York: Scribner's, 1917, edition). This is an admiring survey of her life and work with numerous quotations and sympathetic comments.

605   Böker, Uwe. "Sir Walter Ralegh, Daniel Defoe, und die Namengeblung in Aphra Behn's Oroonoko." Anglia, 90 (1972), 92-104. Historical characters in Oroonoko retain their own names, as Behn's claim to verisimilitude would require, and fictional characters are given names which reveal their personalities and circumstances.

606   Bruce, Donald. Topics of Restoration Comedy. New York: St. Martin's Press, 1974. See item #248.

607   Cameron, W. J. "George Granville and the 'Remaines' of Aphra Behn." N&Q, 204 (1959), 88-92. Behn wrote several poems in the section "Remaines of Belin" appended to The History of Adolphus (1691), others are by George Granville.

608   Cameron, W. J. New Light on Aphra Behn: an investigation into the facts and fictions surrounding her journey to Surinam in 1663 and her activities as a spy in Flanders in 1666. Auckland: U. of Auckland Press, 1961. A detailed study of her life in Surinam and on the continent presents most of the evidence on her activities. The book includes her letters from Flanders.

609   Day, Robert Adams. "Aphra Behn's First Biography." Studies in Bibliography, 22 (1969), 227-240. The three versions of "Life and Memoirs" and a chronology constructed from other printed sources show that the author included almost nothing about her which was not in print. Behn rather than Gildon probably wrote the "Life."

610   Duchovnay, Gerald C. "Aphra Behn's Oroonoko: A Critical Edition." Indiana University dissertation, 1971. The dissertation is an edited text of the novel with an historical and critical introduction and appendices of textual variants.

611   Gagen, Jean E. The New Woman: Her Emergence in English
       Drama, 1660-1730. New York: Twayne, 1954. See item
       #269.

612   Gilder, Rosamund. "Aphra Behn." Theatre Arts Monthly,
       12 (1928), 397-409. A biographical sketch calls her
       "first and foremost" of the women playwrights of the
       Restoration.

613   Graham, C. B. "An Echo of Jonson in Aphra Behn's Sir
       Patient Fancy." MLN, 53 (1938), 278-279. The play
       borrows 2½ lines from Volpone to heighten Wittmore's
       embarrassment in finding his rival instead of a basket
       of gold.

614   Guffey, George. Two English Novelists: Aphra Behn and
       Anthony Trollope. Los Angeles: Clark Library, 1975.
       The critical emphasis on the authenticity of the bio-
       graphical data in Oroonoko has been a barrier to study
       of the novel itself. Oroonoko, like most of Behn's work,
       has significant political elements. Strong parallels
       are intended between James II and Oroonoko, and the book
       argues for the absolute power of hereditary monarchs.

615   Hahn, Emily. Aphra Behn. London: Cape, 1951. This
       is a biography of Behn concentrating on her feminine
       personality.

616   Hahn, Emily. Purple Passage: A Novel about a Lady
       both Famous and Fantastic. Garden City: Doubleday,
       1950. A popular and fictionalized biography develop-
       ing Behn's possible affair with William Scott in con-
       siderable detail.

617   Hamblen, Abigail A. "Lady Who Lived by Her Wit." Dal-
       housie Review, 37 (1957), 52-56. Aphra Behn's reputation
       as a writer rests on Oroonoko. Her life and this work
       still puzzle critics.

618   Hamelius, Paul. "The Source of Southerne's Fatal Mar-
       riage." MLR, 4 (1909), 352-356. Southerne borrows
       extensively from Behn's The Fair Vow-Breaker.

619   Hargreaves, H. A. "The Birth of Mrs. Behn." Humanities
       Association Bulletin, 16 (1965), 19-20. After summariz-
       ing the dispute over Behn's birth, Mr. Hargreaves re-
       ports that A. Purvis found a record of the death of the
       "Afara Amis" previously thought to be Aphra Behn.

620   Hargreaves, H. A. "A Case for Mr. Behn." N&Q, 207
       (1962), 203-205. Joachim Beene, a "hamburgher," may
       have been Aphra Behn's husband.

621   Hargreaves, H. A. "The Life and Plays of Mrs. Aphra
       Behn." Duke University dissertation, 1960. Her work
       is typical of many lesser playwrights' but includes
       other elements which help explain her popularity. Her
       life and ability to use the stage as medium make her
       work distinctive.

622   Hargreaves, H. A. "Mrs. Behn's Warning of the Dutch
       'Thames Plot.'" N&Q, 207 (1962), 61-63. Mrs. Behn
       gave advance warning of a Dutch plan to sink ships in
       the Thames.

623   Hargreaves, H. A. "New Evidence of the Realism of Mrs.
       Behn's Oroonoko." Bulletin of the New York Public Li-
       brary, 74 (1970), 437-444. Much of the realism depends
       upon her claim to being an eye-witness to events in the
       book. The costume which she donated for Mrs. Brace-
       girdle's performance in The Indian Queen adds credence
       to her story.

624   Harris, Brice. "Aphra Behn's 'Bajazet to Gloriana.'"
       TLS, 9 February 1933, p. 92. Evidence suggests that
       the poem should be attributed to Behn.

625   Hill, Rowland M. "Aphra Behn's Use of Setting. MLQ,
       7 (1946), 189-203. She locates eight novels in places
       in which she lived or traveled and claims some degree
       of realism for them. A chronological study of her
       novels shows developing interest in setting and skill
       in linking the credible and romantic.

626   Hogan, Floriana T. "The Spanish Comedia and the English
       Comedy of Intrigue with Special Reference to Aphra Behn."
       Boston University dissertation, 1955. The Spanish co-
       media influenced Behn's plays of intrigue.

627   Johnson, Edwin D. "Aphra Behn's Oroonoko." Journal of
       Negro History, 10 (1925), 334-342. Discusses the his-
       torical validity.

628   Jordan, Robert. "Mrs. Behn and Sir Anthony Love." Res-
       toration and Eighteenth Century Theatre Research, 12
       (1973), 58-59. The plot of Southerne's most successful

comedy is based on Behn's novel, The Lucky Mistake. Southerne may have created two characters, Verole and Ilford, out of Behn's Vernole.

629   Laborde, G. -M. "Du nouveau sur Aphra Behn." Etudes Anglaises, 16 (1963), 364-368. Primarily a survey of scholars' efforts to reconstruct Behn's biography, this article argues that the personality revealed in her letters and novels continually intrigues her readers.

630   Langhans, Edward A. "Three Early Eighteenth-Century Prompt-books." Theatre Notebook, 20 (1966), 142-150. The promptbook for The Rover in the University of London Library is copiously annotated.

631   Leja, Alfred E. "Aphra Behn--Tory." University of Texas dissertation, 1962. The first part of the dissertation gives biographical information, and the next three parts consider her political efforts as spy, playwright, and poet.

632   Lindquist, Carol A. "The Prose Fiction of Aphra Behn." University of Maryland dissertation, 1970. Her appeal in her own time was the result of her ability to incorporate and modify literary conventions and to express the "secular ethos" of her age.

633   Link, Frederick M. Aphra Behn. New York: Twayne, 1968. Mr. Link surveys her plays, poems, translations and novels, giving plot summaries and comments about structure, theme, unity, and technique. The final chapter summarizes her literary reputation and argues that her life and work reflect nearly every facet of her time. An annotated, selected bibliography concludes the volume.

634   Link, Frederick M. Introduction to The Rover. Lincoln: University of Nebraska Press, 1966. The Rover came at a time when Behn was an experienced playwright, skilled in adapting material borrowed from her predecessors. While the play was carefully designed to be popular, it includes a biting attack on forced marriage and a moving heroine.

635   Mathews, Ernst G. "Montfleury's Ecole des Jaloux and Aphra Behn's The False Count." MLN, 54 (1939), 438-439. Behn adapted Montfleury's Ecole for English taste by

eliminating moral elements, adding and changing characters, and complicating the plot.

636   Meyer, Arlin G. "Romance and Realism in the Novels of
       Aphra Behn and Previous Prose Fiction." Ohio University
       dissertation, 1967. Mrs. Behn is a transition figure,
       pivotal between the traditions of romantic and realistic
       conceptions of the Restoration and the combining of
       these traditions in the eighteenth century. Seven of
       her novels are romantic, five realistic, and Oroonoko
       combines the strains.

637   Mignon, Elizabeth. Crabbed Age and Youth: The Old Men
       and Women in the Restoration Comedy of Manners. Dur-
       ham: Duke University Press, 1947. See item #304.

638   Mizener, Arthur. "Poems by Mrs. Behn." TLS, 8 May 1937,
       364. Two poems, not included in the Summers' Works, are
       attributed to her in the 1715 edition of the Works of
       George Villiers, second Duke of Buckingham.

639   More, Paul E. "A Bluestocking of the Restoration." The
       Nation, 103 (1916), 299-302 and 322-323. In a review
       of Summers' Works, the author argues that Mr. Summers'
       zeal outran his judgment in his biography. For example,
       she wrote her plays to add zest to life rather than to
       reform and convert, and she was very much the child of
       Restoration theatre. Her claims to originality rest
       upon her plays.

640   Mundy, P. D. "Aphra Behn (1640?-1689)." N&Q, 200 (1955),
       23. Mrs. Behn may be a descendent of the Amis and Bean
       families of Etham and Elmsted.

641   Mundy, P. D. "Aphra Behn, Novelist and Dramatist (1640-
       89). N&Q, 199 (1954), 199-201. She was probably the
       daughter of a Wye, Kent, barber. The name was fairly
       common in that region.

642   Norman, William. "Mrs. Behn's Emperor of the Moon." N&Q,
       149 (1914), 275. The 1777 production at the Patagonian
       Theatre was a revival.

643   Platt, Harrison G., Jr. "Astrea and Celadon: An Un-
       touched Portrait of Aphra Behn." PMLA, 49 (1934), 544-
       559. Behn went to Surinam with Thomas Scot, shared her
       friends' contempt for Major William Byam, and was asso-
       ciated more with Scot than with the English government

in her secret service work in Holland. This account explains anti-Tory elements and autobiographical discrepancies in Oroonoko and contradicts Gildon's biography.

644   Purvis, A.   "Mrs. Aphra Behn."   Amateur Historian, 1 (1953/54), opposite page 261. Gosse's assertion that Behn was "Aphra Amis" is proved erroneous.

645   Ramsaran, J. A.   "Oroonoko: A Study of the Factual Elements."   N&Q, 205 (1960), 142-145. Elements in Behn's fiction are authentic.

646   S., M.   "Mrs. Behn's Emperor of the Moon."   N&Q, 149 (1914), 394. The sources of the play are Arlequin Empereur and the commedia dell'arte.

647   Sackville-West, Victoria.   Aphra Behn.   The Incomparable Astrea. New York: Viking, 1928; rpt. New York: Russell and Russell, 1970. A popular biography pictures Behn as zestful, light-hearted, reckless, and extravagant. Behn did "not trust her own genius" and seldom cared enough to imbue her works with the realistic portraits of London which she could do so well.

648   Sackville-West, Victoria.   Six Brilliant English Women. London: Howe, 1930. Includes a romantic biography of Behn.

649   Schulte, Edvige.   "L'apporto die traduction alla nascita del romanzo inglese moderno e la tecnica adaltata do Aphra Behn in The Lucky Mistake le forte del romanzo." Riv. di studi salernitani, 1 (1968), 211-238.

650   Scott, Clayton S., Jr.   "Aphra Behn: A Study in Dramatic Continuity." Texas Christian University dissertation, 1972. Her plays indicate the direct influences and continuity of English dramatic traditions operating in the Restoration.

651   Seeber, Edward D.   "Oroonoko and Crusoe's Man Friday." Modern Language Quarterly, 12 (1951), 286-291. Defoe modeled Friday on Oroonoko. The evidence includes passages describing the characters and Oroonoko's reminding the slaves of "Black Friday."

652   Seeber, Edward D. "Oroonoko in France in the Eighteenth
      Century." PMLA, 51 (1936), 953-959. The substance and
      technique of much of the littérature négrophile of the
      eighteenth century and much French abolitionist senti-
      ment came from Oroonoko. Descriptions of Negroes and
      plots in works by such writers as de Staël, La Vallée,
      and Saint-Lambert show direct influence.

653   Seward, Patricia M. "Calderon and Aphra Behn: Spanish
      Borrowings in The Young King." Bulletin of Hispanic
      Studies, 49 (1972), 149-164. Behn borrowed from La
      vida es sueno.

654   Shapiro, Karl, and Robert Baum. A Prosody Handbook.
      New York: Harper & Row, 1965, pp. 169-172. Behn's
      carpe diem song "When Maidens are Young" from The Em-
      peror of the Moon has prosodic imagination which drama-
      tizes the contrast between adult routine and youthful
      joy.

655   Shea, Peter K. "Alexander Pope and Aphra Behn on Wit."
      N&Q, 220 (1975), 12. Her definition of wit in the dedi-
      catory poem to Henry Higdon's A Modern Essay on the
      Tenth Satyr of Juvenal is very similar to Pope's "True
      Wit is Nature to Advantage drest/What oft was Thought,
      but ne'er so well Exprest."

656   Sheffey, Ruthe T. "The Literary Reputation of Aphra
      Behn." University of Pennsylvania dissertation, 1959.
      A detailed assessment of the reputation of Mrs. Behn's
      work begins with her contemporaries and includes a
      recognition of the influence that political, social,
      and literary opinion exerted on their critical judgments.

657   Sheffey, Ruthe T. "Some Evidence for a New Source of
      Aphra Behn's Oroonoko." SP, 59 (1962), 52-63. Her
      friendship with Thomas Tryon and knowledge of his Friend-
      ly Advice to the Gentle-men-Planters of the East and West
      Indies influenced the setting and treatment of slavery in
      Oroonoko.

658   Siegel, Paul. "Aphra Behn's Gedichte und Prosawerke."
      Anglia, 25 (1902), 86-128 and 329-385. This is a biogra-
      phy and survey of her work.

659   Simpson, Joan M. "The Incomparable Aphra." Cornhill
      Magazine, 1067 (1971), 368-371. Aphra Behn used "Astrea"
      as a pseudonym as a writer and as a spy.

660   Stephenson, Peter S.   "Three Playwright Novelists: The
      Contribution of Dramatic Techniques to Restoration and
      Early Eighteenth Century Prose Fiction." University of
      California, Davis, dissertation, 1969. Drama was an im-
      portant influence on the development of the novel and
      especially on the novels of Richardson and Fielding. The
      plays and novels of Behn, Davys, and Congreve serve as
      examples.

661   Summers, Montague. "Aphra Behn and Montfleury." MLN,
      56 (1941), 562. The False Count's source is L'Ecole
      des Jaloux.

662   Summers, Montague. "Memoir of Mrs. Behn" in The Works
      of Aphra Behn. London: Heinemann, 1915. A brief biogra-
      phy evaluating her place in society and in literary his-
      tory quotes letters, periodicals, and critical remarks.

663   Summers, Montague. "A Note on Mrs. Behn and a Dickens
      Parallel." N&Q, 159 (1930), 274-275. Montfleury's
      Ecole des Jaloux provided the plot for The False Count.

664   Suwannabha, Sumitra. "The Feminine Eye: Augustan
      Society as Seen by Selected Women Dramatists of the
      Restoration and Early Eighteenth Century." Indiana Uni-
      versity dissertation, 1973. See item #334.

665   Sypher, Wylie. "A Note on the Realism of Mrs. Behn's
      Oroonoko." MLQ, 3 (1942), 401-405. She described Ko-
      romantin slaves, a distinct type, and punishments which
      are verified by historical accounts.

666   Tucker, Joseph E. "The Earliest English Translation
      of La Rochefoucauld's Maximes." MLN, 64 (1949), 413-
      415. John Davies, not Behn, was the first translator
      of the Maximes.

667   Turner, Margaret. "A Note on the Standard of English
      Translation from the French, 1685-1720." N&Q, 199
      (1954), 516-521. Mrs. Behn outlines the problems of
      translating French contemporary literature in the preface
      to her Entretiens sur la Pluralite des Mondes. Her trans-
      lation of Entretiens is superior to Glanvil's or Gardiner's;
      her translation of La Rochefoucauld's Maximes is freer.

668   Van Lennep, William. "Two Restoration Comedies." TLS,
      28 January 1939, 57-58. Narcissus Luttrell's copy of

the quarto of The Revenge attributes the play to Aphra Behn. Luttrell acquired a copy of The False Count on 17 December 1681 which suggests that the play must have been performed in November or early December of that year.

669 Wagenknecht, Edward. "In Praise of Mrs. Behn." Colophon, 18 (1934), n. pag. This is a summary listing her achievements.

670 Wermuth, Paul C. "Bacon's Rebellion in the London Theatre." Virginia Cavalcade, 7 (1957), 38-39. The author compares The Widow Ranter to Bacon's Rebellion, testing the play's historical accuracy.

671 Witmer, Anne, and John Freehafer. "Aphra Behn's Strange News from Virginia." University of Pennsylvania Library Chronicle, 34 (1968), 7-23. The Widow Ranter is the first English play to be based on an historical event in colonial America. Nathaniel Bacon's life and actions provide plot and character; Aphra Behn's life supplies setting and love interest.

672 Woodcock, George. The Incomparable Aphra. London: Boardman, 1948. This biography evaluates her reputation, the success of her work, and, in the final chapter, her lasting achievements.

673   Hartmann, Cyril H. _Enchanting Bellamy_. London: Heinemann, 1956. A biography without notes is based on her _Apology_ and research and describes theatrical life and personalities in considerable detail.

674   Oman, Carola. _David Garrick_. London: Hodder and Stoughton, 1958. The book includes an account of her relationship to David Garrick.

675   Sewell, Brocard. "George Ann Bellamy." _Wiseman Review_, 235 (1961), 56-69. This biography, based primarily on _An Apology for the Life of George Anne Bellamy_, pays special attention to the influence of her Catholicism.

676   Waldhorn, Arthur. "Charles Churchill and 'Statira.'" _MLN_, 63 (1948), 114-118. Editors Tooke, Hannay, and Laver identify "Statira" in Churchill's _Rosciad_ as the listless actress Miss Pritchard. Bellamy played a better known Statira and is a more likely candidate because of internal evidence, her personality, and Churchill's relationships with her.

ANNE BRACEGIRDLE

677   Hook, Lucyle. "Anne Bracegirdle's First Appearance."
      Theatre Notebook, 13 (1959), 133-136. Her first ap-
      pearance was a child in Otway's The Orphan in 1685.

678   Hook, Lucyle. "Portraits of Elizabeth Barry and Anne
      Bracegirdle." Theatre Notebook, 15 (1961), 129-137.
      See item #286.

679   Hook, Lucyle. Mrs. Elizabeth Barry and Mrs. Anne Brace-
      girdle, Actresses, Their Careers from 1672 to 1695: A
      Study in Influences. New York: New York University
      Press, 1950. See item #285.

680   Howarth, R. G. "Congreve and Anne Bracegirdle." English
      Studies in Africa, 4 (1961), 159-161. See item #287.

681   Noyes, Robert G. "Mrs. Bracegirdle's Acting in Crowne's
      Justice Busy." MLN, 43 (1928), 390-391. A curious com-
      ment on Mrs. Bracegirdle by John Downes in his Roscius
      Anglicanus is explained by reference to the text of a
      song which the famous actress sang from Crowne's Justice
      Busy.

682   Spencer, Hazelton. "Downes's Tribute to Mrs. Bracegirdle."
      MLN, 44 (1929), 375. Although Noyes' discovery concern-
      ing Downe's praise of Mrs. Bracegirdle is interesting,
      it in no way impeaches the gallantry of Downes.

683   Alspach, Russell K.   "Charlotte Brooke: A Forerunner of
      the Celtic Renaissance."   The General Magazine and His-
      torical Chronicle, 40 (1938), 178-183.   Brooke's Reliques
      anticipates modern attention to Irish legends, language,
      and metric difficulties although it had little direct in-
      fluence.

684   Ashley, R. N. Introduction to Reliques of Irish Poetry
      (1789) by Charlotte Brooke and A Memoir of Miss Brooke
      (1816) by A. C. H. Seymour.   Gainesville: Scholars Fac-
      similes & Reprints, 1970.   The introduction gives a brief
      biography, a summary of Brooke's literary career, and
      assesses the contribution her collection and translations
      of Irish poetry made as a "minor national treasure."

685   Gantz, Kenneth.   "Charlotte Brooke's Reliques of Irish
      Poetry and the Ossianic Controversy."   University of
      Texas Studies in English, 20 (1940), 137-156.   Reliques,
      the first book to present any quantity of Irish poetry
      to the public, was a significant factor in the controver-
      sy over Irish literature aroused by James MacPherson.

686   Needham, Gwendolyn B. "Mrs. Frances Brooke: Dramatic
      Critic." TN, 15 (1961), 47-52. The Old Maid includes
      seven numbers devoted to commentary on drama. The reviews
      of plays and discussions of Shakespeare productions are
      unusually full for her time.

687   Noyes, Robert G. The Thespian Mirror; Shakespeare in the
      Eighteenth-Century Novel. Providence: Brown University
      Press, 1955. Brooke's The Excursion contains a lampoon of
      Garrick as theatre manager.

688   Adelstein, Michael E. _Fanny Burney_. New York: Twayne,
       1968. Although she can claim no more than a "secondary
       place in the history of eighteenth century literature,"
       she is significant as the author of one important novel,
       as a notable figure in the development of the novel of
       manners and as an interesting and vigorous if limited
       writer of diaries, letters, and journals. Adelstein at-
       tempts an integrated study of Burney's life and works.

689   Anon. "The Butterfly Becomes a Moth." _TLS_, 15 December
       1972, pp. 1531-1532. The first two volumes of Hemlow's
       Journals and Letters of Fanny Burney show her deleting,
       suppressing, and revising as though she were "remaking
       herself, turning Fanny Burney into Mme. d'Arblay, the
       witty girl into the ponderous literary lady."

690   Anon. "Fanny Burney: An Identification." _N&Q_, 199 (1954),
       359; 368. She visited Mrs. Buxton on 4 August 1789.

691   Anon. "Fanny Burney (1752-1840): A Life in a World of
       Fantasy." _TLS_, 6 January 1940, p. 9. Fanny Burney's
       diaries are a record of fantasy and wish-fulfillment,
       not fact. Unlike the great realist Boswell, she fashioned
       a dramatic incident which pleased her from a basis in fact.

692   Anon. "The Real Fanny Burney." _TLS_, 9 March 1962, p.
       160. In this review of John Wain's edition of selections
       from _Fanny Burney's Diary_, the author emphasizes the "in-
       imitable entertainment" that the diaries provide and
       notes that Fanny Burney's intense interest in vulgarity
       is significant.

693   Benkovitz, Miriam J. "Dr. Burney's Memoirs." _RES_, 10
       (1959), 257-268. An examination of the autobiographical
       fragments left in manuscript by Dr. Charles Burney makes
       it clear that Fanny Burney's _Memoirs of Dr. Burney_ create
       a false and unjust portrait of the man. In her senti-
       mental devotion to her father's memory, she produces a
       biography which is unfaithful to her father's intricate
       character. Among the most serious failures of the
       Memoirs is its inadequate treatment of Dr. Burney's
       professional association with music and the theatre.

694   Benkovitz, Miriam J. Introduction to _Edwy and Elgina_.
       Hamden, Connecticut: Shoestring Press, 1957. The in-
       troduction provides a critical examination of Burney's

tragedy, concluding that it is a failure, but a significantly characteristic failure which exhibits the literary vices which mar Burney's later works.

695   Blakeney, T. S. "A Minor Character in Fanny Burney's Diary Identified." N&Q, 194 (1949), 559. Mr. B----y in Volume I of Burney's Diary (Dobson edition) is identified as Edward Blakeney.

696   Blakeney, T. S. "Queen Charlotte: Fanny Burney's Employer." New Rambler, ser. C 5 (1968), 3-15.

697   Bloom, Edward A. and Lillian D. Introduction to Camilla: Or a Picture of Youth. London: Oxford University Press, 1972. The introduction provides a history of the composition, publication, and early critical fortunes of Burney's third novel.

698   Bracey, Robert. "Hawkins in Madame D'Arblay's Diary." N&Q, 171 (1936), 43. The "Mr. Hawkins" in her Diary is identified as an ex-Benedictine monk who eventually, after his apostasy, married Ann Burney.

699   Bugenot, A. S. "The Wanderer de Fanny Burney: Essai de Rehabilitation." Etudes Anglaises, 15 (1962), 225-232. Her last novel, The Wanderer, though it has been condemned by such critics as Macaulay and Austin Dobson, is nevertheless an interesting and successful novel. Although it possesses the characteristic virtues of Fanny Burney's novels--convincing characters, lively humor and satire, and variety in the scenes and in the portrayal of manners-- only to a limited extent does it approach the other novels. It is the intimate and moving swan-song of a remarkable writer.

700   C., R. W. "A Date in Fanny Burney." N&Q, 189 (1945), 190. A passage in Fanny Burney's Diary dated "Thursday, Feb. 23" should actually be dated 24 July 1783.

701   Cecil, Lord David. "Fanny Burney" in Poets and Storytellers. New York: Macmillan, 1949, pp. 77-96. Evelina signaled the entry of the lady into fiction. She altered the Fielding-esque novel and made it feminine.

702   Cecil, Lord David. "Fanny Burney's Novels" in Essays on the Eighteenth Century Presented to David Nichol Smith in Honour of his Seventieth Birthday. Oxford: Clarendon

Press, 1945, pp. 212-224. Despite her limitations as a novelist, Burney is a significant figure in the history of the English novel because it was she who first attempted to "combine the methods of Richardson and Fielding." In her "feminization of the Fielding type of novel," she helped set the stage for the development of nineteenth century novelistic conventions and concerns.

703   Clifford, James L. "Fanny Burney Meets Edmund Burke." TLS, 23 July 1938, p. 493. Compares her vivid characterization of Burke in her note to Mrs. Piozzi with the account in her Diary.

704   Coolidge, Theresa. "Family Concerns of Fanny Burney." More Books, 21 (1946), 83-86. Notes the Boston Public Library's acquisition of three letters from Fanny Burney to her younger brother Charles. All of the letters concern family matters.

705   Delachaud, Eugénie. "Fanny Burney, Intermédiare Manquée entre l'Angleterre et la France." Revue de Littèrature Comparie, 15 (1935), 381-386. Although her marriage to a Frenchman and her many contacts with France might have made it possible for her to act as an intermediary between French and English culture and literature, her conservative education and outlook, her essentially middle-class attitudes, her distrust of romanticism, and of new trends in thought in general, along with a certain lack of curiosity made her a failure in this role.

706   Dugdale, E. T. S. "Madame D'Arblay." Quarterly Review, 274 (1940), 65-76. A sketch of Fanny Burney's life, literary career, and critical reputation.

707   Eaves, T. C. D. "Edward Burney's Illustrations to Evelina." PMLA, 62 (1947), 995-999. Edward Burney, cousin of Fanny Burney, was an artist and illustrator who, sometime around 1780, produced three illustrations for Evelina. These three illustrations were exhibited at the Royal Academy and one of them was published in a 1791 printing of the novel. It is interesting that two of the three illustrations represent decidedly sentimental scenes from the novel.

708   Edwards, Averyl. Fanny Burney, 1752-1840: A Biography. London: Staples Press, 1948. A short, popular biography with relatively little to say about the novels.

709 Ehrenpreis, Anne Henry. Introduction to Emmeline. The
     Orphan of the Castle. London: Oxford, 1971. The novel
     may have influenced Burney.

710 Erikson, J. P. "Evelina and Betsy Thoughtless." Texas
     Studies in Literature and Language, 6 (1964), 96-103.
     Although the parallels between Eliza Haywood's History
     of Miss Betsy Thoughtless (1751) and Fanny Burney's
     Evelina (1778) are numerous, indeed more numerous than
     has been noted, there are many significant differences
     between the two novels. Thus, while both novels deal
     with young ladies making their first visits to London,
     Betsy continually wonders whether to conform to society
     while Evelina wonders how to conform. Evelina is less
     romantic, less conventional, less episodic, more sophis-
     ticated, more tightly structured, and more truly a novel
     of manners than Betsy Thoughtless.

711 Firth, J. R. "Modes of Meaning." Essays and Studies,
     4 (1951), 118-149. Contains a brief discussion of the
     prose style in Fanny Burney's letters.

712 Gates, William B. "An Unpublished Burney Letter." ELH,
     5 (1938), 302-304. A heretofore unpublished letter from
     Fanny Burney to her brother James makes clear the nov-
     elist's concern over the harsh criticisms of The Wanderer.
     The letter is printed with notes.

713 Gérin, Winifred. The Young Fanny Burney: A Biography.
     London: Nelson, 1961. A biographical sketch aimed pri-
     marily at younger readers which treats Burney's life up
     to the publication of Evelina. Using the Burney diaries,
     Gerin gives special attention to her relationships both
     inside and outside the family. One chapter is devoted
     to Evelina.

714 German, Howard L. "Fanny Burney and the Late Eighteenth
     Century Novel." Ohio State University dissertation, 1958.
     In all of her novels, Burney is concerned primarily with
     manners. Although this concern is consistent throughout
     the novels, she deals with it most successfully in her
     first two novels. The later novels are less successful,
     in part because of an increasing sentimentality and didac-
     ticism. The trend toward greater sentimentality and didac-
     ticism can be explained in terms of both external literary
     influences and her individual development as a personality.

715   Glock, Waldo S. "Appearance and Reality: The Education
      of Evelina." Essays in Literature, (Spring, 1975), 32-
      41. Evelina's continual inability to distinguish between
      appearance and reality adequately would seem to call for
      a process of education in the heroine which would result
      in the final realization concerning deception. Burney's
      refusal to pursue her theme of appearance and reality to
      its logical conclusion --"a permanent change in Evelina"--
      suggests that she was interested less in the serious treat-
      ment of a serious theme than in using the heroine's im-
      perfect perception as a device to develop plot and to pro-
      duce comic situations.

716   Graham, W. H. "Fanny Burney's Evelina." Contemporary
      Review, 171 (1947), 351-354. Evelina is not only a
      novel distinguished by a craftsmanship, a style, and
      a felicity characteristic of the age in which it was
      produced, it is also a vivid picture of upper and middle
      class life in the second half of the century.

717   Hahn, Emily. A Degree of Prudery. London: Arthur Bar-
      ker, 1951. A popular account of Burney's life before
      her marriage.

718   Harris, Harvey R. "Realism in the Fiction of Frances
      Burney." University of Southern California dissertation,
      1957. An examination of realism in her fiction with
      consideration of how closely she approximated contempo-
      rary demands finds that she did conform, modifying her
      psychological realism with demands for decorum.

719   Hemlow, Joyce. A Catalogue of the Burney Family Corres-
      pondence, 1749-1878. New York: New York Public Library
      and McGill, Queens University Press, 1971. The intro-
      duction indicates the nature and extent of the Burney
      family correspondence. There are also discussions of
      the provenance of the Burney manuscripts and of the
      Barrett, Comyn, and Osborn collections of Burney papers.
      A chart graphically illustrates the directions of the
      correspondence.

720   Hemlow, Joyce. "Dr. Johnson and Fanny Burney: Some
      Additions to the Record." Bulletin of the New York
      Public Library, 55 (1951), 55-65. Fanny Burney manu-
      scripts in the New York Public Library shed new light
      on Dr. Johnson's character and behavior and on Burney's
      attitudes toward him.

721 Hemlow, Joyce. "Dr. Johnson and the young Burneys." New Light on Dr. Johnson, F. W. Hilles, ed. New Haven: Yale University Press, 1959, pp. 319-339. Quoting frequently from Burney's diaries, Hemlow traces Johnson's relationship with Charles Burney's various children from his first meeting with them in 1777 to his death.

722 Hemlow, Joyce. "Fanny Burney and the Courtesy Books." PMLA, 65 (1950), 732-761. The courtesy books and other ethical literature of the later eighteenth century were a major influence on the works of Fanny Burney. This influence, which was more and more evident as Burney's career developed, led to an increasingly constricted and narrowly conventional view of art and life, and especially in Camilla, to novels in which the distinctive qualities and felicities of Evelina were conspicuously absent.

723 Hemlow, Joyce. "Fanny Burney: Playwright." University of Toronto Quarterly, 19 (1950), 170-189. Although most of her biographers have known of Fanny Burney's tragedy Edwy and Elgina and her two comedies, Love and Fashion and The Witlings, it is less well known that she wrote two five act tragedies, Herbert De Vere and The Siege of Pevensey, left a draft for a third tragedy, Elberta, wrote two five act comedies, A Busy Day and The Woman-Hater, and had begun another dramatic piece about "Fanny Simper." Each piece is discussed in terms of its outstanding features and its place in Burney's career.

724 Hemlow, Joyce. The History of Fanny Burney. Oxford: Clarendon Press, 1958. A thorough, scholarly, critical biography based largely on unpublished Burney manuscripts. The biographer is especially concerned with the relationship of Burney's life and milieu to her writings.

725 Hemlow, Joyce. "Letters and Journals of Fanny Burney: Establishing the Text." Editing Eighteenth-Century Texts, D. I. B. Smith, ed. Toronto: University of Toronto Press, 1968, pp. 25-43. A survey of Hemlow's efforts to correct the many confusions and distortions wrought by previous editors of the Burney manuscripts.

726 Hemlow, Joyce (ed.). The Journals and Letters of Fanny Burney (Madame d'Arblay). Vols. 1- Oxford: Clarendon Press, 1972- . Each volume has an introduction which includes textual and biographical information. The scope and editorial policy is explained.

727   Hemlow, Joyce. "Preparing a Catalogue of the Burney
       Family Correspondence, 1749-1878." Bulletin of the New
       York Public Library, 71 (1967), 486-495. The author
       describes the preparation for and scope of a catalogue
       of the Burney family correspondence. Special attention
       is given to the nature and provenance of Burney family
       papers housed in the New York Public Library, the Yale
       Beinecke Library, and the British Museum.

728   Hesselgrave, Ruth A. Lady Miller and the Batheaston
       Literary Circle. New Haven: Yale University Press,
       1927. See item # 1472.

729   Hicks, Phyllis D. "Fanny Burney." Spectator, 5 January
       1940, pp. 10-11. Although Evelina and Cecilia now seem
       dated and Camilla and The Wanderer are unreadable, Fan-
       Burney's journals and letters are still interesting and
       vital.

730   Johnson, R. Brimley. Introduction to Fanny Burney and
       the Burneys. London: Stanley Paul, 1926. A collection
       of writings by various members of the Burney family is
       prefaced by a brief introduction discussing the Burney
       family character.

731   Johnson, R. Brimley. The Women Novelists. London: W.
       Collins, 1918. See item #372.

732   Kamm, Josephine M. The Story of Fanny Burney. London:
       Methuen, 1966. A biographical sketch intended for younger
       readers.

733   Laski, Margharita. "Antedatings of OED in Evelina." N&Q,
       207 (1962), 269-270. The first edition of Evelina con-
       tains seventeen words and phrases which antedate the
       earliest examples given in the OED.

734   Lloyd, Christopher. Fanny Burney. London: Longmans,
       1936. A biography.

735   Malone, Kemp. "Evelina Revisited." Papers on English
       Language and Literature, 1 (1965), 3-19. Although the
       plot of Evelina is essentially conventional, Fanny Bur-
       ney manages, by master handling of setting, characters,
       and events to create an admirable and individual novel.

736 Masefield, Muriel. _The Story of Fanny Burney_: _Being_
     an Introduction to the Diary and Letters of Madame
     d'Arblay. Cambridge: University Press, 1927. A popu-
     lar account of Burney's life and times which is designed
     as a general reader's introduction to the diaries and
     letters.

737 Masefield, Muriel. _Women Novelists from Fanny Burney_
     to George Eliot. London: Nicholson and Watson, 1934.
     Brief discussions of novelists including Burney.

738 Mendenhall, John C. "Sophia Burney Mss." _University of_
     Pennsylvania Library Chronicle, 3 (1934), 9-13. Notes
     the acquisition by the Singer Memorial Collection of
     several manuscripts of Sophia Burney, the niece of Fanny
     Burney. The Mss. contain several poems and two plays,
     all written before Sophia's fourteenth year.

739 Moler, Kenneth L. "Fanny Burney's _Cecilia_ and Jane
     Austen's 'Jack and Alice.'" _English Language Notes_, 3
     (1965), 40-42. The masquerade-scene in Jane Austen's
     youthful sketch "Jack and Alice" is probably a good-
     natured satire on the improbability of a similar scene
     in Fanny Burney's _Cecilia_.

740 Montague, Edwine, and Louis L. Martz. "Fanny Burney's
     Evelina" in _The Age of Johnson_: _Essays Presented to_
     Chauncey Brewster Tinker. New Haven: Yale University
     Press, 1949, pp. 171-181. An imaginary conversation
     between "A" and "B" which centers on the art, the values,
     and, finally, the significance of _Evelina_.

741 Morley, Edith J. _Fanny Burney._ London: Oxford Univer-
     sity Press, 1925. A brief survey of Burney's life and works
     with special attention to the **Diaries**.

742 Morrison, Marjorie Lee. "Fanny Burney and the Theatre."
     _DA_, 17 (1957), 2613-2614. Burney was throughout her
     life devoted to the theatre and drama, evident in her
     Diaries and her novels, accounts for some of the best
     and many of the worst elements in her work.

743 Mulliken, Elizabeth Y. "The Influence of the Drama on
     Fanny Burney's Novels." University of Wisconsin disserta-
     tion, 1970. The plots and characters of Burney's novels
     reveal the influence of contemporary sentimental comedy.
     Thus, like eighteenth century comedy, Burney's novels

contain sentimental characters, "mannered" characters, and farcical characters. So, too, her plots follow those of the drama allowing some farcical action, some conversations of the comedy of manners type, and climactic sentimental scenes.

744 Overman, Antoinette A. An Investigation into the Character of Fanny Burney. Amsterdam: H. J. Paris, 1933. A psychological study of Burney which is based primarily upon the theories of character developed by Klages.

745 Patterson, Emily H. "Unearned Irony in Fanny Burney's Evelina." Durham University Journal, 36 (1975), 200-204. Throughout much of Evelina, unintentional ironies develop because of Burney's imperfect control of her materials. This sort of "unearned" irony and this lack of artistic control are particularly evident in the discrepancy between Villars' role as a "wise, high-minded cleric" and his overt actions.

746 Quennell, Peter C. "Bas Bleu." Spectator, 28 March 1958, p. 410. Fanny Burney was, of all the bas bleus of the latter eighteenth century, the only one to make a "definite contribution to the art of literature." While Evelina seems less interesting now than it did to its contemporaries, Burney's famous Diary retains its interest and appeal.

747 Roberts, W. Wright. "Charles and Fanny Burney in the Light of the New Thrale Correspondence in the John Rylands Library." The Bulletin of the John Rylands Library, 16 (1932), 115-136. Among the large collection of letters contained in the Thrale correspondence newly acquired by the John Rylands Library, there are a number of letters from and many letters concerning the Burney family. These shed new light on the professional careers of Charles and Fanny Burney, on the relationship of the Burneys to Dr. Johnson, Mrs. Thrale, and other important figures, and on the relationships within the Burney family. The author provides a chronological survey of and commentary upon the more significant letters.

748 Rubenstein, Jill. "The Crisis of Identity in Fanny Burney's Evelina." New Rambler, 112 (1972), 45-50. Evelina is a novel in which the heroine is caught between the conflicting demands of heredity and environment. She finds her identity by embracing the morality of her upbringing while managing to come to terms with her heredity.

749   Sambrook, A. J. "Fanny Burney's First Letter to Dr.
      Johnson." RES, 14 (1963), 273-275. Burney's first
      letter to Johnson illustrates the "arch and confident"
      manner in which she handled Johnson.

750   Speakman, James S. "Wit, Humor and Sensibility in Eve-
      lina, Belinda, and Northanger Abbey." University of
      California, Davis, dissertation, 1972. See item #406.

751   Tourtellot, Arthur B. Be Loved No More: The Life and
      Environment of Fanny Burney. Boston: Houghton Mifflin,
      1938. A biography which is based largely upon the Bur-
      ney diaries and which emphasizes the particular flavor
      of Burney's times. Tourtellot argues that Burney's de-
      cline as a writer is explicable in terms of her inability
      to deal with the many cultural changes which took place
      during her life.

752   Vopat, James P. "Evelina: Life as Art--Notes toward
      Becoming a Performer on the Stage of Life." Essays in
      Literature, 2 (1975), 42-52. Evelina moves from vulnerable
      innocence through a "journey into experience" which re-
      sults in her mastering the "life of art," the life which
      is based on "prudence, control, limitation." The final
      marriage to Lord Orville symbolizes her final ability to
      perform successfully upon the stage of life.

753   White, Eugene. Fanny Burney, Novelist: A Study in Tech-
      nique. Hamden, Connecticut: Shoestring Press; London:
      Mark Paterson, 1960. A survey of her literary works.

754   Wonchope, A. J. "The D'Arblays in July 1815." Cornhill,
      154 (1936), 25-32. Prints for the first time two letters,
      one from Alex d'Arblay to his mother, another from Locke
      of Norbury to Alex. These letters provide glimpses of
      the d'Arblay family during the exciting days following
      Napoleon's final defeat at Waterloo.

755   Ewert, Leonore H. "Elizabeth Montagu to Elizabeth Car-
       ter: Literary Gossip and Critical Opinions from the Pen
       of the Queen of the Blues." Claremont Graduate School
       dissertation, 1968. See item #1103.

756   Hampshire, G. "Johnson, Elizabeth Carter and Pope's
       Garden." N&Q, 217 (1972), 221-222. She described a
       visit to Twickenham in a 1738 letter. Johnson may have
       accompanied her, and the visit may have inspired "Ad
       Elisam."

757   Ruhe, Edward. "Birch, Johnson, and Elizabeth Carter: An
       Episode of 1738-39." PMLA, 73 (1958), 491-500. Thomas
       Birch was an intimate friend and likely suitor to Eliza-
       beth Carter for ten months. Their relationship and its
       abrupt end help explain Birch and Johnson's later reserve
       toward each other and account in part for Johnson and
       Carter's life long friendship.

758   Sena, John F. "Melancholy in Anne Finch and Elizabeth
       Carter: The Ambivalence of an Idea." YES, 1 (1971),
       108-119. Their works treat melancholy in women and re-
       flect the ambivalent and changing attitudes of English-
       women toward melancholy. The author begins by outlining
       prevailing opinions about the malady and women's suscep-
       tibility to it.

759   Wilson, Mona. These were Muses. London: Sidgwick and
       Jackson, 1924. The book includes many references to
       Carter's opinions and acquaintances.

760 Bickley, Francis. The Cavendish Family. Boston: Houghton Mifflin, 1914. This is a biography of the family
with a lengthy section on William and Margaret.

761 Firth, C. H. Preface to The Life of William Cavendish,
Duke of Newcastle. London: Routledge, 1906. The Life
went through three editions in eight years but received
mixed responses. A survey of the major events and interests of William Cavendish's life as well as the o-
pinions of his contemporaries included in the book demonstrate that Margaret was a "Boswellian" biographer.
Her autobiography explains her ambitions and admits her
handicaps.

762 Gagen, Jean E. "Honor and Fame in the Works of the
Duchess of Newcastle." SP, 56 (1959), 519-538. Her
obsession with achieving enduring fame grew out of Renaissance humanism. Causing conflict within herself and
with her society, her quest combined the traditional
concept of honor crowning virtue and assuring fame with
her raw ambition to compete in an arena usually reserved
for men.

763 Gagen, Jean E. The New Woman. Her Emergence in English
Drama, 1660-1730. New York: Twayne, 1954. See item #
269.

764 Grant, Douglas. Introduction to The Phanseys of William
Cavendish, Marquis of Newcastle, Addressed to Margaret
Lucas, and Her Letters in Reply. London: Nonesuch, 1956.
Margaret answered William's poems in brief letters. The
introduction points out some of the influences on the
contents of poems and letters.

765 Grant, Douglas. Margaret the First: A Biography of
Margaret Cavendish, Duchess of Newcastle, 1623-1673.
London: Hart-Davis, 1957. A biography with generous
quotations, a checklist of her works, and portraits is
designed to show that she deserves to be better known.

766 Goulding, Richard W. Margaret (Lucas) Duchess of Newcastle. Lincoln: Lincolnshire Chronicle Ltd., 1925.
The Cavendishes took every opportunity to praise each

other and affirm their love in print. Selections from
Sociable Letters describe her life and personality. The
second part of the monograph lists her works, editions
of her work, biographies, portraits, and engravings.

767   Meyer, Gerald D. The Scientific Lady in England 1650-
        1760. Berkeley: U. of California Press, 1955. See
        item #123.

768   Mintz, Samuel I. "The Duchess of Newcastle's Visit to
        the Royal Society." JEGP, 51 (1952), 168-176. The
        Duchess was a "virtuoso" whose "restless mind" "would
        never submit to the discipline of scientific procedure."
        Her visit to the Royal Society in 1667 was a landmark
        of virtuoso science. Mr. Mintz describes her visit
        using Pepys', Evelyn's, and Birch's accounts.

769   Perry, Henry Ten Eyck. The First Duchess of Newcastle
        and Her Husband as Figures in Literary History. Boston:
        Ginn and Company, 1918. Biographies of Margaret, and
        secondarily William, include discussions of their friends
        and associates and conclude with chapters on Margaret's
        writings, autobiography, and personality.

770   Perry, Henry Ten Eyck. "The First Duke and Duchess of
        Newcastle as Figures in Literary History." Harvard
        dissertation, 1916. The dissertation was published
        substantially in its original form. See above.

771   Platz, Norbert H. (ed.) English Dramatic Theories, Vol.
        I: From Elyot to the Age of Dryden, 1531-1668. Tubingen:
        Max Niemeyer Verlag, 1973. This is a collection of state-
        ments of theoretical standards for drama including Cav-
        endish's "To the Readers" from Plays.

772   Prasad, Kashi. "Margaret Cavendish's Blazing World: A
        Seventeenth Century Utopia." Essays Presented to Amy G.
        Stock, Professor of English, Rajasthan University, 1961-
        1965, R. K. Kaul, ed. Jaipur, Rajesthan U. Press, 1965.
        Margaret Cavendish's interests shifted according to what
        was in vogue. Blazing World, a fashionable description
        of a new world, is an allegorical adventure tale bringing
        together her interests in government, philosophy, reli-
        gion, and science and revealing her desire for influence
        and respect. Appears on pages 58-67.

773   Stimpson, Dorothy. Scientists and Amateurs. New York:
        H. Schuman, 1948. The Royal Society granted the Duchess's

123

request to attend a meeting and performed a number of experiments for her.

774   Turberville, A. S. _A History of Welbeck Abbey and Its Owners_. 2 vols. London: Faber and Faber, 1938. She was one of the most notable owners in a long line of distinguished residents. She was absorbed in intellectual pursuits and indifferent to the usual interests and pleasures of women. Her writings contain wisdom, beauty, strange speculations, and evidence of a lively, curious mind.

775   Whibley, Charles. "A Princely Woman." _Essays in Biography_. London: Constable, 1913. She was a vain woman, most proud of her philosophical treatises. Her best work, however, was her biography. Several incidents in her life epitomize her personality.

776   Woolf, Virginia. _The Common Reader_. London: Hogarth, 1925. Margaret Cavendish attacked life with energy and extravagance, provoking laughter and admiration from her contemporaries and from posterity.

777 Anderson, Paul B. "Innocence and Artifice: or, Mrs.
     Centlivre and The Female Tatler." PQ, 16 (1937), 358-
     375. Susannah Centlivre probably wrote the numbers of
     the periodical signed"Emilia," "Rosella," "Arabella,"
     and "Sophronia." The discussions of her plays and
     treatment of the theatrical world, parallels between
     the plots of papers and plays, as well as subject matter
     argue for her authorship.

778 Bowyer, John Wilson. The Celebrated Mrs. Centlivre. Dur-
     ham, N. C.: Duke University Press, 1952. This biographi-
     cal study including discussions of her works, her repu-
     tation, and her literary acquaintances sets her in the
     context of contemporary theatre conditions.

779 Bowyer, John Wilson. "The Life and Works of Mrs. Su-
     sanna Centlivre." Harvard University dissertation, 1928.
     Chapter I is a biography. The other chapters examine
     her plays with particular attention to their stage his-
     tory and her dramatic theory.

780 Bowyer, John Wilson. "Susanna Freeman Centlivre." MLN,
     43 (1928), 78-80. Two poems not included in lists of
     Centlivre's works connect her to Holbeach. She is not
     mentioned, however, in Holbeach parish records although
     "Freeman" is a common name. Mr. Bowyer concludes that
     she must have been born in Ireland while her father was
     an exile and appends a list of her works not given in
     the Cambridge history.

781 Boys, Richard C. "A New Poem by Mrs. Centlivre." MLN,
     57 (1942), 361-362. The periodical Caribbeana published
     a poem by Centlivre with a note explaining the circum-
     stances of the poem's composition and that it was an ex-
     tempore effort of interest because it shows "hasty
     Thoughts of so famous a Wit of that Sex."

782 Burke, Terrence W. "Susanna Centlivre's A Bold Stroke
     for a Wife: A Re-evaluation." Case Western Reserve
     dissertation, 1971. Her play reflects almost everything
     going on in the theatre at the turn of the eighteenth
     century. She is a shrewd judge of what the audience will
     like and chooses elements from a variety of sources.

783 Byrd, Jess. Introduction to The Busie Body. Los An-
     geles: Augustan Reprint Society, 1949. This play was
     one of the most successful comedies of intrigue for two
     centuries. The introduction mentions a few statements
     Centlivre made about dramatic theory and gives the
     sources for her plot.

784 Faure, Jacqueline. "Two Poems by Susanna Centlivre."
     Book Collector, 10 (1961), 68-69. The author offers
     two corrections to the 1957 Centlivre bibliography
     which appeared in Book Collector #6, 1957.

785 Jason, Philip K. "The Afterpiece: Authors and Incen-
     tives." Restoration and Eighteenth Century Theatre Re-
     search, 12 (1973), 1-13. During the 1709-1710 theatri-
     cal season, new afterpieces began to have extensive runs.
     Actors were the primary beneficiaries because of the
     opportunities to display their talent.

786 MacKenzie, John H. "Susan Centlivre." N&Q, 198 (1953),
     386-390. Biographical data can be deduced from a number
     of accounts of her life written in the eighteenth century.

787 Maxfield, Ezra K. "The Quaker in English Stage Plays
     before 1800." PMLA, 45 (1930), 256-273. Centlivre is
     among the playwrights depicting Quakers.

788 McKillop, Alan D. "Mrs. Centlivre's The Wonder: -- A
     Variant Imprint." Book Collector, 7 (1958), 79-80. An
     earlier edition of the play is in the Fondren Library
     at Rice.

789 Neill, D. G. "A Poem by Mrs. Centlivre." Book Collector,
     7 (1958), 189-190. The Harvard and Bodleian libraries
     have copies of Political Merriment containing a poem "To
     the Army" attributed to Centlivre.

790 Norton, J. E. "Some Uncollected Authors XIV: Susanna
     Centlivre." Book Collector, 6 (1957), 172-178 and 280-
     285. This bibliography of works has notes and an in-
     troduction.

791 Sherburn, George. "The Fortunes and Misfortunes of Three
     Hours after Marriage." MP, 24 (1926), 91-109. Phoebe
     Clinket was modeled on Centlivre rather than on Anne
     Finch.

792   Stathas, Thalia. "A Critical Edition of Three Plays by
      Susannah Centlivre." Stanford University dissertation,
      1965. The Busie Body, The Wonder, and A Bold Stroke for
      a Wife abound in allusions to social, intellectual, and
      political history, wit, farce, and sentiment. The texts
      of the plays are annotated, editions collated, and an in-
      troduction reviews criticism of her plays.

793   Stathas, Thalia. Introduction to A Bold Stroke for a
      Wife. Lincoln: University of Nebraska Press, 1968.
      After a survey of production history and editions, the
      author discusses the topical wit, "linguistic skill,"
      stage business, concentrated action, and amusing char-
      acters which led to the play's continued popularity.

794   Stratman, Carl J., C. S. V. "Scotland's First Dramatic
      Periodical: The Edinburgh Theatrical Censor." Theatre
      Notebook, 17 (1963), 83-86. The author outlines the
      format and content of The Censor's dramatic criticism,
      including a discussion of the treatment of A Bold Stroke
      for a Wife.

795   Strozier, Robert. "A Short View of Some of Mrs. Cent-
      livre's Celebrat'd Plays, Including a Close Accounting
      of the Plots, Subplots, Asides, Soliloquies, Etcetera,
      Contain'd Therein." Discourse, 7 (1964), 62-80. Her
      plays were immensely popular throughout the eighteenth
      century; for example, The Busy Body outdrew The Way of
      the World. An examination of plots, language, and dra-
      maturgy demonstrates her growing skill and appeal to her
      age.

796   Sutherland, James R. "The Progress of Error: Mrs. Cent-
      livre and the Biographies." RES, 18 (1942), 167-182.
      Biographies of Susannah Centlivre are catalogs of the
      ways unreliable statements are accumulated and propagated.
      Mr. Sutherland begins with obituaries and traces ampli-
      fications and shifts in information through the early
      biographies.

797   ten Hoor, Henry. "A Re-examination of Susanna Centlivre
      as a Comic Dramatist." University of Michigan disserta-
      tion, 1928. A review of her literary reputation and her
      seven comedies explain the characteristics of her art.

798   White, Robert B. "A Study of The Female Tatler (1709-
      1710)." University of North Carolina dissertation, 1966.
      See item #528.

799   Wilson, Mona. <u>These</u> <u>were</u> <u>Muses</u>. London: Sidgwick
      and Jackson, 1924, pp. 1-10. A survey of her plays
      with some discussion of their sources and reception
      follows a summary of the confusion over her early life.

800   Wood, Frederick T. "The Celebrated Mrs. Centlivre."
      <u>Neophilologia</u>, 16 (1931), 268-278. An overview.

801   Case, Arthur E. "Pope and Mary Chandler." RES, 2 (1926),
      343-344 and 466. Mary Chandler's verses beginning "sweet
      solitude" appear to have been written after Pope's Essay
      on Man and to have been first published in 1753 in Cibber's
      Lives of the Poets. On page 466, Mr. Case adds that Wake-
      field never pretended to have any special knowledge of
      Pope's methods of composition. He admits that he and his
      friends "discovered" sources in the course of their reading.

802   Doughty, Oswald. "A Bath Poetess of the Eighteenth Century."
      RES, 1 (1925), 404-420. This biographical survey quotes
      her poetry and finds her a brave, charming woman devoted to
      rationalism. Chandler was an admirer and acquaintance of
      Pope and, in at least one case, influenced his verse.

803   Doughty, Oswald. Comment on Case's article. RES, 2 (1926),
      345. Lacking evidence, Mr. Doughty prefers to believe that
      Wakefield and Elwin were correct in saying that Chandler
      was a source for a few lines in The Essay on Man.

804   Bradbrook, Frank. "Lydia Languish, Lydia Bennett, and
       Dr. Fordyce's Sermons." N&Q, 209 (1964), 421-423. See
       item #246.

805   Hemlow, Joyce. "Fanny Burney and the Courtesy Books."
       PMLA, 65 (1950), 732-761. See item #226.

806   Wilson, Mona. "An Unaffected Blue-stocking." These
       were Muses. London: Sidgwick & Jackson, 1924, pp. 50-
       67. Chapone's Letters on the Improvement of the Mind
       and Miscellanies give little indication of her inter-
       esting personality.

807   Ashley, L. R. N.   Introduction to A Narrative of the
       Life of Mrs. Charlotte Charke. Gainesville: Scholars'
       Facsimiles and Reprints, 1969. A biography concentrating
       on her personality and escapades and an account of the
       publication history of the Narrative preface the reprint.

808   McPharlin, Paul. "Charlotte Charke's Puppets in New York."
       Theatre Notebook, 1 (1947), 111-113. Her materials may
       have been used in New York in 1749.

809   McPharlin, Paul. "Charlotte Clark's Marionette Theatre."
       N&Q, 154 (1928), 316. The author wonders if Colley Cib-
       ber wrote marionette plays for his daughter.

810   Peavy, Charles D. "The Chimerical Career of Charlotte
       Charke." Restoration and Eighteenth Century Theatre Re-
       search, 8 (1969), 1-12. She was an eccentric woman whose
       eonism remains a puzzle. Her theatrical career, plays,
       novels, and Narrative deserve greater attention.

811   Speaight, George. "Charlotte Charke: An Unpublished
       Letter." Theatre Notebook, 12 (1957), 33-34. She wrote
       asking for a benefit in the Haymarket in 1759.

812   Waddell, Helen. "Eccentric Englishwomen: viii Mrs.
       Charke." Spectator, 158 (1937), 1047-1048. This is a
       brief sketch of Charlotte Charke's unusual life.

813   Wingrave, Wyatt. "Charlotte Charke's Marionette Theatre."
       N&Q, 154 (1928), 394. Her Narrative does not mention any
       plays written for her by Colley Cibber.

SARAH CHURCHILL
DUCHESS OF MARLBOROUGH

814   Brown, Beatrice C. "Sarah, Duchess of Marlborough" in
From Anne to Victoria. Essays by Various Hands, Bonamy
Dobrée, ed. London: Cassell, 1937, pp. 41-55. John
Churchill brought out the tenderness and loyalty in Sarah
and inspired the ambition which ruined them both. Sarah
was a rather stupid, impatient woman yet "magnificent" in
her pride, vitality, courage, loyalty, and loneliness.

815   Brown, Richard G. "The Role of the Duchess of Marlborough in Augustan Literature." University of Rochester
dissertation, 1972. The first part of the dissertation
discusses Sarah as a public person and as a patron and
friend. Her Conduct, its publication and reception,
occupy the middle section. The last chapters survey
literary portraits of her with emphasis on those by Swift,
Manley, and Pope.

816   Butler, Iris. Rule of Three: Sarah, Duchess of Marlborough and Her Companions in Power. London: Hodder and
Stoughton, 1967. A detailed biography of Sarah Churchill
emphasizes her friendships, associations, and altercations,
especially her relationships with Queen Anne and Abigail
Masham.

817   Campbell, Kathleen. Sarah, Duchess of Marlborough. London:
Thornton Butterworth; New York: Little, Brown, 1932. This
biography considers personal rather than historical material.

818   Chancellor, Frank. Sarah Churchill. London: Philip Alan,
1932. A biography of Sarah intended to portray her character and personality concluding "Her merits would have out-
weighed her defects but for one important item--she was
completely lacking in sympathy." Appendices include a
table of her accounts as Mistress of the Stole, her will,
and an inventory of her jewels.

819   Colville, Olivia. Duchess Sarah. Being the Social History
of the Times of Sarah Jennings, Duchess of Marlborough. London: Longmans, Green, 1904. A sympathetic biography argues
for "her real goodness of heart." Referring to political
events only when necessary, the book describes her personality, actions, and social life through anecdotes and quotations, many from her letters and her Conduct.

132

820 Dobree, Bonamy. _Sarah Churchill, Duchess of Marlborough_.
London: Gerald Howe, 1927. The energetic girl became
the dangerous woman "sitting on a throne only a little
lower than Queen Anne's" and finally the raging old woman
writing endlessly to justify her life. She was a mag-
netic and arresting figure, with no equal of her sex in
English history except Queen Elizabeth I.

821 Dobree, Bonamy. _Three Eighteenth-Century Figures_: Sarah
Churchill, John Wesley, Giacomo Casanova. London: Oxford University Press, 1962. A brief biography of Sarah
uses anecdotes to characterize her and her relationships
with others.

822 Green, David. "Sarah, Duchess of Marlborough." _Listener_,
63 (1960), 1011-1012. A tercentenary tribute finds her
to have had beauty, integrity, patriotism, common sense,
influence, and a devoted and "Olympian" husband. She
gradually lost the Queen's favor and her personal influence, but she died the richest woman on earth.

823 Green, David. _Sarah, Duchess of Marlborough_. London:
Collins, 1967. This biography is based primarily on the
Blenheim papers and finds Sarah a resilient, courageous
fighter in an important period in English history.

824 King, William. Introduction to _Memoirs of Sarah, Duchess
of Marlborough, together with her characters of contemporaries and her opinions_. London: Routledge, 1930.
The introduction includes a sketch of Sarah and a few
notes on her writings. An index of names mentioned by
Sarah is appended.

825 Kronenberger, Louis. _Marlborough's Duchess: A Study in
Worldliness_. New York: Knopf; London: Weidenfeld &
Nicolson, 1958. A biography of Sarah as a "figure of
politics, a contestant for power, an active promoter of
her husband's interests" demonstrates that her story is
inseparable from John's, from England's, and from Europe's.

826 Molloy, J. Fitzgerald. _The Queen's Comrade. The Life
and Times of Sarah, Duchess of Marlborough_. 2 vols. London: Hutchinson, 1901. The biography fills in the context of her life: the court, the political events, the
people around her, and England during her long life.
There are no notes, but letters and other papers are
quoted as evidence of Sarah's feelings.

133

827   Pratt, Dallas. "The Duchess Speaks Her Mind." *Columbia
       Library Columns*, 14 (1965), 27-42. The letters in the
       Columbia University collection show two kinds of behavior:
       intellectual enjoyment of good friends and ideas, and
       endless disputes and vindications.

828   Reid, Stuart J. *John and Sarah, Duke and Duchess of Marl-
       borough, 1660-1744*. London: John Murray, 1914. The
       complimentary biography is based on Blenheim papers and
       letters.

829   Riely, Elizabeth G. "The Duchess of Marlborough on Swift."
       Scriblerian, 7 (1974), 1-3. Sarah resented Swift's pre-
       ferment in May 1713. Her letters show a gradual change in
       her attitude toward Swift.

830   Rosenberg, Albert. "Prior's Feud with the Duchess of Marl-
       borough." *JEGP*, 52 (1953), 27-30. The quarrel between
       Prior and the Duchess began in early 1704 when she accused
       him of libeling her and the Duke in a lampoon, probably
       Faction Display'd. It appears that Prior did not write
       the lampoon.

831   Snyder, Henry L. "Daniel Defoe, the Duchess of Marlborough,
       and the *Advice to the Electors of Great Britain*." *HLQ*, 29
       (1965), 53-62. She was an active and independent political
       force. She sent money to Defoe through Harley for party
       writings in 1705, and, in 1708, collaborated with Mayn-
       waring in writing *Advice to the Electors*.

832   Thomson, Gladys S. *Letters of a Grandmother, 1732-35:
       being the correspondence of Sarah, Duchess of Marlborough,
       with her granddaughter Diana, Duchess of Bedford*." London:
       Cape, 1943.

833   Wright, Bunker. "A Further Note on Prior and *Faction Dis-
       play'd*." *JEGP*, 52 (1953), 30-31. A letter from Prior to
       Godolphin insists he did not write the lampoon. Prior feared
       displeasing the Queen and the Marlboroughs.

834   Crean, P. J. "Kitty Clive." N&Q, 174 (1938), 309-310.
       A letter which a bookseller's catalogue advertises as
       being from Kitty Clive to David Garrick is almost cer-
       tainly not a letter to Garrick but rather a letter to
       George Colman.

835   Fitzgerald, Percy. The Life of Mrs. Catherine Clive.
       New York: Benjamin Blom, 1971. A reprint of an 1888
       biography.

836   Frushell, Richard C. Introduction to The Case of Mrs.
       Clive Submitted to the Publick. ARS #159. Los Angeles:
       Clark Library, 1973. The introduction describes her
       popularity and influence, her relationship with Fleet-
       wood and Rich, and her Case which puts the players'
       complaints and situations before the public.

837   Frushell, Richard C. "The Cast of Kitty Clive's Sketch
       of a Fine Lady's Return from a Rout." N&Q, 216 (1969),
       350-351. The cast for her farce is given in The London
       Chronicle: or, Universal Evening Post. Clive herself
       played Lady Jenkings.

838   Frushell, Richard C. "Kitty Clive as Dramatist." Dur-
       ham University Journal, 63 (1971), 125-132. Kitty Clive
       wrote four afterpieces between 1750 and 1765. She should
       be recognized as a satiric dramatist of some merit with
       historical and literary importance.

839   Frushell, Richard C. "The Textual Relationship and Bio-
       graphical Significance of Two Petite Pieces by Mrs.
       Catherine (Kitty) Clive." Restoration and Eighteenth
       Century Theatre Research, 9 (1970), 51-58. The Faith-
       ful Irish Woman is based on the earlier A Sketch of A
       Fine Lady's Return from a Rout. A study of the changes
       allows understanding of Clive's compositional techniques.
       Some biographical information can be deduced also.

840   Day, Robert Adams. Introduction to Olinda's Adventures.
       ARS #138. Los Angeles: Clark Library, 1969. Juvenalia
       attributed to Cockburn is a very early, realistic, domes-
       tic novel and a precursor of Defoe's and Richardson's
       work. The character of the heroine is the most signifi-
       cant feature of the somewhat autobiographical novel.

841   Fleming, Alison. "Catharine Trotter--'the Scots Sappho.'"
       Scots Magazine, 33 (1940), 305-314. Her poems and plays
       were second rate, her philosophy merely interpretive, but
       her Letter of Advice and her correspondence are models
       of common sense, fortitude, and striving after a life of
       the mind.

842   Gosse, Edmund. "Catharine Trotter, The First of the
       Bluestockings." Fortnightly Review, 105 (1916), 1034-
       1048. Catharine Trotter, most interesting of the women
       writers between Behn and the Queen Anne writers, was a
       well known playwright for six years. Her own life was
       interesting and provides insight into her time. She was
       "champion of Locke and Clarke, correspondent of Leib-
       nitz and Pope, friend of Congreve, patroness to Farquhar,
       protégée of Marlborough."

843   Gosse, Edmund. "Catharine Trotter: The Precursor of the
       Blue Stockings" in Transactions of the Royal Society of
       Literature. London: Oxford University Press, 1916. Ac-
       quainted with many intellectuals, she wrote letters,
       poetry, and plays which give insight into her unhappy
       life and her repeated attempts to demonstrate the rewards
       of "decency" in theatrical productions.

844   Hook, Lucyle. Introduction to The Female Wits. ARS #124.
       Los Angeles: Clark Library, 1967. The play satirizes
       plays by women, especially those of Manley, Pix, and Cock-
       burn. The satire allows insight into theatrical practices
       and personalities.

845   Weales, Gerald. "A Wycherley Prologue." The Library
       Chronicle, 32 (1966), 101-104. Wycherley wrote the pro-
       logue for Catharine Cockburn's Agnes de Castro.

846   Norton, J. E. "Some Uncollected Authors XVI: Hannah
       Cowley, 1743-1809." Book Collector, 7 (1958), 68-76.
       She was a modest woman whose tragedies are absurd, but
       whose comedies were admired by men like the critic
       Porson and performed regularly for generations. A
       brief biography, an introduction to her works, and
       a bibliography draw together most of the information
       about her.

847   Rhodes, R. C. "The Belle's Stratagem." RES, 5 (1929),
       129-142. The leading character Letitia Hardy was an
       acting test-piece and the ideal of the "fashionable
       female" in the late eighteenth century. The play is
       a good picture of fashionable life, borrows from She
       Stoops to Conquer, and represents textual problems
       familiar to editors of late eighteenth century works.

848   Todd, William B. "Hannah Cowley: Re-Impressions, Not
       Reissues." Book Collector, 7 (1958), 301. Press figures
       suggest corrections in the J. E. Norton bibliography.

MARY DAVYS

849   Day, Robert A. Introduction to <u>Mary Davys</u>, <u>Familiar Let-</u>
        <u>ters</u> <u>Betwixt</u> <u>a</u> <u>Gentleman</u>, <u>and</u> <u>A</u> <u>Lady</u>, <u>1725</u>. Los Angeles:
        Augustan Reprint Society, 1955. The novel is notable for
        its realism, characterization, humor, and workmanlike plot.
        An one hundred, eighty-six item bibliography of epistolary
        fiction, 1660-1740, is appended to the introduction.

850   McBurney, William H. "Mrs. Mary Davys: Forerunner of
        Fielding." <u>PMLA</u>, 74 (1959), 348-355. Her works are realis-
        tic, humorous, and lack excessive sentimentality. They an-
        ticipate Fielding in style and realistic comic emphasis in
        characterization. The preface to the 1725 edition of her
        <u>Works</u> is one of the few early examples of critical theory
        and again, anticipates Fielding.

851   Stefanson, Donald H. "The Works of Mary Davys: A Critical
        Edition." University of Iowa dissertation, 1971. This
        edition of her 1725 <u>Works</u> (both the <u>Works</u> and the disserta-
        tion omit <u>The</u> <u>Accomplish'd</u> <u>Rake</u>) has textual collations, a
        finding list, and an introduction.

CATHERINE HYDE DOUGLAS
DUCHESS OF QUEENSBURY

852   Biddulph, Violet. Kitty, Duchess of Queensbury. London:
Nicholson & Watson, 1935. Kitty Hyde was the object of
admiration and censure all her life. A lively and capri-
cious woman, she knew most of the interesting people and
places in England. This biography quotes letters, poems,
and other contemporary documents extensively.

853   Burgess, C. F. "John Gay and Polly and a Letter to the
King." PQ, 47 (1968), 596-598. She sold subscriptions
to the published edition of the suppressed Polly. When
the King asked her to stay away from court, she sent him
a provocative, deliberate answer probably composed with
either the Duke's or Gay's help.

854   Conolly, L. W. "Anna Margarita Larpent, The Duchess of
Queensbury, and Gay's Polly in 1777. PQ, 51 (1972), 955-
957. Anna Larpent's "Methodized Journal" describes her
going to a revival of Polly with the Duchess. The entry
describes the Duchess's feelings about being dismissed
from George II's court after opposing the suppression of
the play, her involvement in its composition, and notes
that her death was the result of going to the play in
spite of a cold.

855   Sherburn, George. "The Duchess Replies to the King."
Harvard Library Bulletin, 6 (1952), 118-121. The note
includes the texts of the news stories in the Universal
Spectator, the Walpole account, and the Duchess's letter
to the king concerning the Douglases' leaving court.

856   Altieri, Joanne. "Style and Purpose in Maria Edgeworth's
       Fiction." NCF, 23 (1968), 265-278. Her prose style
       gradually became the "flaccid banalities of the polite
       popular novel." She gave up the colloquial, individual-
       ized narrative voice, irregular syntax, lively dialogue
       because of her committment to "the exemplary method."

857   Anon. "Close Looks at Nineteenth Century People." TLS,
       14 January 1972, pp. 39-40. The author reviews Harden's
       Maria Edgeworth's Art of Prose Fiction and Colvin's
       edition of the correspondence Maria Edgeworth: Letters
       from England, 1813-1844. Harden has written a "useful
       summary and criticism;" Colvin is a "sympathetic and
       accomplished editor" who reinforces understanding of char-
       acter by meticulous care for detail.

858   Armytage, W. H. G. "Little Woman." Queens Quarterly,
       56 (1949), 248-257. Castle Rackrent gives us "the finest
       picture of Ireland under the great land-owners." Maria
       Edgeworth's father and Ireland shaped her writing.

859   Buckley, Mary. "Attitudes to Nationality in Four Nine-
       teenth-Century Novelists." Journal of the Cork Historical
       and Archaelogical Society, 78 (1973), 27-34. Her four
       Irish novels express her attitude toward her country and
       her awareness of the divisions and tensions in turn of
       the century Ireland. Inspite of the attention she gives
       to landlord-tenant relations and the lower classes, she
       is eighteenth century in that she belongs to a class,
       not a nation.

860   Butler, Harriet J. and H. E. Butler. "Sir Walter Scott
       and Maria Edgeworth. Some Unpublished Letters." MLR,
       23 (1928), 273-298. This article traces the correspon-
       dence between Scott and the Edgeworths, lists the con-
       tents of a portfolio of letters Maria sent her sister
       Fanny Wilson in 1833, and prints the texts of eleven
       letters.

861   Butler, Marilyn. Maria Edgeworth: A Literary Biography.
       Oxford: Clarendon, 1972. This biography is based on an
       examination of the Edgeworth family's letters and papers
       and later scholars' work. Appendices and bibliography
       include reviews of her works.

862 Butler, Marilyn. "The Uniqueness of Cynthia Kirkpatrick: Elizabeth Gaskell's _Wives and Daughters_ and Maria Edgewroth's _Helen_." _RES_, 23 (1972), 278-290. Cynthia Kirkpatrick, the character who gives much of the excellence to Gaskell's novel is "substantially" derived from the character of Cecilia in Edgeworth's _Helen_. Gaskell's handling of Cynthia in relation to the theme and in her relation to the other characters is also borrowed from Edgeworth.

863 Butler, Ruth F. "Maria Edgeworth." _TLS_, 4 February 1972, p. 129. Permission to use the private memoir by Maria's stepmother was granted by an Edgeworth who had no authority to do so. The prohibition on publication was punctiliously observed until the present generation.

864 Clarke, Isabel C. _Maria Edgeworth, Her Family and Friends_. London: Hutchinson, 1950. A biography largely without notes concentrates on her relationships with her family and friends and on her acquaintance with a number of notable men and women and their influence in her life.

865 Coley, W. B. "An Early 'Irish' Novelist" in _Minor British Novelists_, Charles Hoyt, ed. Carbondale: Southern Illinois Press, 1967. See item #370.

866 Colvin, Christina E. "Maria Edgeworth." _TLS_, 29 September 1972, p. 1157. Surviving locks of her hair prove that it was light brown.

867 Colvin, Christina E. "Maria Edgeworth's Literary Manuscripts in the Bodleian Library." _Bodleian Library Record_, 8 (1970), 196-201. She attached little importance to her manuscripts once they were printed; therefore, only a few survive. The Bodleian owns manuscript copies of _The Bracelets_, _The Double Disguise_, and _Whim for Whim_.

868 Colvin, Christina E. "Maria Edgeworth's Tours in Ireland, III. Connaught." _Studia Neophilologica_, 43 (1971), 474-483. A letter from Maria to her sister-in-law describes her 1836 trip to the Moore's in Connaught. The text of the letter with notes is printed.

869 Colvin, Christina E. "Maria Edgeworth's Tours in Ireland, II. Killarney." _Studia Neophilologica_, 43 (1971), 252-256. A letter from Maria to Joanna Baillie describing her trip to Killarney with Sir Walter Scott and others

illustrates the difference between her letters to family and those to friends.

870   Colvin, Christina E. "Maria Edgeworth's Tours in Ireland, I. Rostrevor." Studia Neophilologica, 42 (1970), 319-329. The trips she took in Ireland provided material for her fiction. Two letters describing her trip to Rostrevor provide a physical setting in Ennui.

871   Colvin, Christina E. "Maria's Father." TLS, 6 January 1966, pp. 9-10. The literary facts in Desmond Clarke's The Ingenious Mr. Edgeworth are not always reliable. The surviving Edgeworth manuscripts do not support his theory that what Maria "lacked was the gift of invention" which Edgeworth supplied for her.

872   Colvin, Christina E. (with Marilyn Butler). "A Revised Date of Birth for Maria Edgeworth." N&Q, 216 (1971), 339-340. Evidence from Maria Edgeworth's letters and existing records suggests that she was born in 1768 rather than in 1767.

873   Craig, Charles R. "Maria Edgeworth and the Common-Sense School." University of Nebraska dissertation, 1971. Her books are expressions of "Scottish Common-Sense philosophy" as espoused by Hugh Blair, Adam Smith, and Dugald Stewart, and her readers would have recognized the affinity. Her treatment of imagination, benevolence, and progress are determined by this position.

874   Edwards, Duane. "The Narrator of Castle Rackrent." SAQ, 71 (1972), 124-129. Thady Quirk is neither completely loyal nor completely calculating. Rather he is sentimental, unreflective, impressionable, money-loving, but learns discrimination by the end of the novel.

875   Evans, Lord. "Maria Edgeworth: A Bicentenary Lecture." EDH, 35 (1969), 40-54. The text of a lecture to the Royal Society of Literature primarily summarizes her life and writings. "All that is best in her work derives from Ireland."

876   Flanagan, Thomas J. The Irish Novelists, 1800-1850. New York: Columbia University Press, 1959. Maria Edgeworth began the development of the Irish novel. Her novels explore the fate of the Anglo-Irish; Castle Rackrent, for example, is a damning description of irresponsibility and abuse of power.

877 Goodman, Theodore. "Maria Edgeworth. Novelist of Reason."
New York University dissertation, 1936. Maria Edgeworth
advocated reason in a variety of ways in her works. Mr.
Goodman isolates influences, her position on such contemporary issues as primitivism and sentimentalism, and
her "ideal characters."

878 Goodman, Theodore. Maria Edgeworth. Novelist of Reason.
New York: New York University Press, 1936. See above.

879 Grey, Rowland. "Heavy Fathers." Fortnightly Review, 92
(1909), 80-89. The fathers of "celebrated authoresses
have been singularly selfish and trying persons." Fanny
Burney's and Maria Edgeworth's were classic examples.

880 Grey, Rowland. "Maria Edgeworth and Etienne Dumont."
Dublin Review, 145 (1909), 239-265. Etienne Dumont's
correspondence with Maria Edgeworth describes Dumont's
suggestion that she write Tales of Fashionable Life,
the experience of her father's death, and an 'Amour d'Au-
tomne.'"

881 Grey, Rowland. "Society According to Maria Edgeworth."
Fortnightly Review, 88 (1907), 296-308. She is a "literary
immortal." Her rendering of Irish life and characters
and her influence on Scott and others may be recognized,
but her ability to create vivid society characters still
has the power to delight.

882 Hawthorne, Mark D. Doubt and Dogma in Maria Edgeworth.
Gainesville: University of Florida Press, 1967. She was
a pioneer in the field of education and a didactic novelist. A study of her work from 1795 to 1817 shows her
educational principles appearing in her novels, a movement of her thought away from her father's, and a reconciliation of themes of passion and reason.

883 Hawthorne, Mark D. "Maria Edgeworth's Unpleasant Lesson:
The Shaping of Character." Studies: An Irish Quarterly
Review of Letters, Philosophy and Science, 64 (1975),
167-177. Belinda was a popular and acclaimed novel in
Edgeworth's time. The revisions in the 1810 edition
delineate her developing artistic techniques.

884 Hemlow, Joyce. "Fanny Burny and the Courtesy Books." PMLA,
65 (1950), 732-761. See item #226.

143

885 Hennig, John. "Goethe and the Edgeworths." MLQ, 15
     (1954), 366-371. Although Richard Lovell and Maria
     Edgeworth's Essay on Irish Bulls probably influenced
     every later Continental mention of the subject, Goethe's
     "Unbehülflichkeit des Geistes" has a definition not
     found in the Essay. His and Maria's writings include
     no references to each other.

886 Hill, Constance N. Maria Edgeworth and Her Circle in
     the Days of Buonaparte and Bourbon. New York: John
     Lane Co, 1909. A description of her travels in France
     and England, 1800-1820, her reactions, and experiences
     portrays her personality and France during these event-
     ful years.

887 Houston, Janetta M. M.   "A Critical Study of the Works
     of Maria Edgeworth." University of Oxford dissertation,
     1964. This is a survey and discussion of her literary
     and education works.

888 Hurst, Michael. Maria Edgeworth and the Public Scene:
     Intellect, Fine Feeling, and Landlordism in the Age of
     Reform. Coral Gables: U. of Miami Press, 1969. A
     study of her contributions to political, social, econ-
     omic, and cultural controversies places her in the con-
     text of the history of ideas and explains why her efforts
     to foster the Anglo-Irish Union were futile.

889 Inglis-Jones, Elisabeth. Great Maria: A Portrait of
     Maria Edgeworth. London: Faber & Faber, 1959. This
     biography has no notes but uses extensive quotations
     from letters and papers.

890 Jeffares, A. Norman. "Early Effort of the Wild Irish
     Girl" in Le romantisme Anglo-Américain: Mélanges offerts
     à Louis Bonnerot, Roger Asselineau, et. al., eds. Paris:
     Didier, 1971. The author points out the characteristics
     of the early Irish novel and compares Edgeworth's fiction
     to Sydney Owenson's.

891 Jeffares, A. Norman. "Maria Edgeworth's Ormond." Eng-
     lish, 18 (1969), 85-90. Castle Rackrent, Ennui, The
     Absentee, and Ormond's Irish material represents the
     changes and complexities of Ireland. Ormond was influ-
     enced by Fielding, and the main character is modeled on
     her father.

892   Kennedy, Sister Eileen. "Genesis of a Fiction: The
       Edgeworth-Turgenev Relationship." ELN, 6 (1969), 271-
       273. Her influence on Turgenev cannot be documented
       and is an example of a widely circulated but unfounded
       opinion. The story probably springs from the spurious
       recollections of "One Who Knew" Turgenev published in
       The London Daily News, 7 September 1883.

893   Lawless, Emily. Maria Edgeworth. London: Macmillan,
       1904. A biography, part of the "English Men of Letters"
       series, without notes, finds Edgeworth kind, youthful,
       and pleasant throughout her life.

894   Leyris, Pierre. "Château-Rackrent." Mercure de France,
       348 (1963), 410-438. The translation of Castle Rackrent
       into French is preceded by a brief biographical sketch
       and an assessment of Edgeworth's achievement.

895   McWhorter, Oleta E. "Maria Edgeworth's Art of Prose
       Fiction." University of Arkansas dissertation, 1965.
       She used her fiction to propagate her father's theories
       which were of special rather than of universal concern.
       Her strengths as a prose writer cannot overcome her
       glaring inadequacies.

896   Michael, Friedrich. "Ein Beitrag zur Geschicte des eth-
       nographischen Romans in England." Koenigsberg disserta-
       tion, 1918. This is a study of Maria Edgeworth's Irish
       novels.

897   Millhauser, Milton. "Maria Edgeworth as a Social Novel-
       ist." N&Q, 175 (1938), 204-205. The primary narrative
       element of The Absentee comes from the economic theme.
       Edgeworth was the only novelist before the Victorians to
       put a social problem before romantic interest.

898   Moler, Kenneth L. "Sense and Sensibility and Its Sources."
       RES, 17 (1966), 413-419. Maria Edgeworth's "Mademoiselle
       Panache" and Jane West's The Advantages of Education as
       well as A Gossip's Story influenced Sense and Sensibility.
       Rather than directly derivative, Austen's novel should
       be seen as working with common conventions.

899   Mood, Robert G. "Maria Edgeworth's Apprenticeship." Uni-
       versity of Illinois dissertation, 1939. This is a study
       of the development of the artist and thinker and the in-
       fluences on her.

900   Murray, Patrick. "Maria Edgeworth and Her Father: The
       Literary Partnership." Eire, 6 (1971), 39-50. Maria
       Edgeworth published only a single novel of any impor-
       tance after her father's death. He contributed his
       knowledge of politics, religion, and literature, his
       experiences, and his critical acumen to her work; she
       became a willing mouthpiece. What is known about her
       method of composition refutes the belief that the
       didacticism was his.

901   Newby, Percy H. Maria Edgeworth. London: Arthur
       Barker, 1950. A biography of Edgeworth with emphasis
       on the influence of her milieu surveys her fiction.

902   Newcomer, James. "Castle Rackrent: Its Structure and
       Irony." Criticism, 8 (1966), 170-179. The novel is
       carefully structured in order to pass judgment on the
       Rackrent family. The first part of the novels estab-
       lishes the themes of recklessness, improvidence, de-
       bauchery, and litigation; the second brings all of these
       together accomplishing the fall of the Rackrent estate
       and the ironic ascendency of the Quirk family.

903   Newcomer, James. "The Disingenuous Thady Quirk." SSF,
       2 (1964), 44-50. Thady Quirk is a realist, calculating
       with his son to exploit and finally ruin the Rackrents.

904   Newcomer, James. Maria Edgeworth. Lewisburg: Bucknell
       University Press, 1973. A brief survey of her life and
       fiction pays some attention to her early educational
       writings.

905   Newcomer, James. Maria Edgeworth, the Novelist, 1767-
       1849, A Bicentennial Study. Fort Worth, Texas: Texas
       Christian University Press, 1967. An appraisal of Edge-
       worth's work begins with a survey of criticism and ex-
       amines the major objections to her fiction. Individual
       chapters are devoted to Patronage, Ormond, her novels of
       manners, and Castle Rackrent.

906   Paterson, Alice. The Edgeworths, A Study of Later Eigh-
       teenth Century Education. London: W. B. Clive, 1914.
       The Edgeworths illustrate the major educational movements
       including demands for changes in methodology, subject
       matter, and student body. A survey of major educational
       topics in Essays on Practical Education shows it to be

the most important work on pedagogy between Locke's
Thoughts and Spencer's Essay on Education.

907   Pollard, M. "The First Irish Edition of Maria Edgeworth's
       Parent's Assistant." The Irish Book, 1 (1962), 85-88.
       The first Dublin printing was in 1798 and followed the
       London second edition. Chambers may have pirated the
       edition.

908   Pollard, M. "Maria Edgeworth's The Parent's Assistant."
       Book Collector, 20 (1971), 347-351. Part II, Volume I
       of the first edition of Edgeworth's book was found on
       an English bookseller's shelf. Correspondence, reviews,
       and notes precede a finding list for the book.

909   Riese, Teut. "Maria Edgeworth's 'Essay on Irish Bulls.'"
       Anglia, 62 (1954), 62-77. The author considers the re-
       lationship between the Essay and her fiction.

910   Ross, Alan S. C. "An Estonian Quotation in Castle Rack-
       rent." N&Q, 220 (1975), 26. Edgeworth quotes an Eston-
       ian poem criticizing "righteousnesses" as a comment on
       Irish "duty work." Mr. Ross identifies her source as
       the 1785 Folk-Lore Journal.

911   Simon, Brian. Studies in the History of Education, 1780-
       1870. London: Lawrence & Wishart, 1960. Practical Ed-
       ucation was "the most significant contemporary work on
       pedagogy." Maria Edgeworth's chapters have less interest.

912   Slade, Bertha C. Maria Edgeworth: A Bibliographical
       Tribute. London: Constable, 1937. An annotated bibliogra-
       phy of editions of Edgeworth's works with notes, brief
       biography, and appendices of press numbers and biographi-
       cal studies of the Edgeworth family includes a number of
       plates of paper labels and title pages of her works.

913   Solomon, Stanley J. "Ironic Perspective in Maria Edgeworth's
       Castle Rackrent." Journal of Narrative Technique, 2 (1972),
       68-73. Thady Quirk's moral insensitivity underscores the
       novel's condemnation of "passive participation in evil."
       Edgeworth's irony, then, encompasses the rise of the Quirk
       family and the general attitude exemplified in the narra-
       tor.

914   Ward, Wilfred. "Moral Fiction a Hundred Years Ago." Dub-
       lin Review, 144 (1909), 245-266. Maria Edgeworth's repu-

tation has unjustly suffered because of the belief that
she wrote unrealistic moral tales. Manoeuvring and
Almeria illustrate her ability to combine moral purpose
with "absolutely truthful" detail.

915   Welsh, Alexander. "Maria Edgeworth and More Dickens."
       Yale Review, 62 (1973), 281-287. In a review essay on
       Butler's Maria Edgeworth and three books on Dickens,
       Mr. Welsh argues that she is an unusually "robust"
       female novelist. Furthermore, the principles of her
       novels were "central to the culture" and earned high
       praise for realism.

ELIZABETH ELSTOB

916   Ashdown, Margaret. "Elizabeth Elstob, The Learned Saxon-
       ist." MLR, 20 (1925), 125-146. Ms. Ashdown gives an ac-
       count of Elstob's life with quotations from letters and
       some assessment of the lasting interest of Elstob's pub-
       lished work.

917   B., J. "The First Home Student." Oxford Magazine, 57
       (1938), 212-13. The piece is a tribute to Elizabeth Elstob
       on the occasion of an exhibit of her works at the Bodleian
       Library. It mentions notable parts of her prefaces, her
       opinions about her sex, and her later life.

918   Collins, Sarah H. "Elizabeth Elstob: A Biography." Indiana
       University dissertation, 1971. The biography assembles in-
       formation about Elstob's life, lists her achievements, and
       points out her life-long precepts and interests. Her opinions
       about education, women, and the Germanic roots of the English
       language place her in a significant position in the history
       of ideas.

919   Douglas, David. English Scholars, 1660-1730. London: Cape,
       1939; 2nd ed. London: Eyre & Spottiswoode, 1951. The sub-
       ject of the book is the legacy and influence of English
       scholars who worked to preserve early English history and
       these scholars' methods and motives. Elstob was a "propa-
       gandist of Old English studies" rather than a scholar of
       the first order. Her introductions are more valuable than
       her texts.

920   Murphy, Michael. "The Elstobs, Scholars of Old English and
       Anglican Apologists." Durham University Journal, 58 (1966),
       131-138. Elizabeth Elstob was a sensible, informed scholar.
       Her English-Saxon Homily on the Birth-Day of St. Gregory
       questions the attitude of English Protestants who refused
       to admit any connection between the Catholic Church and the
       Church of England and uses Old English studies for religious
       polemics, a tradition going back to the 1560's.

921   Peake, Charles. Introduction to An Apology for the study
       of northern antiquities (by Mrs. Elizabeth Elstob). Los
       Angeles: Augustan Reprint Society, 1956. Elstob speaks for
       a group of antiquarian scholars when she answers Swift's
       Proposal for Correcting, Improving and Ascertaining the
       English Tongue. Her objections are well taken. Her defense
       of the English language as a literary medium compiles the
       common arguments, but her scholarship, organization, and use
       of quotations "decisively" bested Swift.

149

SARAH FIELDING

922   Digeon, A. "Fielding a-t-il écrit le dernier chapitre
de 'A Journey from This World into the Next'?" Revue
Anglo-Americaine, 8 (1931), 428-430. Sarah, not Henry,
wrote "A Journey."

923   Grey, Jill E. Introduction to The Governess; or, Little
Female Academy. London: Oxford U. Press, 1968. This
facsimile edition has eighty-two pages of introductory
material including a discussion of influences and significance of The Governess and bibliographies of works,
editions, similar "school stories," and criticism about
the book. The Governess includes important innovations
which became the standard fare of children's books.

924   Johnson, R. Brimley. Introduction to The Lives of Cleopatra and Octavia. London: Scholartis Press, 1928.
While experimenting with a variety of fictional forms,
Sarah was most concerned with the theme of the "natural"
in the midst of a corrupt society. The fictitious autobiographies of Cleopatra and Octavia are representative of much of the writing of her time.

925   Kelsall, Malcolm. Introduction to The Adventures of
David Simple. New York: Oxford U. Press, 1969. A
summary of her acquaintances, learning, and literary career accompanies critical comments on David Simple.

926   Needham, Arnold E. "The Life and Works of Sarah Fielding."
University of California dissertation, 1943. This is a
survey of her life with particular attention to her friendships with an assessment of her literary output.

927   Parrish, Ann. "Eight Experiments in Fiction: A Critical
Analysis of the Works of Sarah Fielding." Boston University dissertation, 1973. Her books are experimental
and often highly original. For example, David Simple is
an "apologue" and the prototype of Rasselas; The Governess
is the first novel for children, and The Countess of
Dellwyn is a psychological study.

928   Raynal, Margaret I. "A Study of Sarah Fielding's Novels."
University of North Carolina dissertation, 1970. A study
of her novels demonstrates an increasing concern with
changes in narrative form, her desire to teach benevo-

lism and religion, and an awareness of the sources of
human suffering.

929   Werner, Herman O., Jr. "The Life and Works of Sarah
       Fielding." Harvard dissertation, 1939. Her life is
       of interest primarily because of her intimacy with
       Henry Fielding and Richardson. Her literary works
       are discussed in detail in the dissertation.

930 Anderson, Paul B. "Mrs. Manley's Texts of Three of Lady
     Winchilsea's Poems." MLN, 45 (1930), 95-99. Delariviere
     Manley printed early versions of three of Finch's poems
     which were remembered by such people as Anna Seward.
     Comparison of the Manley and Scott texts shows Finch's
     judicial changes and attests to the continuing popularity
     of the New Atlantis.

931 Brower, Reuben A. "Lady Winchilsea and the Poetic Tradi-
     tion of the Seventeenth Century." SP, 42 (1945), 61-80.
     Anne Finch's work represents a merging of the elements
     of seventeenth and eighteenth century poetry rather than
     representing pre-Romanticism. Mr. Brower's careful anal-
     ysis places Finch firmly in English poetic traditions.

932 Buxton, John. "The Poems of the Countess of Winchilsea."
     Life and Letters, 65 (1950), 195-204. Her poems are the
     "most elegant," "vivacious," and "delightfully feminine"
     produced by a woman before Wordsworth. Her descriptions
     of love, honor, and external nature are markedly "fem-
     inine." She wrote for friends and shared her love of
     refinement and taste.

933 Buxton, John. A Tradition of Poetry. London: MacMillan;
     New York: St. Martin's, 1967. Chapter VIII is on the
     Countess of Winchilsea. She wrote most of her poems for
     her husband and friends, and her best poems are "the
     most feminine." Her friends and her continuting repu-
     tation with such people as Wordsworth testify to the
     merit of her poetry.

934 Fausset, Hugh I'A. Introduction to Minor Poets of the
     Eighteenth Century. London: Dent; New York: Dutton,
     1930. Anne Finch's poetry is sprightly, witty, and ele-
     gant. Pope "cheapened" what he borrowed from her, and
     Wordsworth praised her. Her poetry is as characteristic
     of the eighteenth century as Pope's.

935 Hughes, Helen S. "Lady Winchilsea and her Friends." Lon-
     don Mercury, 19 (1929), 624-635. A few letters and poems
     discovered in the Wellesley library and in the Duke of
     Northumberland's library are reprinted.

936 Murry, J. Middleton. "Anne Finch, Countess of Winchilsea
     (1661-1720)." New Adelphi, 1 (1927), 145-153. Anne

Kingsmill, though something of a man-hater and a blue-stocking, became a devoted and aristocratic wife. Her piety, love of nature, and deep feeling for her husband combined with her exquisite phraseology make her poetry the "ne plus ultra of feminine poetry," but she was never ashamed of being a writer.

937   Reynolds, Myra. The Poems of Anne, Countess of Winchil-sea. Chicago: University of Chicago Press, 1903. The interest in her poetry comes from the revelation of her personality, her "heretical" religious, social, and literary opinions, and her "Romantic tastes." Biography, friendships, career, reputation, development as a poet, and critical discussion of her poems, classifying them and putting them in literary context are combined in the introduction.

938   Riedenauer, Annemarie M. "Die Gedichte der Anne Finch, Countess of Winchilsea." University of Vienna disserta-tion, 1964. The poems in the Reynolds edition and in the Wellesley collection are grouped into "accidental and spurious," "satirical," "nature and retirement," and "reflective" poetry in order for the author to charac-terize and evaluate her works.

939   Sena, John. "Melancholy in Anne Finch and Elizabeth Carter: The Ambivalence of an Idea." YES, 1 (1971), 108-119. See item #758.

940   Adlard, John. "A Note on Nell Gwyn." Folklore, 83
      (1972), 61-67.

941   B.,G. F. R. "Nell Gwyn." N&Q, 148 (1925), 358. The
      Brighton Public Museum owns her mirror.

942   Bax, Clifford. Pretty Witty Nell; An Account of Nell
      Gwyn and Her Environment. London: Chapman & Hall,
      1932. A biography with a bibliography.

943   C., C. S. "Nell Gwyn." N&Q, 148 (1925), 213. A knife
      and a mirror which belonged to her have been found.

944   Cohen, Selma Jean. "Mr. Pepys Goes to the Theatre."
      Dance Magazine, no. vol. (1956), 36-37, 60-61, and 66.
      Pepys saw a number of dances, including a performance
      by Nell Gwynn.

945   Dasent, A. I. Nell Gwynne. London: MacMillan, 1924.
      A popular account of Nell Gwynn which emphasizes the
      cultural and social life of the Restoration court gives
      special attention to the "topography" of Gwynn's envi-
      ronment (Drury Lane, Whitehall, Pall Mall, and Windsor).

946   Fea, Allan. "Portraits of Nell Gwynn, Moll Davis, and
      Others." Connoisseur, 111 (1943), 29-33. There are many
      problems in identifying their portraits.

947   Goodwin, Gordon, ed. Story of Nell Gwyn. Edinburgh:
      J. Grant, 1908. An edition of a popular biography (1852)
      emphasizing the scandalous in her life and times.

948   Hazelton, George C., Jr. Mistress Nell; a Merry Time
      (Twixt Fact and Fancy). New York: Scribner's, 1901.
      A fictionalized biography.

949   Marshall, Julian. "Royal Tennis Court and Nell Gwyn."
      N&Q, 18 (1902), 136. The Royal tennis court was not
      in Haymarket but in James Street, but there is no rea-
      son to think that Nell Gwynn visited it.

950   Melville, Lewis (pseud. Lewis Saul Benjamin). Nell
      Gwynn, the Story of Her Life. London: Hutchinson, 1923.
      A biography focused on her personal life rather than on
      her career as an actress.

951 Moncada, Ernest J. "The Source of an Epigraph Attributed to Rochester." N&Q, 209 (1964), 95-96. James Howell wrote the obscene epigraph under Gwynn's portrait in the 1718 Works of Rochester.

952 Orr, Lyndon. "Famous Affinities of History." Munsey Magazine, 44 (1910), 73-80. Charles II had an "affinity" for Nell Gwynn.

953 Pierpont, Robert. "Chelsea Hospital, Nell Gwynn, Sir Stephen Fox." N&Q, 146 (1923), 423-425. Gwynn played a part in founding the hospital.

954 Price, F. G. H. "Nell Gwyn, Gwynn, or Gwynne." N&Q, 34 (1900), 350-351. Six variant spellings of "Gwyn" were current.

955 Prideaux, W. F. "Royal Tennis Court and Nell Gwyn." N&Q, 18 (1902), 136. James Street's Royal tennis court was a favorite resort for Charles II and most probably visited by Gwynn.

956 Segre, Carlo. "Una della prime comiche inglesi." Nuova Antologia, 242 (1925), 294-325. A discussion of her career.

957 Todd, William B. "An Unidentified Portrait of Charles II, the Duchess of Cleveland, and Nell Gwyn." N&Q, 199 (1954), 114. Identifies a painting by Lely.

958 Van Lennep, William. "Nell Gwyn's Playgoing at the King's Expense." Harvard Library Bulletin, 4 (1950), 405-408. Prints a bill which shows the plays which Nell Gwyn attended at the Duke of York's playhouse (at the King's expense). This bill shows that over a little more than two seasons Nell Gwynn saw fifty-five plays.

959 Williams, Hugh Noel. Rival Sultanas: Nell Gwyn, Louise de Keroualle, and Hortense Mancini. London: Hutchinson, 1915. A popular account of social life.

960 Wilson, John Harold. "Nell Gwyn as an Angel." N&Q, 193 (1948), 71-72. The author points out that Nell Gwyn played the role of Angelo (an angel) in a 1668 revival of Massinger and Dekker's The Virgin Martyr.

961 Wilson, John Harold. _Nell Gwyn: Royal Mistress_. London: Frederich Muller, 1952. An essentially popular account of Nell Gwyn which nevertheless draws upon a wide range of sources to portray its subject. An appendix prints six letters from Nell Gwyn.

962 Wilson, John Harold. "Nell Gwyn's House in Pall-Mall." _N&Q_, 194 (1949), 143-144. A discussion of five contemporary deeds which make clear the facts concerning Nell Gwynn's residence in Pall Mall.

963 Wilson, John Harold. "Nell Gwyn: Two Portraits." _N&Q_, 201 (1956), 204-206. The evidence suggests the authenticiety of two nude portraits of the actress.

LAETITIA HAWKINS

964 deCastro, J. Paul. "Laetitia Hawkins and Boswell." N&Q,
     185 (1943), 373-4. Hawkins's "Travelling Diary" records
     her visit to the Lichfield bookseller Lomax who showed her
     Johnson memorabilia including correspondence about a damag-
     ing biography by Sir John Hawkins.

965 Skrine, Francis H. Gossip about Dr. Johnson and others,
     being chapters from the memoirs of Miss Laetitia Matilda
     Hawkins. London: Nash and Grayson, 1926. Selections from
     her Anecdotes edited and arranged present her material
     about famous people and their social life.

966   Adams, M. Ray. "Mary Hays, Disciple of William Godwin."
      PMLA, 55 (1940), 472-483. A careful examination of her
      life and works indicates that she does not deserve her
      reputation as a radical. Her ideas in Letters and Essays
      about the monarchy are similar to Paine's, about material-
      ism to Priestley's, about necessity to Godwin's, and about
      feminism and the mind are unoriginal. Her novel, Memoirs
      of Emma Courtney investigates the hypocritical and overly
      modest restrictions on expression of sincere feeling as a
      serious moral dilemma, and, like Wollstonecraft's The
      Wrongs of Woman, was intended to warn women against excess-
      ive sensibility.

967   Adams, M. Ray. Studies in the Literary Backgrounds of
      English Radicalism. Lancaster, Pennsylvania: Franklin
      and Marshall, 1947. Mary Hays was a "free-born" spirit
      whose behavior, friendships, and writing earned her no-
      toriety. Hays sometimes reduced Godwin's ideas to absur-
      dities.

968   Allen, B. Sprague. "The Reaction Against William Godwin."
      MP, 16 (1918), 57-75. Writers such as Mary Hays whose
      Memoirs of Emma Courtney deplores women's economic and
      intellectual dependence aroused greater public outrage
      toward Godwin's Political Justice by providing evidence of
      his influence.

969   Luria, Gina M. "Mary Hays: A Critical Biography." New
      York University dissertation 1972. Mary Hays took part in
      most of the intellectual debates of her time. Her biogra-
      phy, friendships, correspondence, and works document her
      deep involvement in philosophical controversies.

970   Pollin, Burton R. "Mary Hays on Women's Rights in the
      Monthly Magazine." EA, 24 (1971), 271-282. Her writings on
      women's rights echo Godwin's Political Justice. She answered
      a number of letters written to the Monthly Magazine criti-
      cizing that periodical's pro-female essay "Are Literary and
      Scientific Pursuits suited to the Female Character?" In-
      cluded in her letters are a defense of novel writing and
      evidence of her "good heart."

971   Wedd, Annie F. The Love-Letters of Mary Hays (1779-1780).
      London: Methuen, 1925. This is a brief biography with the
      texts of letters.

ELIZA HAYWOOD

972   Elwood, John R. "A Critical Edition of Eliza Haywood's
      The History of Miss Betsy Thoughtless." University of
      Illinois dissertation, 1962. This edition has a biogra-
      phy and an introduction which evaluates influences on
      the novel, its contribution to the development of the
      English novel, and its reputation.

973   Elwood, John R. "Henry Fielding and Eliza Haywood: A
      Twenty Year War." _Albion_, Fall 1973, 184-192. Fielding
      and Haywood exchanged insults periodically between 1730
      and 1752. While Fielding may not have been attacking
      her specifically, his ridicule of novels and translations
      irritated her into making veiled remarks against Field-
      ing. Eventually Fielding tried Betsy Thoughtless in a
      mock trial in the _Covent Garden Journal_.

974   Elwood, John R. "The Stage Career of Eliza Haywood."
      Theatre Survey, 5 (1964), 107-116. This is a biographi-
      cal survey of Haywood's dramatic career (1715-1737).

975   Elwood, John R. "Swift's 'Corinna.'" _N&Q_, 200 (1955),
      529-530. Eliza Haywood, not Delarivière Manley, is a
      more likely "Corinna."

976   Erickson, James Paul. "The Novels of Eliza Haywood."
      University of Minnesota dissertation, 1961. Her develop-
      ment as a novelist parallels popular taste as it shifted
      from early romances, modeled after Behn, to later imi-
      tations of Richardson.

977   Fletcher, Edward G. "The Date of Eliza Haywood's Death."
      _N&Q_, 166 (1934), 385. The Earl of Egmont incorrectly
      records her death in his diary entry for 10 December
      1743.

978   Heinemann, Marcia. "Eliza Haywood's Career in the
      Theatre." _N&Q_, 218 (1973), 9-13. Eliza Haywood acted
      for the Little Theatre in the Haymarket from 1730 to
      1736 where she participated in Fielding's campaign
      against Walpole and played parts suited to her reputa-
      tion.

979   Hodges, James. "_The Female Spectator_: A Courtesy Period-
      ical" in _Studies in the Early English Periodical_, Richmond
      P. Bond, ed. Chapel Hill: University of North Carolina

Press, 1957. See item # 516.

980   Hodges, James. "A Study of the _Female Spectator_ (1744-
       1746). _University of North Carolina Record_, 492 (1951),
       129-131. See item # 517.

981   Hughes, Helen S. "Notes on Eighteenth-Century Fictional
       Translations." _MP_, 17 (1919), 49-55. Eliza Haywood's
       The Fortunate Foundling exemplifies the cavalier use of
       foreign fiction and the practice and influence of trans-
       lations on English fiction. Haywood borrowed from _Les
       Heureux Orphelins_. Later, _The Happy Orphans_, a trans-
       lation with interpretive remarks, appeared.

982   Kent, John P. "Crébillon fils, Mrs. Eliza Haywood and
       Les Heureux Orphelins: A Problem of Authorship." _Ro-
       mance Notes_, 11 (1969), 326-332. Crébillon _fils_ was
       not the author of _Les Heureux Orphelins_. He did not
       know England or English, nor was he as favorably in-
       clined toward English customs as the novelist. By
       claiming the book, he was protecting his wife, the ac-
       tual author, and assuring the book's sale.

983   Mish, Charles C. "Mme. de Gomez and _La Belle Assemblée_."
       Revue de Litterature Comparée, 34 (1960), 212-225. Eli-
       za Haywood translated several of Mme. de Gomez's popular
       works including _La Belle Assemblée_ and _L'Entretien des
       Beaux Esprits_. The former went through eight editions
       and is characteristic of the popular fiction of the 1720's.

984   Priestley, Mary. _The Female Spectator_. London: John
       Lane, 1929. A selection of essays from _The Female Spec-
       tator_ prefaced by a discussion of the periodical as a
       precursor of modern women's magazines.

985   Schulz, Dieter. "The Coquette's Progress from Satire
       to Sentimental Novel." _LWU_, 6 (1973), 77-89. See item
       #399.

986   Suwannabha, Sumitra. "The Feminine Eye: Augustan So-
       ciety as Seen by Selected Women Dramatists of the Res-
       toration and Early Eighteenth Century." University of
       Indiana dissertation, 1973. See item #334.

987   Walmsley, D. M. "Eliza Haywood: A Bicentenary." _TLS_,
       24 February 1956, p. 117. This is a tribute to Eliza
       Haywood as a professional woman.

988 Whicher, George F. "The Life and Romances of Mrs. Eliza
Haywood." Columbia University dissertation, 1915. She
cannot be safely ignored by scholars of the eighteenth
century. Six chapters outline her production and assess
her contribution to such contemporary interests as the
Dancan Campbell case, the domestic novels, and the periodical essays. Chapter one is a biographical summary.

989 Whicher, George F. The Life and Romances of Mrs. Eliza
Haywood. New York: Columbia University Press, 1915.
See above.

990   Albion, Gordon. Charles I and the Court of Rome. London: Burns, Oates, Washbourne, 1935. Henrietta Maria, Charles' Catholic wife was a factor and even took an active part in the negotiations between the Pope and England. She was especially active during negotiations for Papal intervention.

991   Carré, Henri. Henriette de France. Reine d'Angleterre 1609-1669. Paris: Éditions Bernard Grasset, 1947. A biography of Henrietta Maria explains how her Catholic, Bourbon background influenced her behavior and life in England.

992   Hartmann, Cyril H. Charles II and Madame. London: Heinemann, 1934. A study of Charles II and his sister, Henriette-Anne, children of Henrietta Maria based on their letters with printed texts included. The letters describe their mother and their feelings about her.

993   Haynes, Henrietta. Henrietta Maria. London: Methuen; New York: G. P. Putnam, 1912. Henrietta Maria, disliked for her personality, religion, and politics, "hurried Charles to his doom." Because she failed to understand the political realities, her ambitions were thwarted or destructive.

994   Lenanton, Carola Oman. Henrietta Maria. London: Hodde & Stoughton, 1936. This biography outlines the political context of her life and the problems of Charles' reign.

995   Mackay, Janet. Little Madam. A Biography of Henrietta Maria. London: Bell, 1939. Henrietta Maria was a willing political pawn. Her eagerness to please became disagreeable complaining because of Charles' appearance and behavior and her Catholicism. She was, however, an influential figure.

996   Oliver, Jane. Queen of Tears. The Life of Henrietta Maria. London: Collins, 1940. A popular biography of Henrietta Maria traces the increasing difficulty of her life as a devoted queen, wife and mother.

997   Shelmerdine, Joan M. The Secret History of Henrietta, Princess of England. New York: Dutton, 1929. Madame de la Fayette collaborated with the Princess Henrietta, youngest daughter of Charles I, in writing The Secret

<u>History</u> <u>of</u> <u>Henrietta</u>. Queen Henriette-Marie devoted her
life to her daughter's education.

998   Taylor, I. A. <u>The</u> <u>Life</u> <u>of</u> <u>Queen</u> <u>Henrietta</u> <u>Maria</u>. 2 vols.
London: Hutchinson, 1905. Statements of admiration
from her family and of hatred by Englishmen show that
her faults were the results of prejudice and lack of
understanding rather than of intention. Such a distinction is important in judging her regardless of the
results of her behavior.

999 Braund, E. "Mrs. Hutchinson and Her Teaching." _Evangeli-cal Quarterly_, 31 (1959), 72-81. Lucy Apsley Hutchinson shared the excitement and hardships of her husband who was one of the signers of King Charles' death warrant, a member of Parliament, and a prisoner at Sandown Castle. After his death, she wrote his _Memoirs_, the _Principles of the Chris-tian Religion_ and _Of Theology_. She intended the first to guide her daughter in difficult times and the second to ex-pose the weaknesses of philosophy.

1000 Hobman, D. A. "A Puritan Lady." _Contemporary Review_, 176 (1949), 115-118. Lucy Hutchinson's _Memoirs of Colonel Hutchinson_ is more her autobiography than his biography and is filled with incisive characterizations of her con-temporaries.

1001 Mayo, Robert. _Epicurus in England_. Dallas: The Southwest Press, 1934. Her translation of _De Rerum Natura_ is one of only four documents about Epicureanism in England before 1656. She was ashamed of it and, like her contemporaries, feared its influence.

1002 Weiss, S. A. "Dating Mrs. Hutchinson's Translation of Lu-cretius." _N&Q_, 200 (1955), 109. Her translation and letter about Lucretius indicate that Epicureanism was in vogue no earlier than the late 1640's.

ELIZABETH INCHBALD

1003   de Beer, E. S. "Lovers' Vows: 'The Dangerous Insignifi-
        cance of the Butler.'" N&Q, 207 (1962), 421-422. Mrs.
        Inchbald's changes in the character of the butler im-
        prove upon the character as he appears in Das Kind der
        Liebe.

1004   Eva, John. "Mrs. Inchbald and Thomas Holcroft in Canter-
        bury, 1777." N&Q, 199 (1954), 173-174. The files of
        the Kentish Gazette give the parts acted by Elizabeth
        Inchbald in Canterbury in 1777 and correct some minor
        points in Boaden's Memoirs of Mrs. Inchbald.

1005   Gosch, Marcella. "'Translaters' of Kotzebue in England."
        Monatshefte für deutschen Unterricht, 31 (1939), 175-
        183. August von Kotzebue's plays influenced stagecraft
        and "middle class drama." Inchbald translated Das Kind
        der Liebe modifying characters as she felt necessary to
        make the play acceptable to English audiences.

1006   Hamnet, Ian. "Elizabeth Inchbald." Blackfriars, 35 (1954),
        215-220. Her best plays are never more than mediocre, but
        they serve as useful apprentice pieces for her novels.
        The Catholicism in the book has "popular" elements and
        takes second place to her social criticism. Her forte,
        however, is dramatic scenes in which there are strong,
        emotional confrontations between characters.

1007   Joughin, George L. "An Inchbald Bibliography." Univer-
        sity of Texas Studies in English, 14 (1934), 59-74. The
        bibliography locates the items and tabulates reprintings.

1008   Joughin, George L. "The Life and Works of Elizabeth
        Inchbald." Harvard University dissertation, 1932. A
        study of her novels, plays, and literary criticism is
        prefaced with a biography. Her rationalism, religion,
        and financial problems influenced her work.

1009   Joughin, George L. The Life and Works of Elizabeth
        Inchbald. London: Brown, 1916. See above.

1010   Littlewood, Samuel R. Elizabeth Inchbald and Her Circle.
        London: O'Connor, 1921. Inchbald was a "bright and
        noble spirit" and a charming woman whose life has all
        the elements of a good novel: romance, hardship, striv-
        ing, achievement, and contact with interesting personali-
        ties.

1011   McKee, William. "Elizabeth Inchbald, Novelist." Catho-
       lic University of America dissertation, 1935. Beginning
       with a biography, the author defines the influences on
       her novels with special attention to her Catholicism
       and the demands on her time. He assesses the novels'
       quality and contribution to the development of fiction.

1012   Moreux, Francoise. Elizabeth Inchbald et La Comédie
       "Sentimentale" Anglaise au XVIIIᵉ Siècle. Paris: Au-
       bier-Montaigne, 1971. Texts and translations of I'll
       Tell You What and Appearance is Against Them are prefaced
       by biographical notes, tables dating her works, and a
       critical discussion of plot, themes, and character.

1013   Park, Bruce R. "Thomas Holcroft and Elizabeth Inch-
       bald: Studies in the Eighteenth-Century Drama of Ideas."
       Columbia University dissertation, 1952. Inchbald and
       Holcroft presented a world view poised on current "modes
       of apprehension" (rationalism and sentimentalism) in
       their plays. Many of their difficulties are explained
       by incompatible aspects of their philosophies.

1014   Strachey, G. L. Introduction to A Simple Story. London:
       Henry Frowde, 1908. The novel is superior to Evelina
       but has been neglected because it is so different from
       the nineteenth century novel in subject and style.

1015   Tobler, Clara. Mrs. Inchbald: eine vergessene eng-
       lische Bühnendichterin and Romanschriftstellerin des
       18 Jahrhunderts. Berlin: Mayer & Müller, 1910. This
       appreciation of the life, dramatic works, and novels
       points out the strengths of her literary output. It
       also considers the translations of her work.

1016   Tompkins, J. M. S. Introduction to A Simple Story. Lon-
       don: Oxford, 1967. While sharing many of the character-
       istics of the late eighteenth century novel by women, the
       novel is unusual because of Inchbald's ability to use
       Catholic elements, dramatic techniques, and to create
       good minor characters.

1017   Anon. "Swift's _Journal_ _to_ _Stella_." _TLS_, 24 September
        1925, pp. 605-606. The _Journal_ was Swift's private
        chamber where, away from the company of great men who
        praised him, he could speak a "little language" to a
        woman who understood better than anyone how he could
        be at once coarse and delicate, cynical and yet cherish
        such a depth of feeling.

1018   Davis, Herbert. _Stella,_ _A_ _Gentlewoman_ _of_ _the_ _Eighteenth_
        Century. New York: Macmillan, 1942. A brief review
        of the known facts concerning Stella's relationship with
        Swift.

1019   Deford, Miriam Allen. "Swift and Stella. An Unsolved
        Mystery Story." _Modern_ _Age_, 11 (1967), 400-406. A
        rather sentimental account of Swift's friendship with
        Esther Johnson and his acquaintance with Hester Van-
        homrigh.

1020   Ehrenpreis, Irvin. "The Pattern of Swift's Women." _PMLA_,
        70 (1955), 706-716. Swift sought parental authority over
        firstborn, fatherless women. He praised women for "mas-
        culine" traits.

1021   Ehrenpreis, Irvin. "Swift's 'Little Language' in _The_
        Journal _to_ _Stella_." _SP_ , 45 (1948), 80-88. The special
        vocabulary reveals Swift did not address Stella as a wife.

1022   England, A. B. "Private and Public Rhetoric in the _Jour-_
        nal _to_ _Stella_." _Essays_ _in_ _Criticism_, 22 (1972), 131-
        141. The contrast between the apparently spontaneous
        and free style and the more formal style in his _Journal_
        dramatizes Swift's concern with the theme of private
        versus public self. Ultimately, however, "Pdfr's style,"
        Swift's "spontaneous" style is very nearly as self-con-
        scious as the artful, obviously highly wrought style of
        the "other I," and this fact points finally and ironically
        to the indivisibility of the "two" Swifts.

1023   Fischer, John I. "The Uses of Virtue: Swift's Last Poem
        to Stella" in _Essays_ _in_ _Honor_ _of_ _Esmond_ _Linworth_ _Marilla_,
        Thomas A. Kirby, ed. Baton Rouge: Louisiana State Uni-
        versity Press, 1970. Far from being simply a graceful
        versified compliment, Swift's last poem to Stella is a

complex treatment of the "advantages, nature, and purposes of a virtuous life," and, more specifically, a treatment of the relationship of virtue to salvation.

1024 Gold, Maxwell B. _Swift's Marriage to Stella, Together with Unprinted and Misprinted Letters_. Cambridge: Harvard University Press, 1937. A scholarly investigation of the mysteries surrounding Swift's supposed marriage to Stella. New evidence is presented and an appendix contains previously unpublished or misprinted documents.

1025 Gregory, Alyse. "Stella, Vanessa, and Swift." _Nineteenth Century_, 113 (1933), 755-764. A popular account of Swift's relationships with Stella and Vanessa.

1026 Hand, George. "Swift and Marriage" in _Essays and Studies by the Members of the Department of English, University of California_. _University of California Publications in English_, 14 (1943), 73-93.

1027 Hearsey, Marguerite. "New Light on the Evidence for Swift's Marriage." _PMLA_, 42 (1927), 157-161. Supports the possibility of Swift-Stella marriage on the basis that Berkeley could have been told of it by the Bishop of Clogher.

1028 Jackson, Robert W. "Stella: her relationship with Jonathan Swift" in _North Munster Studies: Essays in Commemoration of Monsignor Michael Moloney_, Etienne Rhynne, ed. Limerick: Thomond Archaeological Society, 1967, pp. 375-394. Speculates about their relationship.

1029 Jackson, Robert W. _Swift and his Circle: A Book of Essays_. Dublin: The Talbot Press, 1945. See item # 97.

1030 Kirkpatrick, T. Percy C. "Swift and Stella." _TLS_, 19 June 1937, p. 464. If the alleged private marriage of Swift and Stella did take place, it was not only illegal but also in violation of important Church Canons.

1031 Paulson, Ronald. "Swift, Stella, and Permanence." _ELH_, 27 (1960), 298-314. In Swift's poems to Stella, he treats the subject of the proper relationship of soul to body. His contention in these poems that the spiritual alone is of ultimate significance is analogous to his emphasis

on "spiritual victory" in the poems which he wrote as
personal apologias.

1032   Petitjean, A. M. "Swift et Stella." Cahiers du Sud,
        24 (1937), 720-733. A survey of their relationship.

1033   Pons, E. "Du nouveau sur le 'Journal à Stella.'" Etudes
        Anglaises, 1 (1937), 210-229. A description of British
        Museum journal-letters.

1034   Rice, J. A. Jun. "A Letter from Stella." TLS, 29 May
        1930, p. 457. Notes the discovery of a letter from
        Stella to Captain Dingley and of a letter from Rebecca
        Dingley to the same correspondent.

1035   Rodgers, Katherine M. "'My Female Friends:' The Misogyny
        of Jonathan Swift." TSLL, 1 (1959), 366-379. Swift at-
        tacks women's physical functions as well as the romantic
        ideal in "a deep unconscious revulsion against Woman as
        Animal."

1036   Tyne, James L. "Swift and Stella: The Love Poems" in
        Quick Springs of Sense: Studies in the Eighteenth Cen-
        tury, Larry S. Champion, ed. Athens: University of
        Georgia Press, 1974. The poems to Esther Johnson are
        love poems "of considerable distinction" and originality.

1037   Uphaus, Robert W. "Swift's Stella and Fidelity to Ex-
        perience." Dublin Magazine, 8 (1970), 31-42. His poems
        to Stella consistently demonstrate Swift's determination
        to confront the facts of experience, especially the
        facts of aging, without self-deception. Through this
        fidelity to experience, he is able to point out the per-
        manence and worth of virtue.

1038   Uphaus, Robert W. "Swift's Stella Poems and Fidelity
        to Experience." Eire, 5 (1970), 40-52.

1039   Williams, Harold. Introduction to Journal to Stella.
        2 vols. Oxford: Clarendon Press, 1948. The introduc-
        tion sketches the biographical and historical backgrounds
        of the Journal and also provides a brief discussion of
        bibliographical and stylistic points concerning the Jour-
        nal.

1040   Williams, Harold. "Stella's Friends." TLS, 9 May 1936,
        p. 400. Notes and prints the poem discovered in the

British Museum addressed to Stella during her last ill-
ness. The poem is in the hand of Thomas Sheridan and
is signed by a number of Stella's friends.

DOROTHY JORDAN

1041 Aspinall, Arthur, ed. Mrs. Jordan and Her Family: being the unpublished correspondence of Mrs. Jordan and the Duke of Clarence. London: Barker, 1951.

1042 Fothergill, Brian. Mrs. Jordan: Portrait of an Actress. London: Faber & Faber, 1965. A biography of Dorothy Jordan.

1043 Jerrold, Clare. The Story of Dorothy Jordan. New York: Benjamin Blom, 1969. A biography.

1044 Lawrence, W. J. "Mrs. Jordan in Dublin." N&Q, 17 (1901), 221-222. Her debut could not have been earlier than 1779.

1045 Lawrence, W. J. "Mrs. Jordan in Dublin." N&Q, 19 (1903), Describes her as Phoebe in As You Like It.

1046 Lawrence, W. J. "The Portraits of Mrs. Jordan." Connoisseur, 26 (1910), 143-150. Discusses portraits and gives a biographical sketch.

1047 M, P. D. "Dorothy Jordan, Actress, 1762-1816." N&Q, 182 (1942), 232. Her father's name was Bland.

1048 Sergeant, Philip W. Mrs. Jordan, Child of Nature. London: Hutchinson, 1913. Biography based largely on contemporary sources.

1049 Woods, Charles B. "The 'Miss Lucy' Plays of Fielding and Garrick." PQ, 41 (1962), 294-310. See item #356.

1050   Fulford, Roger, ed. Introduction to The Autobiography
       of Miss Knight, Lady Companion to Princess Charlotte.
       London: Kimber, 1960. The introduction contains a
       sketch of Knight's life and character and a note on her
       papers and Autobiography.

1051   Luttrell, Barbara. The Prim Romantic: A Biography of
       Ellis Cornelia Knight, 1758-1837. London: Chatto and
       Windus, 1965. Drawing from Knight's diary and a wide
       range of contemporary sources, Luttrell constructs a
       scholarly account of Knight's life and times. Contains
       appendices and bibliography.

1052   Riely, John C. "Lady Knight's Role in the Boswell-Piozzi
       Rivalry." PQ, 51 (1972), 961-965. Lady Knight (the
       mother of Cornelia) claimed to have prevented Mrs. Piozzi
       from making a scandalous attack on Boswell. This claim
       has been accepted by at least two modern scholars. An
       investigation of the evidence shows, however, that Lady
       Knight was not, in fact, instrumental in preventing Piozzi's
       attack.

1053   Anon. "Authorship of the Political Quixote." Johnsonian
        News Letter, 13 (1953), 4-5. Miriam Small ascribed The
        History of Sir George Warrington: or the Political Quixote
        to Lennox in her 1935 biography. She offers evidence that
        The History was the work of Jane Purbeck.

1054   Dalziel, Margaret. Introduction to The Female Quixote; or
        The Adventures of Arabella. London: Oxford University
        Press, 1970. The introduction explains Lennox's burlesque
        of French romances, differences from Cervantes' purposes,
        the satire of the morality of romances, and the novel's
        high contemporary reputation. There is an appendix and
        chronology table by Duncan Isles.

1055   Eddy, Donald D. "John Hawkesworth: Book reviewer in the
        Gentleman's Magazine." PQ, 43 (1964), 223-238. Hawkesworth's
        reviews can be identified by their similarities to his signed
        reviews of the same works which appeared in the Monthly
        Review. His reviews of Lennox's The Sister discuss her repu-
        tation and display knowledge of her works while reviewing
        the comedy and its reception.

1056   Fyvie, John. Some Famous Women of Wit and Beauty. A
        Georgian Galaxy. London: Constable, 1905. See item #66.

1057   Hayes, Elizabeth G. "Charlotte Ramsay Lennox: The Female
        Quixote; or, The Adventures of Arabella." Stanford disser-
        tation, 1964. This annotated edition of the novel has an
        introduction including an assessment of the extent and
        nature of Cervantes' influence, bibliographies, and appen-
        dices.

1058   Holman, D. L. "Mrs. Lennox and Dr. Johnson." Chambers Jour-
        nal, March 1947, pp. 183-186. Mrs. Lennox was disliked by
        the women in Johnson's circle and many of her contemporaries.
        because of her poverty, her ambition, and her favor with
        Johnson. Her talents declined and even Johnson would have
        pitied The Memoirs of Henry Lennox.

1059   Isles, Duncan. "Johnson and Charlotte Lennox." New Ram-
        bler, 19 (1967), 34-48. Johnson assisted Charlotte Lennox's
        literary career more than that of any other writer. The
        relationship, spanning thirty-four years, epitomizes John-
        son's manner of supporting writers. Descriptions of her
        life, her work, her personality, and of the specific help
        Johnson gave her make up the bulk of the essay.

1060   Isles, Duncan. "The Lennox Collection." HLB, 18 (1970),
       317-344; HLB, 19 (1971), 36-60; 165-186; and 416-435. A
       collection of forty-two letters written to or about Char-
       lotte Lennox with introduction, chronology, bibliography,
       and notes are printed in full. The appendix locates two
       other letters.

1061   Kauver, Elaine M. "Jane Austen and The Female Quixote."
       SNNTS, 2 (1970), 211-221. Lennox uses the conventions of
       the coming-of-age and quixotic novels to burlesque romances
       and to bring Arabella to a realistic acceptance of life
       and to a happy marriage. Jane Austen adapted and refined
       a number of Lennox's techniques.

1062   Kynaston, Agnes M. "The Life and Writings of Charlotte
       Lennox, 1720-1804." University of London thesis, 1936.
       This is a biography and survey of her work.

1063   Maynadier, Gustavu s H. The First American Novelist? Cam-
       bridge: Harvard University Press, 1940. Charlotte Lennox
       had been in American and had first hand knowledge of New
       York and some of the frontier settlements. She was proba-
       bly born in the colonies in 1720, but she may have mis-
       represented details about her life.

1064   Price, Jonathan R. "Measure for Measure and the Critics:
       Toward a New Approach." Shakespeare Quarterly, 20 (1969),
       179-204. Lennox and others wrote criticism on Shakespeare's
       comedy.

1065   Séjourné, Philippe. The Mystery of Charlotte Lennox: First
       Novelist of Colonial America (1727?-1804). Aix-en-Provence:
       Publications des Annales de la Faculté des Lettres, 1967.
       The mystery of her early years was a shadow which kept her
       from being completely accepted in society. Her novels,
       Harriot Stuart and Euphemia, are quite "American" and clear
       up some of the questions about her youth. A bibliography
       and critical treatment of information about her years in
       England are included.

1066   Slomen, Judith. "The Female Quixote as an Eighteenth Cen-
       tury Character Type." Transactions of the Samuel Johnson
       Society of the Northwest. Ed. Robert H. Carnie. Calgary,
       Alberta: Samuel Johnson Society of the Northwest, 1972.
       IV, 86-101.   Arabella is a sympathetic version of a common
       heroine, the unprotected young lady, formed by her novel
       reading and in need of rescue by a prudent man. She lives
       in a world in which excitement must be created, but she

manufactures a system by which she orders reality and in-
terprets all experience. The way men in the novel react
to Arabella is very similar to the condescending way they
treat all women. The romances have provided Arabella with
useful models for behavior.

1067   Small, Miriam R. Charlotte Ramsey Lennox: An Eighteenth
        Century Lady of Letters. Hamden, Connecticut: Archon,
        1969; rpt. of New Haven: Yale University Press, 1935.
        A biography of Lennox concentrating on her literary career
        finds her a versatile and prolific writer, highly respected
        in her own time. Her Female Quixote and Shakespear Illus-
        trated are lasting contributions. There are appendices on
        James Ramsey, texts of poems, works by and attributed to
        Lennox.

1068   Small, Miriam R. "The Life and Literary Relations of Char-
        lotte Lennox." Yale University dissertation, 1925. The
        dissertation was published in revised and expanded form
        in 1935.

1069   Staves, Susan. "Don Quixote in Eighteenth Century England."
        CL, 24 (1972), 193-215. The eighteenth century interpreted
        Cervantes' Don Quixote as an Augustan satire. This inter-
        pretation influenced such writers as Henry Fielding and
        Charlotte Lennox; later in the hands of Charlotte Smith
        and others, Quixote became a romantic figure.

1070   Todd-Naylor, Ursula. "Charlotte Lennox." Oxford University
        dissertation, 1931. This is a biography and description
        of her work.

1071   Wilson, Mona. These were the Muses. London: Sidgwick &
        Jackson, 1924. The chapter "The Female Quixote" (pp. 11-
        26) surveys Lennox's life and literary output with special
        attention to her relationship with Johnson and to Henrietta
        and The Female Quixote.

SARAH LENNOX

1072 Curtis, Edith R. Lady Sarah Lennox, an Irrepressible
      Stuart, 1745-1826. New York: Putnam & Sons, 1946. A
      popular biography describes her private life and roman-
      tic involvements including her relationship with George
      III.

1073 Ilchester, Mary, and Lord Stavordale. The Life and Let-
      ters of Lady Sarah Lennox, 1745-1826. 2 vols. London:
      John Murray, 1901. This collection of writings and let-
      ters by and about Sarah Lennox begins with a biography.

1074 King-Hall, Magdalen. Lady Sarah. A Novel. London:
      Peter Davies, 1939. The fictionalized biography is based
      on Ilchester's book. Sarah's "romps" with King George,
      her marriage, and her social life depict English life
      and the experience of a prominent woman.

1075   Anderson, Paul B. "Delarivière Manley's Prose Fiction."
        PQ, 8 (1934), 168-188. After a summary of Manley's lit-
        erary career and contemporary reputation, Mr. Anderson
        examines her presentation of the varieties of female
        experience in her fiction, finding realistic detail,
        capacity to experiment with fictional techniques, and
        considerable understanding of female responses to her
        time.

1076   Anderson, Paul B. "The History and Authorship of Mrs.
        Crackenthorpe's Female Tatler." MP, 28 (1931), 354-
        360. See item # 506.

1077   Anderson, Paul B. "La Bruyère and Mrs. Crackenthorpe's
        Female Tatler." PMLA, 52 (1937), 100-103. See item #
        507.

1078   Anderson, Paul B. "Mary de la Rivière Manley, a Cava-
        lier's Daughter in Grub Street." Harvard University
        dissertation, 1931. This biography connects her per-
        sonal, literary and political lives, finding her the
        foremost woman of letters in the early eighteenth
        century.

1079   Anderson, Paul B. "Mistress Delarivière Manley's Biogra-
        phy." MP, 33 (1936), 261-278. She is the "most repre-
        sentative professional" woman of her time. Her works
        and biographical data record the life of an early woman
        writer and her self-concept.

1080   Anderson, Paul B. "Mrs. Manley's Texts of Three of Lady
        Winchilsea's Poems." MLN, 45 (1930), 95-99. See item #
        930.

1081   Anderson, Paul B. "'Splendor out of Scandal.' The Lucin-
        da-Artesia Papers in The Female Tatler." PQ, 15 (1936),
        286-300. See item #508.

1082   Bennett, Gilbert. "Conventions of the Stage Villain."
        The Anglo-Welsh Review, 14 (1964), 92-102. See item
        # 240.

1083   Duff, Dolores D. "Materials toward a Biography of Mary
        Delarivière Manley." Indiana University dissertation,
        1965. The dissertation examines her early life, four
        important, close relationships, and her literary career.

1084   Elwood, John R. "Swift's 'Corinna.'" N&Q, 200 (1955),
        529-530. See item # 975.

1085   Gagen, Jean E. The New Woman: Her Emergence in English
        Drama, 1660-1730. New York: Twayne, 1954. See item #
        269.

1086   Graham, Walter. "Thomas Baker, Mrs. Manley, and The Fe-
        male Tatler." MP, 34 (1937), 267-272. See item # 514.

1087   Hook, Lucyle. Introduction to The Female Wits. ARS #
        124. Los Angeles: Clark Library, 1967. See item #285.

1088   Kline, Richard B. "Anne Oldfield and Mary de la Rivière
        Manley: The Unnoticed Reconciliation." RECTR, 14 (1975),
        53-58. By 1720, Mrs. Manley called Mrs. Oldfield "gra-
        cious," and Mrs. Oldfield agreed to speak an epilogue
        written by Prior for a benefit night for Manley.

1089   Köster, Patricia. "Humanism, Feminism, Sensationalism:
        Mrs. Manley vs. Society" in Transactions of the Samuel
        Johnson Society of the Northwest, Robert H. Carnie, ed.
        Calgary: U. of Alberta Press, 1972, vol. 4, 42-53. Al-
        myna, or the Arabian Vow (1706) argues for the education
        of women. Other works by Manley demonstrate the ruinous
        consequences of an inadequate education.

1090   Köster, Patricia. The Novels of Mary Delarivière Manley.
        2 vols. Gainesville, Florida: Scholars' Facsimiles and
        Reprints, 1971. The introduction includes a brief biogra-
        phy, a discussion of the works included, and an outline
        of critical work about Manley.

1091   Milford, R. T. "The Female Tatler." MP, 29 (1932), 350-
        351. The Bodleian has complete sets of the original and
        rival Female Tatlers.

1092   Needham, Gwendolyn B. "Mary de la Rivière Manley: Tory
        Defender." HLQ, 12 (1949), 253-288. A survey of the
        secret histories, Examiners, and pamphlets demonstrates
        that she was an effective political propagandist, recog-
        nized and respected as such by her contemporaries.

1093   Needham, Gwendolyn B. "Mrs. Manley: Eighteenth-Century
        Wife of Bath." HLQ, 14 (1951), 259-284. She was not
        only the first political journalist, the first author of
        a best seller, but also the "first to assail by deed and
        word the double standard of morality." Her behavior and

reactions to her are similar to the story of and responses to the Wife of Bath. Manley's writings contain numerous "feminist declarations" and passages pointing out her sex's achievements.

1094   Sergeant, Philip. "Rivella the Reckless" in Rogues and Scoundrels. London: Heinemann, 1924. A popular biography emphasizes her unconventional behavior.

1095   Snyder, Henry L. "New Light on Mrs. Manley." PQ, 52 (1973), 767-770. She may have spent at least the year 1706 in Newgate for debt. The evidence, including a recently discovered petition to Queen Anne signed "Maria Williamina Manley," and the summary of biographical facts raise other issues.

1096   Winton, Calhoun. "Steele, Mrs. Manley and John Lacy." PQ, 42 (1963), 272-275. Delarivière Manley, not Lacy, was the author of the 1714 pamphlet The Ecclesiastical and Political History of Whig-Land of Late Years which parodies a Whig book bearing Steele's name. The pamphlet attacks Steele by innuendo and scandalous anecdotes.

1097   Zbinden, E. O. "Mrs. Mary Manley's Leben und dramatische Tätigkeit. Basel dissertation, 1916. This is a survey of her career and dramatic works based on sketchy material.

ELIZABETH MONTAGU

1098   Blunt, Reginald. _Elizabeth Montagu, "Queen of the Blues:"
        Her Letters and Friendships from 1762 to 1800._ Boston:
        Houghton Mifflin, 1923. Beginning where the Climenson
        book ends, Mr. Blunt selects and edits to display her
        interests and to describe important people and events.

1099   Boulton, James T. "Mrs. Elizabeth Montagu (1720-1800)."
        Burke Newsletter, 3 (1961-62), 96-98. Her friendships
        with such men as Burke, Johnson, and Reynolds testify
        to her ability and personality.

1100   Busse, John. _Mrs. Montagu, Queen of the Blues._ London:
        Howe, 1928. Because she achieved no fame for conversation
        or for her literary productions, her lasting reputation
        is the more remarkable. Her letters record the lives
        and friendships of the interesting and important people
        of her time.

1101   Climenson, Emily J. _Elizabeth Montagu, the Queen of the
        Bluestockings: Her Correspondence from 1720-1761._ 2
        vols. London: John Murray, 1906. Her letters are se-
        lected and edited to describe her ordinary life rather
        than her opinions about literature and current events.
        Her wide circle of acquaintances and her social life
        put her in close touch with English culture.

1102   deCastro, J. Paul. "Elizabeth Robinson Montagu (1720-
        1800)." _N&Q_, 181 (1941), 305 and 347. Her first known
        letter was written when she was eleven in 1731. Her
        editors have added to the confusion in dating her letters.

1103   Ewert, Leonore H. "Elizabeth Montagu to Elizabeth Carter,
        Literary Gossip and Critical Opinions from the Pen of
        the Queen of the Blues." Claremont Graduate School dis-
        sertation, 1968. Elizabeth Montagu's letters to Miss
        Carter contain numerous literary references. Her comments
        on books and literary figures such as Johnson, Gray, and
        Burke show her to be a common sense critic, alert to
        literary tastes and issues. She wrote about patronage,
        publishing, subscriptions, and reviewing revealingly.

1104   Fyvie, John. _Some Famous Women of Wit and Beauty. A
        Georgian Galaxy._ London: Constable, 1905. See item #
        66.

1105   Harmsen, Tyrus G. "Elizabeth Montagu." N&Q, 203 (1958),
        88. Her papers were purchased for the Huntington Library
        in 1925.

1106   Hegeman, Daniel V. "Three English Bluestockings Visit
        Germany." Kentucky Foreign Language Quarterly, 4 (1957),
        57-73. The first literary form in which women distin-
        guished themselves was letter writing. As they began
        to travel, their letters catalogue feminine interests and
        judgments and the changing tastes in society at large.
        Lady Mary Wortley Montagu illustrates the "Age of Rea-
        son," Elizabeth Montagu the "Era of Sensibility," and
        Dorothy Wordsworth the "Triumph of the Middle Class."

1107   Hornbeak, Katherine. "New Light on Mrs. Montagu"in The
        Age of Johnson: Essays Presented to Chauncey Brewster
        Tinker. New Haven: Yale University Press, 1949, pp.
        349-361. James Woodhouse's The Life and Lucubrations of
        Crispinus Scriblerus provides unflattering information
        about Elizabeth Montagu's pride, ambition, and parsimon-
        iousness. Her correspondence discusses Woodhouse's work
        and their changing feelings toward one another.

1108   Huchon, René L. Mrs. Montagu and Her Friends, 1720-1800.
        London: Murray, 1907. An examination of Mrs. Montagu's
        moral and intellectual character, her Essay on the
        Genius of Shakespeare and its reception, and her literary
        acquaintances concludes that her insight and parties were
        inferior to those of Frenchwomen such as Mme. du Deffand
        but her learning and ostentation were superior.

1109   Jones, Claude E. "Johnson and Mrs. Montagu: Two Letters."
        N&Q, 191 (1946), 102-103. Herbert Croft solicited infor-
        mation about Edward Young for Johnson's Lives of the Poets.

1110   Jones, W. Powell. "Elizabeth Montagu: Her Letters."
        N&Q, 203 (1958), 182. The collection of letters used
        by Climenson and Blunt contains much unpublished ma-
        terial and is at the Huntington Library.

1111   Jones, W. Powell. "The Romantic Bluestocking, Elizabeth
        Montagu." HLQ, 12 (1948), 85-98. Elizabeth Montagu's
        letters reveal not only the hostess, the intimate of the
        famous, and the female savant, but also the woman, a "ro-
        mantic and impressionable woman who was keenly sensitive
        to the newer intellectual fashions of her day." Her in-
        terest in the picturesque in nature, in Ossian, and in the
        sublime balances the portrait of her personality.

1112   McElderry, B. R. "Boswell in 1790-91: Two unpublished
        comments." N&Q, 207 (1962), 266-68. Two letters to
        Mrs. Montagu contain gossip about Boswell.

1113   Phillips, George L. "Mrs. Montagu and the Climbing-
        Boys." RES, 25 (1949), 237-244. She entertained the
        London chimney-sweepers' apprentices at a dinner every
        May Day. This gesture of generosity startled her con-
        temporaries and provoked stories explaining her action.

1114   Ross, Ian. "A Bluestocking over the Border: Mrs. Eliz-
        abeth Montagu's Aesthetic Adventures in Scotland, 1766."
        HLQ, 28 (1965), 213-233. Her letters during her four
        week tour of Scotland give her reactions to people,
        places, and ideas. She sought out and took an especial
        pleasure in the "wild and romantick" and primitive.

1115   West, Rebecca. "Elizabeth Montagu" in From Anne to Vic-
        toria, Bonamy Dobree, ed. London: Cassell, 1937. She
        "conformed completely to the masculine notion of what a
        woman should be." Because of this, she was popular, but
        she knew her life was less than she wanted and that her
        intellectual abilities were slight. Her authority in
        society and her Essay on Shakespeare, however, were not
        contemptible achievements.

LADY MARY WORTLEY MONTAGU

1116   Baker, C. H. C. "Lady Mary Wortley Montagu's Fiance."
        TLS, 4 September 1937, p. 640. Baker identifies the
        "odious fiance" whom the youthful Lady Mary was very
        nearly forced to marry as Clotworthy Skeffington.

1117   Drew, Elizabeth. _The Literature of Gossip_. New York:
        Norton, 1964. Lady Mary's letters are frequently quoted
        in a biographical sketch (pp. 68-89).

1118   Dufrenoy, Marie-Louise. "Lady Mary Wortley Montagu et
        la satire orientale" in _Proceedings from the IVth Con-_
        gress of the International Comparative Literature Asso-
        ciation in Fribourg, 1964, Francois Jost, ed. 2 vols.
        The Hague: Mouton, 1966. The essay is concerned pri-
        marily with Lady Mary's introduction of small pox vac-
        cination into England.

1119   Franke, Wolfgang. "Elizabeth Lady Craven on Lady Mary
        Wortley Montagu: Some Eighteenth-Century Hints on the
        Authorship of the Five Spurious Letters." _N&Q_, 218
        (1973), 417-420. Lady Craven's attacks on the authen-
        ticity of Lady Mary's published correspondence, while
        invalid, provide some evidence that the authors of the
        spurious letters in the first printing might have been
        Horace Walpole, a Mr. Acland, and an unnamed "clever
        man."

1120   Gibbs, Lewis (pseud. for Joseph W. Cove). _The Admirable_
        Lady Mary: The Life and Times of Lady Mary Wortley Mon-
        tagu (1689-1762). London: Dent; New York: Morrow, 1949.
        A popular biography of Lady Mary which gives special at-
        tention to her quarrel with Pope and to her mysterious
        departure from England in 1739.

1121   Grundy, Isobel M. "A Moon of Literature: Verse by Lady
        Mary Wortley Montagu." _New Rambler_, 112 (1972), 6-22.
        This survey of Lady Mary's verse emphasizes the deriva-
        tive nature of most of her poetry and divides her poetic
        efforts into "personal" and "dramatic" categories. The
        article includes many examples of Lady Mary's verse which
        are quoted from her manuscripts.

1122   Grundy, Isobel M. "New Verse by Henry Fielding." _PMLA_,
        87 (1972), 213-245. Some heretofore unpublished poetry
        by Henry Fielding consisting of three parts of an un-
        finished burlesque epic (1729) and a separate verse-epistle

(1733) reflect the influence of Lady Mary's literary opinions and are a defense of Lady Mary against the satiric attacks of Pope respectively. The verse is printed with notes.

1123   Grundy, Isobel M. "Ovid and Eighteenth-Century Divorce: An Unpublished Poem by Lady Mary Wortley Montagu." RES, n.s. 23 (1972), 417-428. In her "Epistle from Mrs. Y--- to her Husband, 1724," published in this article for the first time, Lady Mary adopts the Ovidian heroic epistle for the purpose of creating a poem which deals sympathetically with a woman who had been divorced for adultery. The result is not only an interesting fusion of literary and topical materials, "but also an accomplished piece of poetry." The poem is printed with notes.

1124   Halsband, Robert. "Addison's Cato and Lady Mary Wortley Montagu." PMLA, 65 (1950), 1122-1129. Lady Mary's critique of Addison's Cato demonstrates her versatility as a woman of letters and her interest in drama. Also, it is evident that Lady Mary's critique, which was written at the request of her husband and circulated in manuscript, was not only read by Addison but used by him as the basis for several changes in the versification, the diction, and sentiments of his tragedy.

1125   Halsband, Robert. "Algarotti as Apollo: His Influence on Lady Mary Wortley Montagu." Friendship's Garland: Essays Presented to Mario Praz on his Seventieth Birthday, Vittorio Gabrieli, ed. 2 vols. Roma: Edizioni di Storia e Letteratura, 1966. Lady Mary was infatuated with him in later life and wrote love letters to him.

1126   Halsband, Robert. "An Imitation of Perrault in England: Lady Mary Wortley Montagu's Carabosse." Comparative Literature, 3 (1951), 174-177. Lady Mary's Carabosse is perhaps a unique example of an early eighteenth century English imitation of the French contes de fies. In this recasting of Perrault's "La Belle au Bois Dormant," Lady Mary makes several important changes which transform Perrault's conte into what is essentially a personal essay which provides a spiritual self-portrait of its author.

1127   Halsband, Robert. "Lady Mary Wortley Montagu and Eighteenth Century Fiction." PQ, 45 (1966), 145-156. Although Lady Mary's greatest fame is quite justly founded upon her letters, she also was a writer of fiction, producing prose

romances, fairy tales, and "essays employing fictional devices." Moreover, Lady Mary was an avid, if often unap-
proving, reader of novels, and she has left many critical
comments on the popular novels of her day. In general, she
approves of didacticism and realism, and objects to "romanticism." She was, for the most part, unimpressed by the
novels of both Richardson and Fielding.

1128   Halsband, Robert. "Lady Mary Wortley Montagu as a Friend
        of Continental Writers." John Rylands Library Bulletin,
        39 (1956), 57-74. Lady Mary was acquainted with numerous
        continental men of letters, including Jean-Baptiste Rous-
        seau, Antonio Conte, Scipione Maffei, Voltaire, and Mon-
        tesquieu.

1129   Halsband, Robert. "Lady Mary Wortley Montagu as Letter-
        Writer." PMLA, 80 (1965), 155-163. Reprinted in The
        Familiar Letter in the Eighteenth Century, H. Anderson,
        P. Daghlian, and I. Ehrenpreis, eds. Lawrence: U. of
        Kansas Press, 1966. Her correspondence is notable for
        an astonishing variety which includes love letters, witty
        pictures of upper-class English life, serious if not pro-
        found moral reflections, and acute descriptions of foreign
        lands and customs. Her letters are distinguished by frank-
        ness and reasonableness, sometimes by cynicism and urban-
        ity, sometimes by passionate extravagance, and not infre-
        quently by a style which is at once concise and unaffected.

1130   Halsband, Robert. "Lady Mary Wortley Montagu: Her Place
        in the Eighteenth Century." History Today, 16 (1966),
        94-102. Mr. Halsband sketches Lady Mary's career as
        traveller, feminist, political writer, and woman of
        letters.

1131   Halsband, Robert. "Lady Mary Wortley Montagu's Answer
        to Dorset's Ballad." HLQ, 13 (1950), 409-413. A poem
        discovered in the manuscripts of Margaret Campbell,
        Countess of Loudoun, is Lady Mary's imitation of and
        answer to Charles Sackville, the Earl of Dorset's fa-
        mous ballad beginning "To all you ladies now at hand.

1132   Halsband, Robert. "'The Lady's Dressing Room' Explicated
        by a Contemporary" in The Augustan Milieu, Henry K. Miller,
        Eric Rothstein, and G. S. Rousseau, eds. Oxford: Claren-
        don, 1970. Lady Mary wrote an answer to a poem by Swift.

1133 Halsband, Robert. The Life of Lady Mary Wortley Montagu. Oxford: Clarendon, 1956 (corrected, 1960). A scholarly and full, completely documented life of Lady Mary is based on previously unpublished material.

1134 Halsband, Robert. "The Literary Career of Lady Mary Wortley Montagu." Northwestern University dissertation, 1948. This is a survey of her writing.

1135 Halsband, Robert. "A 'New' Lady Mary Letter." PQ, 44 (1965), 180-184. One of Lady Mary's letters from Constantinople was printed in the Parisian periodical, Le Nouveau Mercure (October 1718).

1136 Halsband, Robert. "New Light on Lady Mary Wortley Montagu's Contribution to Smallpox Inoculation." Journal of the History of Medicine and Allied Sciences, 8 (1953), 390-405. Lady Mary helped the vaccination become accepted in a number of ways.

1137 Halsband, Robert. Introduction to The Nonsense of Common-Sense, 1737-1738. Evanston: Northwestern University Press, 1947. Lady Mary wrote the essays to support the Walpole ministry.The essays are interesting because of the political arguments and the social satire.

1138 Halsband, Robert. "Pope, Lady Mary and the Court Poems, 1716." PMLA, 68 (1953), 237-250. On the basis of external evidence, it is possible to determine that, of the three "Court Poems" published by Curll in 1716, two were by Lady Mary and one by Gay. Further, it is evident that Pope's revenge on Curll, which followed the publication of these poems, was not, as has been supposed, in defense of Lady Mary, but rather in defense of Gay and, secondarily, of Pope himself.

1139 Halsband, Robert. Introduction to The Selected Letters of Lady Mary Wortley Montagu. London: Longman, 1970. The editor supplies brief biographical sketches of her principal correspondents, an introduction which treats her as a personality and as a letter-writer, and brief prefatory notes to the chronological divisions into which the letters are arranged.

1140 Halsband, Robert. "Two New Letters from Lady Mary Wortley Montagu to Alexander Pope." PQ, 29 (1950), 349-352. Two

brief, unsigned letters, deposited among Pope's Homer
MSS. in the British Museum, are in the hand of Lady
Mary. Although the letters are without dates, they
can be assigned to the latter part of 1723 and the
fall of 1724, thus showing that Pope and Lady Mary were
on friendly terms later than has been supposed.

1141   Halsband, Robert. "Walpole versus Lady Mary" in Horace
        Walpole: Writer, Politician, and Connoisseur, W. H.
        Smith, ed. New Haven: Yale, 1967, pp. 215-226. Al-
        though Horace Walpole generally demonstrated a deep and
        vigorous dislike for Lady Mary as a woman, he had great
        respect for her as a woman of letters. Appendix III
        (p. 339) of this volume reprints Walpole's annotations
        to Lady Mary's poems.

1142   Hughes, Helen S. "A Letter from Lady Mary to Mr. Wort-
        ley Montagu." RES, 4 (1928), 327-330. A heretofore
        unpublished letter discovered in the Wellesley College
        Library suggests that the relations between Lady Mary
        and her husband were, at the time of her 1739 departure
        for Italy, at least amicable, thus making it unlikely
        that Lady Mary's "self-imposed exile" was brought about
        by marital difficulties.

1143   Jacobs, Elijah L. "The Amiable Lady Mary." South Atlan-
        tic Quarterly, 58 (1959), 381-392. It is a mistake to
        picture Lady Mary Wortley Montagu as essentially warm
        hearted and gracious. Such a portrait does little jus-
        tice to her real personality, which was revealed in her
        quarrels with Pope and which was distinguished by clever-
        ness, wit, cynicism, and toughness.

1144   Kauf, Robert. "Der Brief der Lady Mary Wortley Montagu:
        Ein Tadel der Wiener Hanswurstkomödie." Mashe und Kothurn,
        13 (1967), 109-113.

1145   Melville, Lewis (pseud. for Lewis S. Benjamin). Lady
        Mary Wortley Montagu: Her Life and Letters. Boston:
        Houghton-Mifflin, 1925. This popular biography makes
        extensive use of her letters.

1146   Miller, Henry K. "Fielding and Lady Mary Wortley Montagu:
        A Parallel." N&Q, 203 (1958), 442-443. The same couplet
        appears in a poem by Fielding and one by Lady Mary. It
        is impossible to date either poem or to determine who
        borrowed from whom.

1147   Miller, Henry K. "Lady Mary Wortley Montagu's Fiction."
       TLS, 16 August 1928, p. 596. A sale at Sotheby's in-
       cluded approximately three hundred volumes from Lady
       Mary's library along with several hundred autograph
       letters.

1148   Oppel, Horst. "Lady Mary Wortley Montagu." Die neueren
       Sprachen, Heft 3 (1958), 97-103.

1149   Parreaux, André. "L'Angleterre de Lady Montagu." Etudes
       Anglais, 20 (1967), 24-28. Although Lady Mary is justly
       celebrated as a commentator on foreign lands, her letters
       reveal a deep understanding of her native England, an
       understanding which is not without significance for the
       student of civilization.

1150   Penning, C. P. J. "Lady Mary Worthley /sic/ Montagu en
       de variolatie." Bijdragen tot de geschiedenis der gen-
       eeskunde, 20 (1940), 8-15.

1151   Pilon, Edmond. "Lady Mary Wortley Montagu." Revue
       Bleue, 76 (1938), 256-258. Pilon surveys Lady Mary's
       talents and early life and characterizes her as "une
       grande dame Anglaise au xviii^e siecle."

1152   Ransom, Harry H. "Mary Wortley Montagu's Newspaper."
       University of Texas Studies in English, 26 (1947), 84-
       89. The Nonsense of Common Sense had to compromise
       its ideals for popular taste. Public indifference ended
       her efforts.

1153   Sykes, W. J. "Letters of Lady Mary Wortley Montagu."
       Dalhousie Review, 23 (1943), 415-423; 24 (1944), 21-30.
       Lady Mary Wortley Montagu's career as a letter-writer
       may be divided into four periods: (1) 1708-1716, the
       letters of courtship and early married life, (2) 1716-
       1718, her letters from Turkey, (3) 1719-1738, a period
       of comparatively few letters, the most important of
       which were written to her sister, Lady Mar, in Persia,
       and (4) 1739-1762, the letters to her daughter, the
       Countess of Bute, from Italy. A survey of these various
       letters reveals an interesting though hardly amiable per-
       sonality, distinguished by liveliness, intelligence, and
       cynicism.

1154   Tillotson, Geoffrey. "Lady Mary Wortley Montagu and
       Pope's Elegy to the Memory of an Unfortunate Lady." RES,

12 (1936), 401-412. Tillotson argues that Pope's _Elegy_ was in part inspired by the poet's emotional attachment to Lady Mary.

1155 Williams, A. L. "Pope's Duchesses and Lady Mary's." _RES_, n.s. 4 (1954), 359-361. A passage in Pope's _Dunciad_ (Book II, 123-132) which has been assumed to contain an example of purely personal satire against Lady Mary Wortley Montagu is more significant for its general satire on prostitutes.

1156   Aikin-Sneath, Betsy. "Hannah More." London Mercury, 28 (1933), 528-535. Although appearing contradictory, Hannah More's fondness for London social life and religious service unites to form a stable and happy personality. Her suggestions for reform were common sense and progressive.

1157   Aldridge, Alfred Owen. "Madame de Staël and Hannah More on Society." Romanic Review, 38 (1947), 330-339. Hannah More answered Madame de Staël's criticisms of English society in "English Opinions of French Society."

1158   Bennett, C. H. "The Text of Horace Walpole's Correspondence with Hannah More." RES, 3 (1952), 341-345. Correlating the scattered correspondence between More and Walpole shows the misdating, misplacing, and editing of the Berry and Roberts' editions of her letters. The editing which More did confirms her jealousy of Ann Yearsley.

1159   Bracey, Robert. "Hannah More and Joseph Berington." Eighteenth Century Studies and Other Papers. Oxford: Blackwell, 1925. Hannah More's conversion and rebuke by Joseph Berington is described.

1160   Bradbrook, Frank. "Lydia Languish, Lydia Bennett and Dr. Fordyce's Sermons." N&Q, 209 (1964), 421-423. See item #246.

1161   Child, Philip. "Portrait of a Woman of Affairs--Old Style." University of Toronto Quarterly, 3 (1933), 87-102. A collection of the most amusing anecdotes from More's long life end with her feverishly scribbling a tribute to the king after her life of "practical piety," energy, and achievement.

1162   Courtney, Luther W. "Hannah More's Interest in Education and Government." University of Iowa dissertation, 1925. Her absorption in educational and political reform developed until they were the controlling forces in her life.

1163   Courtney, Luther W. "Hannah More's Interest in Education and Government." Baylor Bulletin, 32 (1929), 3-68. Her works on government and education express the opinions of her contemporaries. Her family and friends influenced her considerably, and she was an influential force in educational reform.

1164   Forster, E. M. "Mrs. Hannah More." New Republic, 45 (1925), 106-109, reprinted in Nation and Athenaeum, 38 (1926), 493-494. Percy was a successful five act tragedy. Biographical sketch.

1165   Harland, Marion (pseud. Mary Virginia Hawes Terhune). Hannah More. New York: Putnam's, 1900. This somewhat sentimental biography describes her growing from a sweet, precocious, but sickly child who told everyone stories and then pretended to go to London to deliver the manuscript into the popular society woman and tireless educator of the poor.

1166   Hemlow, Joyce. "Fanny Burney and the Courtesy Books." PMLA, 65 (1950), 732-761. See item # 226.

1167   Hopkins, Mary A. Hannah More and her Circle. New York: Longmans, 1947. A biography devoted to describing her relationship with her family and well known contemporaries. Her personality and her work were shaped to a large extent by her acquaintances.

1168   Johnson, R. Brimley. The Letters of Hannah More. London: John Lane, 1925. A "characterization" of More describes her ability to use mass psychology, journalism, and depicts her tenacity and energy.

1169   Jones, Mary G. The Charity School Movement: A Study of eighteenth-century Puritanism in Action. Cambridge: University Press, 1952; Hamden: Archon, 1964. The book contains scattered discussions of Hannah More who, with others like her, earned the epithet "The Age of Benevolence"for the eighteenth century through their work with educational reform and the poor.

1170   Jones, Mary G. Hannah More. Cambridge: University Press, 1952. A biography based on memoirs and correspondence describes her personality, principles, influence and reactions to her by admirers and detractors. More was concerned with redemption, a fact her pre-French Revolutionary ideas obscure.

1171   Knox, E. V. "'Percy' (The Tale of a Dramatic Success)."
        London Mercury, 13 (1926), 509-515. Percy was a success-
        ful blank verse tragedy.

1172   Liebert, Herman W. "'We Fell upon Sir Eldred'" in New
        Light on Dr. Johnson: Essays on the Occasion of his
        250th Birthday, Frederick Hilles, ed. New Haven: Yale
        University Press, 1959. The only poem for which John-
        son's revisions are definitely known is More's Sir El-
        dred of the Bower. His revisions testify to his high
        regard for More's poem and to his poetic practices.

1173   Malim, M. C. "Hannah More: 1745-1833." Contemporary
        Review, 144 (1933), 329-336. She influenced the educa-
        tion and care of children and established philanthropy
        as a vocation through her various writings.

1174   Meakin, Annette M. B. Hannah More, A Biographical Study.
        London: John Murray, 1919. A biography intended to
        debunk such unflattering opinions as More's being in-
        different to natural beauty and being excessively Cal-
        vinistic. The biography gives a detailed account of
        her energetic life.

1175   Newell, A. G. "Early Evangelical Fiction." Evangelical
        Quarterly, 38 (1966), 3-21 and 81-98. See item #389.

1176   Pearson, Norman. "The Lighter Side of Hannah More."
        Nineteenth Century, 59 (1906), 842-858. Although she
        has the reputation for stern morality, she wrote novels
        and plays, took part in London high life, and enjoyed
        good conversation to the end of her life.

1177   Shaver, Chester L. "The Publication of Hannah More's
        First Play." MLN, 62 (1947), 343. A letter from William
        Eddis dated 8 November 1773 dates publication of A Search
        After Happiness 10 May 1773 and comments on its reception.

1178   Snodgrass, A. E. "Dr. Johnson's Petted Lady." Cornhill
        Magazine, 148 (1933), 336-342. Johnson liked her for
        her charm, industry, and common sense.

1179   Sparke, Archibald. "Author Wanted." N&Q, 155 (1928),
        52-53. Gives details of performances of Percy.

1180   Spector, Robert D. "William Roberts' 'Memoirs of the
        Life and Letters of Hannah More.'" N&Q, 197 (1952), 140-

141. There were three London editions of the Memoirs in 1835 and another in 1838.

1181   Tinker, Chauncey B. Nature's Simple Plan. A Phase of Radical Thought in the Mid-Eighteenth Century. Princeton: Princeton University Press, 1922. Hannah More discovered Ann Yearsley, commended her to her bluestocking friends, and saw her poetry published. A quarrel over Yearsley's money ended the patronage, and Yearsley sunk into oblivion. The incident shows the women's desire to advance poetry and their lack of critical acumen.

1182   Tompkins, J. M. S. Polite Marriage. Cambridge: University Press, 1938. See item # 185.

1183   Trumbull, H. Clay. Yale Lectures on the Sunday School. New York: Scribner's, 1904. There are a few pages in this history of the formation and development of Sunday schools which describe More's work and observations on the lack of Christian knowledge among the poor.

1184   Weiss, Harry B. "Hannah More's Cheap Repository Tracts in America." Bulletin of the New York Public Library, 50 (1946), 539-549 and 634-641. The Cheap Repository Tracts were published between 1795 and 1798 to replace the penny books and street ballads and pamphlets which the social reformers judged to be corrupting influences. By 1800, they were being printed, sold and distributed in America with slight changes. Mr. Weiss summarizes the contents of several typical stories and concludes with a finding list. Part II is a checklist of the tracts published in America, 1797-1826, with notes.

1185   Bond, W. L. "Amelia Opie. Novelist and Quaker." English, 3 (1940), 62-66. This biographical sketch describes Amelia Opie as a spirited woman whose zest for life was only slightly tempered by her conversion to Quakerism.

1186   MacGregor, Margaret E. Amelia Alderson Opie: Worldling and Friend. Northampton, Massachusetts: Smith College Studies in Modern Languages, 1933. A carefully annotated biographical study with a critical introduction prepared by four of MacGregor's friends after her death finds Opie's subjects to be lovers and domestic life presented with morals and grounded in currect social and political ideas.

1187   Menzies-Wilson, Jacobine and Helen Lloyd. Amelia, The Tale of a Plain Friend. London: Oxford University Press, 1937. This biography is based on Amelia Opie's letters and describes characteristic and important events in her life in detail. Her personality, like her letters and handwriting, was honest, sprightly, and sensitive.

1188   Povey, Kenneth. "Amelia and the Hermit." The Sussex County Magazine, 3 (1929), 37-44. Her novel Temper, or Domestic Scenes led to a friendship with William Hayley and marked her transformation into a practical moralist.

1189   Matthews, Arnold G. Mr. Pepys and Nonconformity. London:
        Independent Press, 1954. Osborne's letters to William
        Temple include news and gossip as well as personal endear-
        ments. Her descriptions of Puritan ministers were accurate
        and lively.

1190   Parry, Edward A. Letters from Dorothy Osbourne to William
        Temple (1652-1654). London: Dent, 1914. Mr. Parry ar-
        ranges Dorothy Osbourne's letters into chapters prefaced
        by an introduction which quotes Macauley. Appendices give
        biographical and historical information.

1191   Smith, G. C. Moore, ed. The Letters of Dorothy Osborne to
        William Temple. Oxford: Clarendon, 1928. Her letters give
        a vivid description of her courtship and of England. The
        introduction praises the literary quality, describes the
        Osborne-Temple lives, and traces the way the letters came
        down to us. Notes to letters, appendices, and geneological
        charts follow the text.

1192   Woolf, Virginia. The Common Reader, Second Series. London:
        Hogarth, 1932. Osborne practiced the kind of writing per-
        mitted genteel women, essay writing disguised as letter
        writing. She wrote such good letters that even today her
        character and Temple's emerge. Her ironic humor is still
        fresh.

1193   Alspach, Russell K. "The Matchless Orinda." MLN, 52
        (1937), 116-117. Thomas Newcomb's poem "Bibliotheca"
        includes twenty-six uncomplimentary lines about Philips
        and her verse.

1194   Elmen, Paul. "Some Manuscript Poems by the Matchless
        Orinda." PQ, 30 (1951), 53-57. The manuscript poems
        and fragments of poems in the National Library of Wales
        show that variants from the published versions (all un-
        authorized) are "numerous and important."

1195   Hiscock, W. G. "Friendship: Francis Finch's Discourse
        and the Circle of the Matchless Orinda." RES, 15 (1939),
        466-468. Francis Finch wrote a little treatise setting
        guidelines for friendship to Anne Owen and Katherine
        Philips and their close friends. The treatise provides
        information about her poetry and "Platonic Circle."

1196   Roberts, William. "The Dating of Orinda's French Trans-
        lations." PQ, 49 (1970), 56-67. Katherine Philips
        translated poems by Saint-Amant and Scudéry in the early
        sixties. Her translations may have become an influential
        part of literary pictorialism.

1197   Roberts, William. "Saint-Amant, Orinda, and Dryden's
        Miscellany." ELN, 1 (1964), 191-196. "On Solitude" in-
        cluded in the Dryden-Tonson Miscellany (1716) is by
        Philips and first appeared in Poems (1667). Mr. Roberts
        explains its anonymous inclusion and its popularity.

1198   Souers, Philip W. The Matchless Orinda. Cambridge, Mass:
        Harvard University Press, 1931. This biography of Philips
        includes numerous quotations. The selections from Letters
        from Orinda to Poliarchus are especially complete. Appen-
        dices and bibliography follow the text.

1199   Barry, Iris. Introduction to <u>Memoirs</u> <u>of</u> <u>Mrs</u>. <u>Letitia</u>
       <u>Pilkington</u> <u>1712</u>-<u>1750</u>. New York: Dodd, Mead, 1928; Lon-
       don: Routledge, 1928. The introduction treats her al-
       most exclusively in relation to Swift until her divorce.
       "There is something brave about her," and she intended
       to give her readers their money's worth. Bibliographical
       notes with texts of prefaces, newspaper notices, and a
       dedication by J. Isaacs are included.

1200   Jerrold, Walter and Clare. <u>Five</u> <u>Queer</u> <u>Women</u>. London:
       Brentano's, 1929. A brief biography of her, with quota-
       tions from her <u>Memoirs</u>, explains her fight to keep up
       appearances while suffering deeply.

1201   Ponsonby, Lord. "Laetitia Pilkington (1712-1750)--a Cu-
       riosity of Literature." <u>English</u>, 1 (1937), 297-306. She
       was distinguished by her "effrontery," her acquaintance
       with eminent people, her "peculiar talents," and her
       record of early eighteenth century life. Her <u>Memoirs</u>
       and what is known of her life show a spirited, dextrous,
       but not profound person.

1202   Woolf, Virginia. <u>The</u> <u>Common</u> <u>Reader</u>. London: Hogarth,
       1925. She was a cross between Moll Flanders and Lady
       Ritchie who managed life with courage and humor.

1203   Allentuck, Marcia C. "Thraliana: A Correction." N&Q,
        199 (1954), 208. In Katherine Balderston's edition,
        Henry Fuseli (1741-1825) is incorrectly indexed as Jean
        Gaspar Fuseli (1706-1782), Henry's father.

1204   Allison, James. "Mrs. Thrale's Marginalia in Joseph
        Warton's Essay." Huntington Library Quarterly, 19 (1956),
        155-164. Mrs. Thrale thought very highly of Joseph War-
        ton's Essay on the Genius and Writings of Pope and, in
        the marginalia of her copy of this work, she expresses
        interesting opinions on Gray, Thomson, Congreve, Pope,
        and Johnson.

1205   Balderston, Katherine C. (ed.) Thraliana: The Diary of
        Mrs. Hester Lynch Thrale (later Mrs. Piozzi), 1776-1809.
        Oxford: Clarendon Press, 1942. The introduction argues
        that Thraliana reveals Mrs. Piozzi as a woman of complex
        and divided personality, a woman at once intelligent and
        narrow, reasonable and sentimental, witty and dull, know-
        ing and vain. In addition, Thraliana, perhaps the first
        English book of its type, is an important source for the
        study of Johnson and Piozzi's relations with him.

1206   Belloc, Hilaire. "Mrs. Piozzi's Rasselas." Saturday Re-
        view of Literature, 15 August 1925, pp. 37-38. Mrs. Piozzi
        annotated her copy of Rasselas. Some passages bear wit-
        ness to the book's speaking directly to her.

1207   Burnim, Kalman A. (ed.) "The Letters of Sarah and William
        Siddons to Hester Lynch Piozzi in the John Rylands Li-
        brary." Bulletin of the John Rylands Library, 52 (1969),
        46-95. Although the Siddons' correspondence to Mrs.
        Piozzi is not significant as literary art, it provides
        an intimate view of two important families linked by
        friendships.

1208   C/hapman/, R. W. "Did Johnson Destroy Mrs. Thrale's Let-
        ters?" N&Q, 185 (1943), 133-134. Evidence seems to con-
        firm accounts that Johnson destroyed a number of letters
        from Hester Thrale in 1784.

1209   C/hapman/, R. W. "Johnson's Letters to Mrs. Thrale." N&Q,
        185 (1943), 18. A series of queries concerning details
        in Johnson's letters to Mrs. Thrale.

1210   C/hapman/, R. W. "Mrs. Piozzi's Omissions from Johnson's
        Letters to Thrales." RES, 22 (1946), 17-28. A study of
        Piozzi's omissions of and deletions from Johnson's cor-
        respondence in her 1788 edition of his letters to the
        Thrale family concludes that, as an editor, Piozzi was
        at least "indifferent honest" and, in general, trustworthy.

1211   C/hapman/, R. W. "Mrs. Thrale's Letters to Johnson Pub-
        lished by Mrs. Piozzi in 1788." RES, 24 (1948), 58-61.
        The letters from Mrs. Thrale to Johnson which were pub-
        lished by her in 1788 were printed not from the originals
        but rather from transcripts which she had edited.

1212   C/hapman/, R. W. "Piozzi on Thrale." N&Q, 185 (1943),
        242-247. A series of notes concerning the suppressed
        proper names in Piozzi's edition of Johnson's letters to
        her.

1213   Clifford, James L. From Puzzles to Portraits: Problems
        of a Literary Biographer. Chapel Hill: University of
        North Carolina Press, 1970. Using his own experiences
        as a biographer of Piozzi and Johnson, the author gives
        an informal and anecdotal account of the difficulties and
        pleasures of biographical research.

1214   Clifford, James L. Hester Lynch Piozzi (Mrs. Thrale).
        Oxford: Clarendon Press, 1941. A full and scholarly ac-
        count of her life providing both a detailed portrait of
        the subject and a thoroughgoing account of her literary
        and personal relationships.

1215   Clifford, James L. "Hester Thrale-Piozzi." Bath Weekly
        Chronicle and Herald, 10 June 1950, p. 16. A number of
        diary entries record her pleasure in her last home, #8
        Gay Street, Bath.

1216   Clifford, James L. "Hester Thrale-Piozzi." Bath Weekly
        Chronicle and Herald, 17 June 1950, p. 16. She has been
        sentimentalized or censured by most critics. Recent re-
        lease of manuscripts and papers, especially of her letters
        and her "Children's Book," allows a more just portrait.

1217   Clifford, James L. "Mrs. Piozzi's Letters" in Essays
        on the Eighteenth Century Presented to David Nichol Smith.
        Oxford: Clarendon Press, 1945. Although Piozzi is per-
        haps the least well known of the major letter writers of
        the eighteenth century, her letters are remarkable for

                                    199

their humor, colloquial energy, anecdotal charm, and,
most of all, for their clear revelation of a distinctive
personality. The essay is on pages 155-167.

1218   Clifford, James L. "The Printing of Mrs. Piozzi's Anecdotes of Dr. Johnson." Bulletin of the John Rylands Library, 20 (1936), 157-172. Records the history of two
important changes which Mrs. Piozzi made in her Anecdotes
during its preparation for publication. Both changes involved Boswell, although the second change, which amounted
to a direct attack on him, was deleted before the final
printing.

1219   Esdaile, Arundell. "Hester Thrale." Quarterly Review,
284 (1946), 179-194. A biographical sketch describes her
as "only an amateur" in literature and intellectually "of
the second order," but concludes her to have been one of
the great salonnieres, a faithful and important friend
to Johnson, and, all in all, a "most remarkable woman."

1220   Ewing, Majl. "Mrs. Piozzi Peruses Dr. Thomas Browne."
PQ, 22 (1943), 111-118. Mrs. Piozzi's marginalia in her
copy of Browne's works reveal no interest in his style
or his more serious reflections but do show her spontaneous response to his discussion of vulgar errors.

1221   Fletcher, Edward G. "Mrs. Piozzi on Boswell's and Johnson's Tour." University of Texas Studies in English, 32
(1953), 45-58. Comments on marginalia in Piozzi's copy
of Boswell's Tour.

1222   Gilmour, J. "Mrs. Piozzi and the Metres of Boethius."
N&Q, 200 (1955), 488. The "Metres of Boethius," which
were translated by Dr. Johnson and Mrs. Piozzi, are printed
in her Letters to and from the Late Samuel Johnson in such
a way as to conceal "the nature of the translators' collab-
oration."

1223   Hyde, Mary. The Impossible Friendship: Boswell and Mrs.
Thrale. Cambridge: Harvard University Press, 1972. In
this account of the friendship, rivalry, and final enmity
between Boswell and Piozzi, the author uses unpublished
documents in her personal collection of Johnsoniana.

1224   Keast, William R. "The Two Clarissas in Johnson's Dictionary." SP, 54 (1957), 1932. Dictionary entries.

1225   Knapp, O. G. (ed.). The Intimate Letters of Hester Piozzi
and Penelope Pennington, 1788-1821. London: John Lane,

1914. Printing the correspondence of Piozzi and Penelope Pennington with connecting narrative and commentary, the author tells the story of Piozzi's later life.

1226   Lustig, Irma. "Boswell at Work: The 'Animadversions' on Mrs. Piozzi." MLR, 67 (1972), 11-30. During Johnson's life, Boswell was not seriously jealous of Mrs. Piozzi. A series of events after Johnson's death including the publication of the Anecdotes containing material considered damaging to Johnson's reputation and of Johnson's letters to Mrs. Piozzi revealing their great intimacy motivated Boswell's resentment.

1227   M. "Piozzi on Boswell and Johnson." Harvard Library Notes, 17 (1926), 104-111. Notes the Harvard Library's acquisition of a Boswell's Life of Johnson (8th edition, 1816) and a Boswell's Journal of a Tour to the Hebrides (2nd edition, 1785) from the collection of Amy Lowell. Both items belonged to Hester Piozzi and both contain her annotations.

1228   Merritt, Percival (ed). Piozzi Marginalia, comprising some extracts from the manuscripts of Hester Lynch Piozzi and annotations from her books. Cambridge: Harvard University Press, 1925. The first two chapters of the book sketch Hester Piozzi's life. The last four print her marginalia with connecting and explanatory commentary.

1229   Merritt, Percival. The True Story of the So-called Love Letters of Mrs. Piozzi: "In Defence of an elderly Lady." Cambridge: Harvard University Press, 1927. The seven "love letters" supposedly written from the elderly Piozzi to a young actor named William Augustus Conway are fraudulent.

1230   Pottle, Frederick A., and Charles H. Bennett. "Boswell and Mrs. Piozzi." MP, 29 (1942), 421-430. A generally favorable review of Clifford's Hester Lynch Piozzi disagrees with Clifford's contention that Boswell distorted his record of Johnson's talk in order to attack Piozzi.

1231   Quennell, Peter C. Singular Preference. New York: Viking, 1953. Contains a brief popular sketch of Piozzi's life and character with particular emphasis on her complex relationship with Johnson.

1232   Riely, John C. "Bozzy and Piozzi: The History of a
        Literary Friendship and Rivalry." University of Penn-
        sylvania dissertation, 1972. A study of their rela-
        tionship.

1233   Riely, John C. "Johnson's Last Years with Mrs. Thrale:
        Facts and Problems." Bulletin of the John Rylands Li-
        brary, 57 (1974), 196-212. A detailed account of John-
        son's relationship with Hester Piozzi from the time of
        Henry Thrale's death in 1781 to Johnson's own death in
        1784.

1234   Riely, John C. "Lady Knight's Role in the Boswell-
        Piozzi Rivalry." PQ, 51 (1972), 961-965. See item #
        1052.

1235   Riely, John C., and Alvaro Ribeiro. "'Mrs. Thrale' in
        the Tour: A Boswellian Puzzle." Publications of the
        Bibliographical Society of America, 69 (1975), 151-163.

1236   Roberts, W. Wright. "Charles and Fanny Burney in the
        Light of the new Thrale Correspondence in the John Ry-
        lands Library." The Bulletin of the John Rylands Li-
        brary, 16 (1932), 115-136. See item #747. The letters
        shed new light on the relationship between Thrale and Burney.

1237   Spacks, Patricia M. "Scrapbook of a Self: Mrs. Piozzi's
        Late Journals." Harvard Library Bulletin, 18 (1970),
        221-247. Her late journals show an obsessive desire for
        self-justification and a "temptation to elaborate" which
        make her judgments and writings suspect.

1238   Takada, Mineo. "Hester Lynch Piozzi (Thrale)." Doshisha
        Women's College of Liberal Arts Annual Reports of Studies,
        vol. 21. Kyoto: Doshisha Women's College, 1970, pp.
        248-270. An unsympathetic view of her life.

1239   Thorpe, James. "Friend to Mrs. Piozzi: Penelope Pen-
        nington in Miniature." Princeton University Library
        Chronicle, 21 (1960), 105-110. Although Penelope Pen-
        nington did not meet Mrs. Piozzi until 1788, their
        friendship as revealed in their considerable correspon-
        dence was an intimate and significant one.

1240   Tyson, Moses, and Henry Guppy (ed.). The French Journals
        of Mrs. Thrale and Dr. Johnson. Manchester: University
        Press, 1932. The introduction offers a brief critical

comparison of Johnson's and Thrale's "French Journals"
and a biographical sketch of Piozzi. There are shorter
sketches of those who accompanied Johnson in France.

1241 Vulliamy, C. E. Mrs. Thrale of Streatham. London: Cape,
1936. A popular life which attempts to give an account
of Piozzi's "true position in the social history of
literature."

1242 Wecter, Dixon. "Johnson, Mrs. Thrale, and Boswell:
Three Letters." MLN, 56 (1941), 525-529. Two letters
from Johnson to Hester Thrale and one from James Boswell to his uncle John are published for the first time.

1243 Weinbrot, Howard D. "Samuel Johnson's 'Short Song of
Congratulation' and the Accompanying Letter to Mrs.
Thrale: The Huntington Library Manuscripts." Huntington Library Quarterly, 34 (1970), 79-80. These two
documents deserve closer attention than they have received.

1244 Yung, K. K. "The Association Books of Johnson, Boswell,
and Mrs. Piozzi in the Birthplace Museum." New Rambler,
112 (1972), 23-44. Essentially an annotated list of
the "association books" of Johnson, Boswell, and Mrs.
Piozzi to be found in the Johnson Birthplace Museum.
The author is curator of the Museum.

1245 Zamick, M. (ed.). Three Dialogues by Hester Lynch Thrale.
Manchester: University Press, 1932. The introduction
includes a brief critical consideration of the manuscripts' qualities as literature, a biographical note
on Piozzi, and a series of notes on the personalities
mentioned in the Dialogues.

1246 Allen, M. L. "The Black Veil: Three Versions of a Symbol." ES, 47 (1966), 286-289. The black veil is a central symbol in Ann Radcliffe's The Mysteries of Udolpho. Moreover, the veil "constitutes a simple but effective symbol of 'mystery' itself." Dickens' The Black Veil (1836) and Hawthorne's The Minister's Black Veil (1837) are two short works which were written in response to the Gothic mode represented by the Radcliffe novel and which are constructed upon a single mystery in which the veil plays a part.

1247 Arnaud, Pierre. "Un Document Inedit: Le Contrat des Mysteries of Udolpho." Etudes Anglais, 20 (1967), 55-57. The publishing contract for The Mysteries of Udolpho makes it clear that she was paid five hundred pounds for her novel. Also, the contract demonstrates that, contrary to what has been supposed by several critics and scholars, the novel was composed and corrected prior to her visit to the Rhine. The contract is photographically reproduced and printed in the article.

1248 Beaty, Frederick L. "Mrs. Radcliffe's Fading Gleam." PQ, 42 (1963), 126-129. In her romance, The Mysteries of Udolpho, Radcliffe twice depicts characters who associate the process of aging with "the fading of an illusion that once enveloped the beauties of nature." Her treatment of this theme most certainly influenced Coleridge and very probably influenced Wordsworth.

1249 Bland, D. S. "Endangering the Reader's Neck: Background Description in the Novel." Criticism, 3 (1961), 121-139. Natural description in Mrs. Radcliffe's novels is usually a more or less unintegrated attempt to paint "mood" landscapes, to provide, in other words, a literary equivalent to the paintings of Salvator Rosa. This inorganic type of description, although it influenced Scott to some extent, was justly mocked and rejected by Jane Austen.

1250 Coolidge, Archibald C., Jr. "Charles Dickens and Mrs. Radcliffe: A Farewell to Wilkie Collins." Dickensian, 58 (1962), 112-116. Many devices used by Dickens were probably derived from Gothic novels. Radcliffe's influence seems most apparent in The Old Curiosity Shop and Barnaby Rudge.

1251 Decottignies, Jean. "A l'occasion centenaire de la naissance d'Anne Radcliffe: Un domaine 'maudit' dans les lettres françaises aux environs de 1800." Revue des sciences humaines, (1964), 447-475. This is a study of Radcliffe's reception, reputation, and influence in late eighteenth and early nineteenth century France.

1252 Durant, David S., Jr. "Ann Radcliffe's Novels: Experiments in Setting." University of North Carolina dissertation, 1972. The various fictional strategies—including reliance on moralizing, action, landscape description, and historical setting—used in Radcliffe's six novels are reflected in the prose style of each work.

1253 Epstein, Lynne. "Ann Radcliffe's Gothic Landscape of Fiction and the Various Influences Upon it." New York University dissertation, 1972. This study of the influences on her Gothic novels emphasizes the influences on her treatment of landscape.

1254 Epstein, Lynne. "Mrs. Radcliffe's Landscapes: The Influence of Three Landscape Painters on Her Nature Descriptions." Hartford Studies in Literature, 1 (1969), 107-120. In her descriptions of nature, she is influenced by Salvator Rosa, Claude Lorrain, and Nicholas Poussin. The Romance of the Forest and Udolpho in particular demonstrate the influence of these three painters.

1255 Havens, Raymond D. "Ann Radcliffe's Nature Descriptions." MLN, 66 (1951), 251-255. Although Radcliffe's novels are remarkable for nature descriptions which emphasize "wild, melancholy, and sublime scenes," her unpublished journals make it clear that, when writing for herself, she preferred "cheerful" and "smiling" scenes of nature. Instead of the grandiose, sublime, and Johnsonian style so characteristic of the descriptive passages of her novels, her journal descriptions are notable for their stylistic clarity and simplicity.

1256 Humphrey, George. "Victor au l'enfant de la forêt et le roman terrifant." FR, 33 (1959), 137-146. Ducray-Duminil was very possibly influenced by Radcliffe's Udolpho.

1257 Keebler, Lee E. "Ann Radcliffe: A Study in Achievement." University of Wisconsin dissertation, 1968. This is a

study of her artistic development from her earliest
work through The Italian.

1258 McKillop, Alan D. "Mrs. Radcliffe on the Supernatural
in Poetry." JEGP, 31 (1932), 352-359. In a piece intended to be part of an introduction to her Gaston de
Blondville but which was printed posthumously in 1826
under the title "On the Supernatural in Poetry," Ann
Radcliffe develops a theory of the supernatural which
emphasizes the importance of obscurity and uncertainty,
which argues against supernaturalism which shocks the
understanding, and which distinguishes between horror
and terror. The essay reflects Radcliffe's knowledge
of Shakespeare and her indebtedness to Burke.

1259 Mayo, Robert D. "Ann Radcliffe and Ducray-Duminil."
MLR, 36 (1941), 501-505. Radcliffe's Romance of the
Forest was influenced by Ducray-Duminil's Alexis, ou
la Maisonnette dans les bois.

1260 Murray, E. B. Ann Radcliffe. New York: Twayne, 1972.
There is one chapter on Radcliffe's "Life and Times,"
and one devoted to the Gothic tradition. Separate chapters treat her novels from The Castles of Athlin and
Dunbayne to The Italian. The emphasis is on the artistic form and content of the novels.

1261 Nettels, Elsa. "'The Portrait of a Lady' and the Gothic
Romance." South Atlantic Bulletin, 39 (1974), 73-82.
Although The Portrait of a Lady is neither a satire nor
a burlesque of the Gothic novel, James ".achieves . . .
a critical view of the Gothic romance, of its picture of
life, and its effect upon readers." In addition, James
uses "Gothic imagery" to depict the consciousness of
Isabel Archer.

1262 Pound, Edward F. "The Influence of Burke and the Psychological Critics on the Novels of Ann Radcliffe." University of Washington dissertation, 1964. Contemporary aesthetic and psychological theories influenced her novels.
The study concentrates on Udolpho and the influence of
Kames, Blair, Beattie, Alison, and Burke.

1263 Ronald, Margaret A. "Functions of Setting in the Novel:
From Mrs. Radcliffe to Charles Dickens." Northwestern
dissertation, 1971. The dissertation traces the increasingly complex uses of setting from Radcliffe's Udolpho to

Scott's The Heart of Mid-Lothian to Bronte's Jane Eyre and, finally, to Dickens' Bleak House.

1264   Ruff, William. "Ann Radcliffe, or, The Hand of Taste" in The Age of Johnson: Essays Presented to Chauncey Brewster Tinker. New Haven: Yale University Press, 1949, pp. 183-193. True to her age, Ann Radcliffe's fiction is the very "embodiment of good taste." Indeed it may be said that, despite her "gothic trimmings," her real contribution to English literature is the "novel of taste." In her concern with good taste—elegance, moral propriety, and proper etiquette—Radcliffe looks forward to Jane Austen.

1265   Sadleir, Michael. "Poems by Ann Radcliffe." TLS, 29 March 1928, p. 242. The format and preface of "The Poems of Mrs. Ann Radcliffe" (1816) seem to suggest that Radcliffe was, by this date, regarded by her editor as either dead or no longer active as a writer. An explanation for this assumption is perhaps to be found in the rumors that she suffered a mental collapse sometime after 1802.

1266   Smith, Nelson C. "The Art of Gothic: Ann Radcliffe's Major Novels." University of Washington dissertation, 1967. A study of her specific contributions to the development of the Gothic novel emphasizes Radcliffe's interest in "defining and developing" the emotion of fear.

1267   Smith, Nelson C. "Sense, Sensibility, and Ann Radcliffe. SEL, 13 (1973), 577-590. Despite the fact that Radcliffe is often regarded by modern critics as the "high priestess of sensibility," her novels show not only that she was capable of distinguishing between sense and sensibility, but also that she was capable of pointing out "flaws" and "weaknesses" of excessive sensibility. In short, she uses the techniques of the gothic novel to demonstrate the dangers of sentimentality and to advocate the importance of common sense.

1268   Stoler, John A. "Ann Radcliffe: The Novel of Suspense and Terror." University of Arizona dissertation, 1972. Her ability to fuse her characters, plots, and settings into one atmospheric whole allows her to achieve a remarkable unity of effect in her novels which is perfectly suited to the requirements of the tale of terror.

1269   Sypher, Wylie. "Social Ambiguity in a Gothic Novel."
       Partisan Review, 12 (1945), 50-60. The "bourgeois
       romanticism" of Radcliffe's Udolpho reveals an inherent
       vulgarity which results from an art that "half retains"
       and "half rejects bourgeois standards." Her fiction is
       significant in that it "so inadequately conceals the
       naked contradictions intrinsic in bourgeois romanticism,
       a revolt so radically inhibited that it failed to be in
       a deep social sense creative."

1270   Swigart, Ford H., Jr. "Ann Radcliffe's Veil Imagery"
       in Studies in the Humanities, W. F. Grayburn, ed. In-
       diana: Indiana University of Pennsylvania Press, 1969,
       pp. 55-59. Veil imagery, which is found in all of
       Ann Radcliffe's novels, emphasizes the novelist's "in-
       terest in visual effects that focus on picturing and
       seeing."

1271   Thomas, Donald. "The First Poetess of Romantic Fiction:
       Ann Radcliffe, 1764-1823." English, 15 (1964), 91-95.
       The author surveys Ann Radcliffe's career as a novelist
       and her contributions to the development of the gothic
       novel.

1272   Thompson, L. F. "Ann Radcliffe's Knowledge of German."
       MLR, 20 (1925), 190-191. Passages in her Journal through
       Holland and Germany suggest that she had some knowledge
       of German, and, thus, could have read Schiller's Geister-
       seher (a possible influence on Udolpho) before its ap-
       pearance in English in 1795.

1273   Tompkins, J. M. S. "Ramond de Carbonnières, Grosley, and
       Mrs. Radcliffe." RES, 5 (1929), 294-301. Ann Radcliffe
       was influenced by Ramond de Carbonnières' Observations
       fortes dans les Pyrenees (1789) and P. J. Grosley's New
       Observations on Italy and its Inhabitants (1769) in the
       composition The Mysteries of Udolpho. Grosley also in-
       fluenced The Italian.

1274   Ware, Malcolm. "Mrs. Radcliffe's 'Picturesque Embellish-
       ment.'" Tennessee Studies in English, 5 (1960), 67-71.
       Although her descriptions of sublime scenery were often
       attacked by contemporary critics for their "frequency,
       length, and sameness," these descriptions were the result
       of a conscious adherence to artistic principle and were
       recognized and praised as such by Dr. Nathan Drake in his
       essay entitled "On Objects of Terror" (1820).

1275   Ware, Malcolm. <u>Sublimity</u> <u>in</u> <u>the</u> <u>Novels</u> <u>of</u> <u>Ann</u> <u>Radcliffe</u>.
         Upsala & Copenhagen: Lindequist Munksgaard, 1963. This
         is a study of passages in Radcliffe's novels which reflect
         Burke's theories of the sublime.

1276   Wieten, A. A. S. <u>Mrs</u>. <u>Radcliffe--Her</u> <u>Relation</u> <u>Towards</u>
         <u>Romanticism</u>. Amsterdam: H. J. Paris, 1926. This study
         concentrates on Ann Radcliffe's poetry and on its in-
         fluence on Romantic authors.

MARY ROBINSON

1277   Adams, M. Ray. Studies in the Literary Backgrounds of
       English Radicalism. Lancaster, Pennsylvania: Franklin
       and Marshall, 1947. See item # 967.

1278   Barrington, E. (pseud. Lily Adams Beck). The Exquisite
       Perdita. New York: Dodd, Mead, 1926. This is a fic-
       tionalized account of Mary Robinson's life.

1279   Makower, S. V. Perdita: A Romance in Biography. Lon-
       don: Hutchinson, 1908. This is a biography with a
       bibliography.

1280   Mendenhall, John C. "Mary Robinson." University of
       Pennsylvania Library Chronicle, 4 (1936), 2-10. Her
       Memoirs, begun two years before her death and finished
       by her daughter, are candid and egotistical. She cap-
       tivated the Prince of Wales with her performance of
       Perdita in A Winter's Tale. Her poetry was praised by
       her contemporaries although she also wrote plays and
       Gothic tales.

1281   Steen, M. The Lost One. A Biography of Mary--Perdita--
       Robinson. London: Methuen, 1937. This biography traces
       her life from her school days through her successful
       stage career beginning in 1776.

1282   Hughes, Helen S. "Elizabeth Rowe and the Countess of
       Hertford." PMLA, 59 (1944), 726-746. The Countess
       encouraged Elizabeth Rowe to incorporate imagination,
       elegance, and romantic sentiments in her work. The
       women corresponded for twenty years.

1283   Hughes, Helen S. The Gentle Hertford: Her Life and
       Letters. New York: MacMillan, 1940. See item #
       1345.

1284   Richetti, John. "Mrs. Elizabeth Rowe: The Novel as
       Polemic." PMLA, 82 (1967), 522-529. Elizabeth Rowe's
       Friendship in Death was quite popular. An accommoda-
       tion of fiction to the idealogical needs of the time,
       her book shows death conquered by true love in a series
       of tales based on the clichés of novellas and scandalous
       memoirs.

1285   Stecher, Henry F. Elizabeth Singer Rowe, the Poetess of
       Frome: A Study in Eighteenth Century English Pietism.
       Bern: Lang, 1973. She led a pious life in a decadent
       age. Her literary connections were wide and her early
       work reflects their taste. Her work was popular and
       influential.

1286   Wright, H. Bunker. "Matthew Prior and Elizabeth Singer."
       PQ, 24 (1945), 71-82. Although only Prior's letters
       survive, their correspondence clarifies the nature of
       their relationship and gives some insight into their
       characters. Elizabeth appears rather vain and bad tem-
       pered and Prior seems to tease her.

1287   Crittenden, Walter M. Introduction to A Description
        of Millenium Hall by Mrs. Sarah Scott, an Eighteenth-
        Century Novel. New York: Bookman Associates, 1955.
        The introduction relates Scott to publishing and fic-
        tional practices of her time. Her biography and her
        interest in education illumine parts of the novel.

1288   Crittenden, Walter M. "The Life and Writings of Mrs.
        Sarah Scott, Novelist (1723-1795)." University of
        Pennsylvania dissertation, 1931. This biography and
        survey of her works finds her to be a "typical product
        of the century's sentimental and didactic ideals" and
        a representative novelist.

1289   Grow, L. M. "Sarah Scott: A Reconsideration." Coranto,
        9 (1973), 9-15. Her letters to her sister Elizabeth Mon-
        tagu have a livelier, more varied style than her novels.
        She is at her best when she describes people.

1290   Onderwyzer, Gaby E. "Sarah Scott's Agreeable Ugliness,
        a Translation." MLN, 70 (1955), 578-580. Agreeable
        Ugliness was a very literal translation of La Laideur
        Aimable, et les dangers de la Beauté rather than an
        original work of Scott's.

1291   Onderwyzer, Gaby E. "Sarah Scott: Her Life and Works."
        University of California, Berkeley, dissertation, 1957.
        This is a survey of her life, friendships, and publica-
        tions.

ANNA SEWARD

1292   Addleshaw, S. "The Swan of Lichfield: Anna Seward
and her Circle." Church Quarterly Review, 124 (1937),
1-34. Anna Seward and her acquaintances.

1293   Ashmun, Margaret. The Singing Swan: An Account of Anna
Seward. New Haven: Yale University Press: London: Milford, Oxford University Press, 1931. A scholarly biography treats Seward's career as a social lioness and bluestocking and provides a commentary on later eighteenth-
century literary life. The preface is by Frederick
Pottle.

1294   Clifford, James L. "The Authenticity of Anna Seward's
Correspondence." MP, 39 (1941), 113-122; reprinted in
Studies in the Literature of the Augustan Age: Essays
Collected in Honor of Arthur Ellicott Case, Richard C.
Bays, ed. Ann Arbor: George Wahr, 1952. The 1811 edition of Seward's letters, long thought to be a reliable
source for commentary on life and letters in the late
eighteenth century, represents not a printing of original
letters, but rather a printing of late and self-serving
revisions by Seward and, thus, cannot be trusted as evidence in controversial matters.

1295   Hanford, James H. "A Letter from the Swan of Lichfield
Introduced and Annotated by James Holly Hanford." New-
berry Library Bulletin, 4 (1957), 201-210. Prints, with
a commentary, a heretofore unpublished letter from Anna
Seward to William Hayley.

1296   Hesselgrave, Ruth A. Lady Miller and the Batheaston
Literary Circle. New Haven: Yale University Press,
1927. See item # 1472.

1297   Kent, Muriel. "A Lichfield Group." Cornhill Magazine,
158 (1938), 347-358. An essay on several notable figures
(Anna Seward, Richard Lovell Edgeworth, Thomas Day) associated with Lichfield. The discussion of Anna Seward
concentrates on her relationship with Samuel Johnson.

1298   Laithwaite, P. "Anna Seward and Dr. Johnson." TLS, 7
January 1932, p. 12. In the marginal notes in her copy
of Mrs. Piozzi's "Letters to and from the late Samuel
Johnson," we see further evidence of her antipathy for
Johnson.

1299   Lucas, E. V. _A Swan and Her Friends_. London: Methuen,
        1907. A popular, detailed biography which argues for
        Seward's importance as a pioneer blue stocking and
        which gives much space to her personal and literary re-
        lationships.

1300   Monk, Samuel Holt. "Anna Seward and the Romantic Poets:
        A Study in Taste" in _Wordsworth and Coleridge: Studies
        in honor of George McLean Harper_, Earl Leslie Griggs, ed.
        Princeton: Princeton University Press, 1939, pp. 118-134.
        The comments on poetry in Anna Seward's letters provide
        an index to "characteristic pre-romantic taste," a taste
        which was equally uneasy with Augustan and Romantic poetry,
        but which relished the sentimental, rhetorical, "sublime,"
        and sometimes Gothic verse of such poets as Akenside,
        Gray, Collins, and Chatterton.

1301   Myers, Robert Manson. _Anna Seward: An Eighteenth-Century
        Handelian_. Williamsburg, Virginia: Manson Park Press,
        1947. Anna Seward was characteristic of her age in her
        ardent and sentimental love of Handel's music.

1302   Pearson, Hesketh. "The Swan of Lichfield." _Life and
        Letters Today_, 15 (1936), 67-79. A brief popular biogra-
        phical sketch of Anna Seward.

1303   Pearson, Hesketh. _The Swan of Lichfield. Being a Se-
        lection from the Correspondence of Anna Seward_. London:
        Hamilton, 1936. The introduction provides a popular
        account of her life which emphasizes her romantic at-
        tachments, her literary enthusiasms, and her uneasy re-
        lationship with Johnson.

1304   Rewa, Michael. "Johnson, Anna Seward, and Tacitus." _A-
        merican Notes and Queries_, 7 (1969), 134-135. Anna Seward's
        celebrated response to Johnson's contention that he was
        prepared to love anyone "except an American" ("sir, this
        is an instance that we are always most violent against
        those whom we have injured") is a somewhat altered quota-
        tion from Tacitus.

1305   Rousseau, G. S. "Anna Seward to William Hayley: A Let-
        ter from the Swan of Lichfield." _Harvard Library Bulletin_,
        15 (1967), 273-280. Prints for the first time the long
        letter written in 1785 from Seward to Hayley. The letter
        is most interesting for its revelation of the deep respect

she felt for Hayley and for its comments on Cowper's
then new poem The Task.

1306   Scudder, Harold H.   "Anna Seward and the Mathias Fami-
       ly."   N&Q, 184 (1943), 184-187.   A heretofore unpublished
       letter identifies the Mathiases who entertained Anna
       Seward during a London vacation in 1786 as the family
       of T. J. Mathias, sub-treasurer to the Queen.

1307   Woolley, James D.   "Johnson as Despot: Anna Seward's
       Rejected Contribution to Boswell's Life."   MP, 70 (1972),
       140-145. Anna Seward described Johnson's disapproval
       of Jane Harry's becoming a Quaker in detail.   In John-
       son's conversation with Mary Knowles, he called Jane
       a fool and an "odious wench" and became agitated.   The
       letter is printed with bibliographical discussion.

FRANCES SHERIDAN

1308   Chew, Samuel P. "The Life and Works of Frances Sher-
       idan." Harvard dissertation, 1937. A biography in-
       cludes a description and evaluation of her writings.

1309   Chew, Samuel P. "The Dupe: A Study of the 'Low.'"
       PQ, 18 (1939), 196-203. Audience reactions to the
       play indicate the great influence of the public's de-
       mands for decorum.

1310   Russell, Norma. "Some Uncollected Authors XXXVIII:
       Frances Sheridan, 1724-1766." Book Collector, 13 (1964),
       196-205. For years, Frances Sheridan's Memoirs of Miss
       Sidney Bidulph (1761) was the most widely read sentimen-
       tal novel. Her Eastern novel, Nourjahad, and her play,
       The Discovery, were also acclaimed.   The annotated check-
       list of her works is preceded by a sketch of her life,
       mention of her acquaintances, notes on the reception of
       her works, and Richard Brinsley's borrowings from her
       play Journey to Bath.

1311   Wilson, Mona. "The Mother of Richard Brinsley Sheri-
       dan." These were Muses. London: Sidgwick & Jackson,
       1924, pp. 27-49. Frances Sheridan was an amiable and
       charming woman who became a fairly popular writer. She
       wrote because of economic need.

SARAH KEMBLE SIDDONS

1312   Anon. "Mrs. Siddons." Theatre Arts Monthly, 9 (1925),
       485.

1313   C., C. S. "Ann of Swansea." N&Q, 6 (1920), 45. Ann of
       Swansea was Ann Kemble, Sarah Siddons' sister.

1314   Clark, W. S. "The Siddons in Dublin." Theatre Notebook,
       9 (1955), 103-111. A description of her three visits to
       Dublin with accounts of the parts she played, her acting
       technique, and her reception.

1315   de la Torre, Lillian. Actress: Being the Story of Sarah
       Siddons. New York: Nelson, 1957. This is a popular
       biography for younger readers.

1316   Donohue, Joseph W., Jr. "Kemble and Mrs. Siddons in Mac-
       Beth: The Romantic Approach to Tragic Character." The-
       atre Notebook, 22 (1967/68), 65-86. By examining the
       acting techniques, the author concludes that "theatri-
       cal performance faithfully mirrors an age."

1317   Eaton, Walter P. "Professor is Thrilled." Theatre Arts
       Monthly, 10 (1926), 472-478. An account of Sarah Siddons'
       career centered around Professor G. J. Bell's description
       of her acting.

1318   ffrench, Yvonne. Mrs. Siddons, Tragic Actress. London:
       Derek Verschoyle, 1954. This is a biography with some
       information about the theatre during her career.

1319   Morris, Clara. "Sarah Siddons' Tryst." McClure's Maga-
       zine, 19 (1902), 78-83. A fictional, romantic tale.

1320   Parsons, Florence Mary. The Incomparable Siddons. London:
       Methuen; New York: Putnam, 1909. A biography without
       notes concentrating on her personality and artistic life.

1321   Swale, Ellis. "Mrs. Siddons's Residence in Paddington."
       N&Q, 188 (1945), 108. Locates her residence.

1322   Turberville, Arthur S. English Men and Manners in the
       Eighteenth Century. New York: Oxford University Press,
       1926. This is a social history which includes some notes
       on Mrs. Siddons.

1323   van Lennep, William (ed.). The Reminiscences of Sarah
       Kemble Siddons, 1773-1785. Cambridge: Widener Library,
       1942. Mrs. Siddons wrote her Reminiscences when she
       was seventy-five. She includes a season at Drury Lane,
       her meeting with Johnson, and other events in her life.

1324   Warde, Thomas. "Gainsborough's Original 'Siddons.'" N&Q,
       148 (1925), 260. The author wants information about the
       painting.

1325   Ehrenpreis, Anne Henry. Introduction to Charlotte Smith's
        The Old Manor House. London: Oxford University Press,
        1969. A popular novel in its own time, The Old Manor
        House is considered her best novel. It conforms to the
        tastes of her time and exhibits unusual skill in dialect
        and characterization. The text has notes.

1326   Ehrenpreis, Anne Henry. Introduction to Emmeline. The
        Orphan of the Castle. London: Oxford, 1971. Emmeline
        was widely acclaimed although Mary Wollstonecraft and
        Anna Seward criticized it. The novel had considerable
        influence on the Gothic novel and perhaps on Burney and
        Austen. The edition includes notes and a bibliography.

1327   Ehrenpreis, Anne Henry. "Northanger Abbey: Jane Austen
        and Charlotte Smith." NCF, 25 (1970), 343-348. Ethelinde
        was a direct influence on Austen's Catharine and shows
        that Catharine was a preliminary sketch for Northanger
        Abbey.

1328   Foster, James R. "Charlotte Smith, Pre-Romantic Novelist."
        PMLA, 43 (1928), 463-475. Her novels are the descendents
        of Richardson's but add the influence of Prevost's and
        D'Arnaud's pictorial style. Her descriptive landscapes
        influenced Radcliffe, Helen Maria Williams, Mary Robinson,
        and others. Her novels are typical of the sentimental
        adventure narrative and "are dead, and justly so."

1329   Fry, Carrol L. "Charlotte Smith, Popular Novelist." Uni-
        versity of Nebraska dissertation, 1970. Smith was a sen-
        timental novelist whose work shows increasing emphasis
        on social injustice. Interesting elements are use of set-
        ting, Gothic elements, awareness of slavery and issues of
        the French Revolution.

1330   Graham, John. "Character, Description and Meaning in the
        Romantic Novel." Studies in Romanticism, 5 (1966), 208-
        218. A part of her basic technique of characterization
        was the description of facial expressions which became a
        guide to sensibility in her novels. Lavater's Essays on
        Physiognomy testify to great interest in the subject.

1331   Hilbish, Florence M. A. "Charlotte Smith, Poet and Novel-
        ist (1749-1806)." University of Pennsylvania dissertation,

1941. A detailed study of her life and works concludes
with an assessment of the influences on and innovations
in her work. She popularized the English sonnet form,
introduced a number of innovations in setting, and wrote
psychological novels.

1332   McKillop, Alan D. "Charlotte Smith's Letters." HLQ, 15
(1952), 237-255. The Huntington Library has forty-five
letters written by Charlotte Smith in which she describes
her family situation, her writing, her arrangements for
publishing her works, and her literary isolation.

1333   Pollin, Burton R. "Keats, Charlotte Smith, and the
Nightingale." N&Q, 211 (1966), 180-181. Charlotte
Smith's "On the Departure of the Nightingale" influenced
Keats'"Ode to the Nightingale." She enjoyed some fame
in her time.

1334   Staves, Susan. "Don Quixote in Eighteenth Century England."
CL, 24 (1972), 193-215. The eighteenth century interpreted
Don Quixote as an Augustan satire. This interpretation
influenced such writers as Henry Fielding and Charlotte
Lennox; later, in the hands of Charlotte Smith and others,
Quixote became a romantic figure.

1335   Turner, Rufus P. "Charlotte Smith (1749-1806): New Light
on her Life and Literary Career." University of Southern
California dissertation, 1966. Her letters prove that
her literary works were produced under financial exigency
and include biographical elements, express opinions about
literary immortality, and describe her dislike of England.
The dissertation includes a finding list of correspondence
and works in United States libraries.

1336   Whiting, George W. "Charlotte Smith, Keats, and the
Nightingale." Keats-Shelley Journal, 12 (1963), 4-8.
Keats echoes her widely reprinted and popular sonnet
"Farewell to the Nightingale."

1337　Adams, Robert M. "Joanna and the Poets." Virginia Quarterly Review, 27 (1951), 55-74. Her dreams and visions led her to write nearly 12,000 pages of prophecies and "spiritual truth," to "enroll saints," and to declare herself pregnant by the Spirit at age sixty-four. The wide popular appeal of her movement can be explained by the context of contemporary thought.

1338　Balleine, George R. Past Finding Out: The Tragic Story of Joanna Southcott and Her Successors. London: SPCK, 1956; New York: Macmillan, 1956. Her biography describes an influential and controversial woman, the beginning of many prophetic movements in the late eighteenth century Protestant Church, and religion among the lower classes.

1339　Officer, G. H. "Joanna Southcott." Church Quarterly Review, 159 (1958), 106. Her box was opened on 11 July 1927 and contained a night cap, a lottery ticket, a 1772 medal, a dice box, a pistol, a few coins, a 1793 calendar of the French court, and a novel. There are speculations that this was not the right box.

1340　Wright, Eugene P. A Catalogue of the Joanna Southcott Collection at the University of Texas. Austin: U. of Texas Press, 1968. Descriptions including such information as author, date, and number of pages for the autograph manuscripts, pamphlets, books, portraits, and miscellaneous items (personal effects, scrolls) for Southcott, her followers, and critics in the University of Texas's Stark Library are catalogued.

1341　Wright, Eugene P. "A Descriptive Catalogue of the Joanna Southcott Collection at the University of Texas." University of Texas dissertation, 1966. See above.

FRANCES THYNNE
COUNTESS OF HERTFORD

1342   Campbell, Hilbert H. "Thomson and the Countess of Hert-
        ford Again." MP, 67 (1970), 367-369. Yale University's
        library owns a "Song" by Thomson which differs from the
        published version and which shows that the Countess was
        one of the most important women to "charm his suscepti-
        ble heart."

1343   Campbell, Hilbert H. "Thomson's Seasons, the Countess
        of Hertford, and Elizabeth Young: A Footnote to The
        Unfolding of the Seasons." TSLL, 14 (1972), 435-444.
        Thomson expressed intense personal feelings about both
        women in disguised forms in his poetry.

1344   Hughes, Helen S. "Elizabeth Rowe and the Countess of
        Hertford." PMLA, 59 (1944), 726-746. The two women
        corresponded throughout their lives. The Countess en-
        couraged Elizabeth Rowe to incorporate imagination,
        elegance, and romantic sentiments in her work.

1345   Hughes, Helen S. The Gentle Hertford: Her Life and
        Letters. New York: Macmillan, 1940. A full and scholar-
        ly life of the woman who was patroness and friend of James
        Thomson, John Dyer, and other eighteenth century poets.
        The author's account incorporates many letters, journals,
        and other documents.

1346   Hughes, Helen S. "John Dyer and the Countess of Hertford."
        MP, 27 (1930), 311-320. Lady Hertford owned a manuscript
        copy of Gronger Hill which throws light on Dyer's compo-
        sitional methods. She may have had some personal acquain-
        tance with Dyer.

1347   Hughes, Helen S. "Thomson and the Countess of Hertford."
        MP, 25 (1928), 439-468. The author discredits Johnson's
        story that Thomson offended her by failing to assist her
        "poetical operations" and was never invited back to the
        country estate. The Countess never lost interest in
        Thomson and they continued to be friends until his death.

1348   Hughes, Helen S. "Thomson and Lady Hertford Again." MP,
        28 (1931), 468-470. Adds to the list of poetic tributes
        from Thomson to Lady Hertford.

222

1349   Rousseau, G. S. "Pineapples, Pregnancy, Pica, and
        Peregrine Pickle. Tobias Smollett. Ed. G. S. Rousseau
        and P. G. Boucé. New York: Oxford University Press,
        1971. See item #497.

1350   Seligman, S. A. "Mary Toft--The Rabbit Breeder." Medi-
        cal History, 5 (1961), 349-360. She delivered bits and
        pieces of rabbits and other animals over a period of
        several months, deceiving several eminent medical men.
        Sir Thomas Douglas intimidated her into confessing to
        fraud; she was sent to Bridewell and became the object
        of obscene ballads. A list of contemporary pamphlets
        on the subject concludes the essay.

1351   Thomas, K. Bryn. James Douglas of the Pouch and his
        Pupil, William Hunter. Springfield, Illinois, Thomas,
        1964; London: Pitman Medical Publishing Co., 1964.
        The sixth chapter of this biography of Douglas discusses
        the Toft case and lists a number of the resulting satires.

1352   Brailsford, Mabel P. Susanna Wesley, The Mother of Methodism. London: Epworth Press, 1938. A laudatory, popular biography emphasizes Susanna Wesley's long-suffering, indefatigable efforts as a mother.

1353   Doughty, W. L. Introduction to The Prayers of Susanna Wesley. London: Epworth Press; New York: Philosophical Library, 1956. The meditations of Susanna Wesley (here transposed into prayers) give insight into her "mind and heart." A brief biography largely drawn from Clarke's Memoirs of the Wesley Family prefaces the prayers.

1354   Harmon, Rebecca L. Susanna, Mother of the Wesleys. Nashville, Tennessee: Abingdon Press, 1968. A detailed biography divided roughly into sections on Susannah Wesley's contributions: educating and maintaining her children, holding "kitchen meetings" for her family and neighbors, and advising John and Charles in the Methodist movement. She helped establish the lay ministry. Chapters on her times, the position of women, her children and her husband are included.

1355   Harrison, G. Elsie. Son to Susanna. The Private Life of John Wesley. London: Ivor Nicholson and Watson, 1937. Beginning with the fire at Epworth rectory, the course of JohnWesley's life would be directed by his mother. Throughout his life, Susanna educated him, forged his faith, and instilled the principles in him which became Methodism.

1356   Newton, John A. Susanna Wesley and the Puritan Tradition in Methodism. London: Epworth Press, 1968. A biography reconstructing the Puritan environment which shaped Susanna Wesley's character and beliefs points out the Puritan influence on her philosophy of child-rearing and on the development of Methodism.

1357   Rogal, Samuel J. "John Wesley's Women." Eighteenth Century Life, 1 (1974), 7-10. Most of the essay lists women who preached Methodism and describes Wesley's cautious and politic behavior toward them. Wesley's opinion of women was directly influenced by his mother's words and example.

1358   Melander, Martin. "An Unknown Source of Jane Austin's
       Sense and Sensibility." Studia Neophilologica, 22
       (1950), 146-170. A Gossip's Story is the source dis-
       cussed.

1359   Moler, Kenneth L. "Sense and Sensibility and Its
       Sources," RES, 17 (1966), 413-419. Austen could have
       been influenced by the theme of the need for discretion
       in judgment and affection and for reason to govern the
       heart in The Advantages of Education.

1360   Tompkins, J. M. S. "Elinor and Marianne: A Note on
       Jane Austen." RES, 16 (1940), 33-43. Jane West's A
       Gossip's Story was the starting point for Sense and
       Sensibility.

1361   Daly, Augustin. <u>Woffington</u>: <u>A</u> <u>Tribute</u> <u>to</u> <u>the</u> <u>Actress</u>
        <u>and</u> <u>Woman</u>. New York: Benjamin Blom, 1972. A reprint
        of the 1891 appreciation.

1362   de Castro, J. P. "'Peg Woffington's Cottages,' Tedding-
        ton." <u>N&Q</u>, 183 (1942), 84. There seems to be no evi-
        dence that certain cottages at Teddington, reputed to be
        almshouses supported by Peg Woffington's charity, were
        built or supported by Peg Woffington. Indeed, these
        buildings, which were not finished during her lifetime,
        seem never to have been intended for almshouses.

1363   Dobson, Austin. "Mrs. Woffington" in <u>Side-Walk</u> <u>Studies</u>.
        London: Oxford University Press, 1902. A short biography.

1364   Dobson, Austin. "Peg Woffington" in <u>Side-Walk</u> <u>Studies</u>.
        London: Milford, 1924. A biographical sketch.

1365   Dunbar, Janet. <u>Peg</u> <u>Woffington</u> <u>and</u> <u>her</u> <u>World</u>. London:
        Heineman, 1968. A detailed life of the actress gives
        considerable attention to the history and character of
        the eighteenth century theatre and to the relationship
        of that theatre to general society. A list of her roles
        is included.

1366   Hanbury-Williams, John. "Peg Woffington and her Por-
        traits." <u>Connoisseur</u>, 106 (1940), 227-233. A sampling
        of the portraits and poems about her.

1367   L., F.F. "Peg Woffington's Letter." <u>N&Q,</u> 10 (1904), 124.
        The author doubts that the letter is genuine.

1368   Lawrence, W. J. "The Woffingtons of Dublin, Some Records
        of an Old Musical Family." <u>The</u> <u>Musical</u> <u>Antiquary,</u> 3 (1911/
        12), 215-219. Speculates about the "Miss Woffington" who
        performed on musical glasses and traces the musical mem-
        bers of her family from 1720 to 1836.

1369   Lucey, Janet C. <u>Lovely</u> <u>Peggy</u>: <u>The</u> <u>Life</u> <u>and</u> <u>Times</u> <u>of</u>
        <u>Margaret</u> <u>Woffington</u>. London: Hurst & Blackett, 1952.
        A fictionalized biography.

1370   Scott, W. S. "Peg Woffington and Her Circle." <u>New</u> <u>Rambler,</u>
        ser. C 2 (1967), 14-23. A brief biography.

1371   Seton-Anderson, James. "Peg Woffington and Mrs. Cholmon-
        deley." N&Q, 183 (1942), 264-265. Peg Woffington and
        Mrs. Cholmondeley (Mary Woffington) were the daughters
        of one Arthur Woffington, "said to have been a bricklayer
        in Dublin."

1372   Allen, B. Sprague. "The Reaction Against William God-
       win." MP, 16 (1918), 57-75. See item #968.

1373   Bradbrook, Frank. "Lydia Languish, Lydia Bennet and Dr.
       Fordyce's Sermons." N&Q, 209 (1964), 421-423. See item
       #246.

1374   Durant, Clark. Preface and supplement to Memoirs of
       Mary Wollstonecraft. London: Constable, 1927. The
       preface summarizes the criticism on Wollstonecraft and
       argues her affinity with Blake. The supplement adds
       material about her life and discusses and prints some
       of her letters.

1375   Ehrenpreis, Anne Henry. Introduction to Emmeline. The
       Orphan of the Castle. London: Oxford, 1971. See item
       #1326.

1376   Flexner, Eleanor. Mary Wollstonecraft. New York: Coward,
       1972. This detailed life emphasizes Wollstonecraft's
       character as a thinker.

1377   George, Margaret. One Woman's "Situation," A Study of
       Mary Wollstonecraft. Urbana: University of Illinois
       Press, 1970. A biography which sees Wollstonecraft as
       the model of "modern woman," a model which can only be
       understood through a comprehension not only of her com-
       plex psychological character but also of the extent to which
       her life provided a classic definition of what Simone de
       Beauvoir called woman's "situation."

1378   Hare, Robert R. "Charles Brockden Brown's Ormond: the
       Influence of Rousseau, Godwin, and Mary Wollstonecraft."
       University of Maryland dissertation, 1968. Ormond is "an
       allegorized roman-à-clef in which Brown dramatizes con-
       flicts between Rousseauistic, Wollstonecraftian, and God-
       winian ideas of education, love, and marriage." The four
       female characters represent four aspects of Mary Woll-
       stonecraft. The principal male characters of the novel
       are likewise representations of men who figured in Mary
       Wollstonecraft's life. It was the "Wollstonecraftian"
       content of Brown's work which interested Shelley.

1379   Hare, Robert R. Introduction to The Emigrants. Gainesville:
       Scholars Facsimile Reprints, 1964. Mary Wollstonecraft, not
       Gilbert Imlay wrote The Emigrants.

1380   Harper, George Mills. "Mary Wollstonecraft's Residence
        with Thomas Taylor the Platonist." N&Q, 207 (1962),
        461-463. It is probable that Mary Wollstonecraft's
        residence with Thomas Taylor can be dated as having be-
        gun in August and ended in November of 1782.

1381   Hayden, Lucy K. "A Rhetorical Analysis of Mary Woll-
        stonecraft's A Vindication of the Rights of Woman." Uni-
        versity of Michigan dissertation, 1972. A study of the
        major ideas, the rhetorical methods, and the contemporary
        reception of the Vindication.

1382   James, H. R. Mary Wollstonecraft: A Sketch. Oxford:
        University Press, 1932. A brief biography emphasizes
        her personality rather than her literary achievements.

1383   Janes, Regina. "Mary, Mary Quite Contrary, Or, Mary As-
        tell and Mary Wollstonecraft Compared"in Studies in Eigh-
        teenth Century Culture, Ronald C. Rosbottom, ed., vol.v.
        Madison: University of Wisconsin Press, 1976, pp. 121-
        139. See item #566.

1384   Jeffrey, Sydney. "Fuseli and Mary Wollstonecraft." TLS,
        15 February 1941, p. 81. Among the William Roscoe papers
        in the Picton Library there are letters to Roscoe from
        Mary Wollstonecraft, one of which mentions Fuseli.

1385   Kurtz, Benjamin P. and Carrie C. Autrey. Introduction to
        Four New Letters of Mary Wollstonecraft and Helen Maria
        Williams. Berkeley: University of California Press, 1937.
        The introduction traces the history of the letters and
        praises Wollstonecraft extravagantly.

1386   Linford, Madeline. Mary Wollstonecraft. London: Leo-
        nard Parsons, 1924. A popular biography dwells almost
        exclusively on her "place in history as the great pio-
        neer of the feminist movement."

1387   McGavran, Margaret R. "Mary and Margaret: The Triumph
        of Woman." Cornell University dissertation, 1973. Psy-
        chobiographies of Mary Wollstonecraft and Margaret Fuller
        interpret their lives as attempts to reduce emotional
        turmoil by attaining sexual equality.

1388   Nicholes, Eleanor L. Introduction to A Vindication of the
        Rights of Men. Gainesville: Scholars' Facsimiles &
        Reprints, 1959. The introduction compares editions of A
        Vindication of the Rights of Men and The Rights of Men

to The Rights of Woman.

1389 Nicholes, Eleanor L. "Mary Wollstonecraft" in Romantic
      Rebels, Essays on Shelley and His Circle, Kenneth Neill
      Cameron, ed. Cambridge: Harvard University Press, 1973.
      The biographical sketch includes a consideration of her
      literary works as extensions of her personality.

1390 Nitchie, Elizabeth. "An Early Suitor of Mary Wollstone-
      craft." PMLA, 58 (1943), 163-169. It is probable that
      Joshua Waterhouse, then a Fellow at Cambridge and later
      the eccentric Rector of Little Stukeley, was a suitor
      of Mary Wollstonecraft.

1391 Nixon, Edna. Mary Wollstonecraft, Her Life and Times.
      London: Dent, 1971. This is a popular life.

1392 Perigault-Duhet, P. M. "Du Nouveau sur Mary Wollstone-
      craft: L'oeuvre Litteraire de George Imlay." Etudes
      Anglais, 24 (1971), 298-303. Although it appears likely
      that the novel The Emigrants, supposedly by George Im-
      lay, was actually the work of Mary Wollstonecraft, ar-
      guments concerning her authorship of A Topographical
      Description of the Western Territory of North America,
      also attributed to Imlay, are less convincing.

1393 Poston, Carol H. "Mary Wollstonecraft's A Vindication
      of the Rights of Woman: A Critical and Annotated Edi-
      tion." University of Nebraska dissertation, 1973. A
      preface to the critical edition discusses the historical
      and intellectual milieu of Wollstonecraft's Vindication,
      the structure, themes, and arguments of the book, its
      importance as an educational tract, and the biography
      and influence of its author.

1394 Preedy, George R. (pseud. for Gabrielle M. V. C. Long).
      This Shining Woman: Mary Wollstonecraft Godwin, 1757-
      1797. London: Collins, 1937. This is a fictionalized,
      popular biography.

1395 Roper, Derek, "Mary Wollstonecraft's Reviews." N&Q, 203
      (1958), 37-38. Although at least four hundred twelve
      articles in Johnson's Analytical Review (1788-1799) have
      been attributed to Mary Wollstonecraft, only two hundred
      four of these are signed and, therefore, may be safely
      attributed to her, while two hundred eight others are
      of varying and doubtful authenticity.

1396   Ruksheena, K. S. "Mary Wollstonecraft—artist." _Filo-
        logiceskie Nauki_, 11 (1968), 29-40. Mary Wollstonecraft,
        whom bourgeois writers treat primarily as a founder of
        the woman's movement, is of exceptional interest as a
        creative artist for students of the working class move-
        ment and of the radical democratic movement and as a cor-
        roborator of Lenin's thought. A survey of Marxist work
        on Wollstonecraft recognizes her insight into the mean-
        ing of events in her own time.

1397   Sunstein, Emily W. _A Different Face: The Life Of Mary
        Wollstonecraft_. New York: Harper & Row, 1975. A de-
        tailed biography concentrates on her psychological com-
        plexity and her importance as a feminist.

1398   Sunstein, Emily W. "Mary Wollstonecraft: Another Bro-
        ther, and Corrected Dating." _N&Q_, 220 (1975), 25-26.
        Henry Wollstonecraft, Mary's younger brother, was born
        in 1761 and was still alive in 1787. Thus, although
        his life was somewhat mysterious, he did not, as has
        been reported, die in infancy. The author also offers
        new dates for several events in Wollstonecraft's life.

1399   Taylor, G. R. Stirling. _Mary Wollstonecraft. A Study
        in Economics and Romance_. London: Martin Secher, 1911.
        A popular life of Wollstonecraft which attempts to come
        to grips with her personality concentrates on her liter-
        ary works as the means to understanding her.

1400   Tomalin, Claire. _The Life and Death of Mary Wollstone-
        craft_. London: Weidenfeld and Nicolson, 1974. A scho-
        larly biography concentrates on her importance as a fem-
        inist and provides a detailed account of her personal
        relationships and intellectual milieu. There are illus-
        trations, a "family tree," and an annotated bibliography.

1401   Tomkievicz, Shirley. "The First Feminist." _Horizon_, 14
        (1972), 115-119. A biographical sketch argues that Mary
        Wollstonecraft did not found the feminist movement but
        was its inspiration.

1402   Wardle, Ralph M. Introduction to _Godwin and Mary: Letters
        of William Godwin and Mary Wollstonecraft_. Lawrence: Uni-
        versity of Kansas Press, 1966. The introduction describes
        the first meeting of Godwin and Wollstonecraft, their
        courtship, and their marriage.

1403   Wardle, Ralph M.   "Mary Wollstonecraft, _Analytical Re-_
       viewer."   _PMLA_, 62 (1947), 1000-1009.   Her articles
       written for the _Analytical Review_ between 1788 and 1796
       are an index to their author's "growth in self confi-
       dence, studiousness, and critical perception."

1404   Wardle, Ralph M.   _Mary Wollstonecraft, A Critical Biogra-_
       phy.   Lawrence: University of Kansas, 1951.   A full,
       scholarly treatment of her life and works based, to a
       considerable extent, upon new information contained in
       the unpublished papers of Godwin and Wollstonecraft.

1405   Woolsey, Dorothy B.   "Mary Wollstonecraft."   _New York_
       Herald Tribune Books, 26 September 1937, p. 18.   An
       attack on the accuracy of _This Shining Woman_ by George
       Preedy .

1406 Bennett, C. H. "The Text of Horace Walpole's Correspondence with Hannah More." RES, 3 (1952), 341-345.
Walpole praised Ann Yearsley's poetry in letters to
Hannah More; before allowing Mary Berry to publish the
letters More removed most of the praise.

1407 Tinker, Chauncey B. Nature's Simple Plan. A Phase of
Radical Thought in the Mid-Eighteenth Century. Princeton:
Princeton University Press, 1922. Hannah More "discovered"
Ann Yearsley, commended her to her bluestocking friends,
and saw her poetry published. A quarrel over the poet's
money ended the patronage and Yearsley sunk into oblivion.
The incident shows the women's desire to advance poetry
and their lack of critical acumen.

1408 Tompkins, J. M. S. Polite Marriage. Cambridge: University
Press, 1938. The dispute over the deed in trust had literary circles agog.

1409   Anon. The Library of Mrs. Elizabeth Vesey, 1715-1791.
        Newcastle-on-Tyne: William H. Robinson, 1926.

1410   Anon. "Private Libraries--xxvii. The Marquess of
        Cholmondeley." TLS, 23 November 1940, p. 596. Hough-
        ton came to the Cholmondeley family through the marriage
        of Sir Robert Walpole's daughter Mary to the present
        Lord Cholmondeley's ancestor. The library contains a
        substantial collection of the classics and eighteenth
        century books purchased by Sir Robert himself, most of
        which appear to have been bound by the same binder.

1411   Arkell, Ruby Lillian. Caroline of Ansbach. London:
        Oxford University Press, 1939. A scholarly biography
        which affords a documented account of the life and
        times of George II's consort.

1412   Armstrong, Martin. Lady Hester Stanhope. New York:
        Viking, 1928. Hester Stanhope, an irrepressible and
        dauntless woman, never found love or influence.

1413   Ashley-Montagu, M. F. "Imaginary Conversations." TLS,
        27 January 1940, p. 45. Landor may have borrowed the
        form for his "Imaginary Conversations" from Clara Reeve's
        "The Progress of Romance."

1414   Aspinall-Oglander, Cecil. Admiral's Wife, being the
        Life and Letters of the Honourable Mrs. Boscawen from 1719
        to 1761. London: Longmans, 1940. A biography of one of
        "the best known figures" of Johnson's time. Uses her
        letters extensively.

1415   Athill, Lawrence. "Eccentric English Women: v. Hannah
        Snell." Spectator, 158 (1937), 899-900. She served as
        a soldier for four years. In the course of her adven-
        tures, she was flogged, wounded in action, and distin-
        guished herself for her cooking.

1416   Beatty, Joseph M., Jr. "Mrs. Montagu, Churchill, and Miss
        Cheere." MLN, 41 (1926), 384-386. Identifies the father
        of the girl Churchill debauched as Sir Henry Cheere.

1417   Bentley, G. E., Jr. "Blake, Hayley, and Lady Hesketh."
        RES, 7 (1956), 264-286. The correspondence between William

Hayley and Lady Hesketh reveals, contrary to general
scholarly opinion, that, although she was limited in
her appreciation of Blake's mind and art, Lady Hesketh
was well-meaning and enthusiastic in her efforts on his
behalf.

1418   Bernbaum, Ernest. The Mary Carleton Narratives, 1663-
1673. Cambridge: Harvard, 1914. Mary Carleton, tried
and acquitted for bigamy and hanged for theft, wrote
and inspired a number of pamphlets. These pamphlets
shed light on the development of journalism and fiction.

1419   Bessborough, Vere B. Ponsonby, 9th earl of. Georgiana:
Extracts from the Correspondence of Georgiana, Duchess
of Devonshire. London: Murray, 1955. A brief introduction prefaces the edited letters of Georgiana Cavendish.

1420   Bessborough, Vere B. Ponsonby, 9th earl of, with A. Aspinall. Lady Bessborough and Her Family Circle. London: Murray, 1940. An introduction provides biographical information concerning Lady Bessborough and her
family.

1421   Bevan, Bryan. "Queen Anne 1665-1714." Contemporary Review, 205 (1964), 432-435. A biographical sketch of
Queen Anne describes her as a fairly effective queen,
an ungrateful child, and a "latent lesbian."

1422   Bevan, Bryan. "Queen Catharine of Braganza, 1638-1705."
Contemporary Review, 207 (1965), 308-312. This biographical sketch concentrates on her troubled days at court.

1423   Biddulph, Violet. The Three Ladies Waldegrave (and Their
Mother). London: Peter Davies, 1938. Maria, illegiti-
mate daughter of Dorothy Clement and Edward Walpole, wife
of James, Lord Waldegrave, and her three daughters are
the subject of this study set in political and social
context.

1424   Black, Frank G. "Miss Smythies." TLS, 26 September 1935,
p. 596. Evidence is offered that the novel The Brothers
(1758) is by the Colchester writer, Miss Smythies.

1425   Bor, Margot, and Lamond Clelland. Still the Lark: A
Biography of Elizabeth Linley. London: Merlin Press,
1962.

1426   Bowen, Marjorie (Pseud. for Gabrielle Margaret Vere Camp-
        bell Long). The Third Mary Stuart, Mary of York, Orange
        and England, being a Character study with memoirs and
        letters of Mary II of England, 1662-1694. London: John
        Lane, 1929. A popular portrait of Mary II which is based
        largely on her diaries and letters and which deals with
        politics only "where absolutely necessary."

1427   Bradbrook, M. C. "The Elegant Eccentrics." MLR, 44 (1949),
        184-198. A biographical essay on the eccentrics Lady
        Eleanor Butler and Miss Sarah Ponsonby who ran away to
        Llangollen Vale. The Vale was made famous by Anna Seward's
        1795 poem.

1428   Bronson, Bertrand H. "Chattertoniana." MLQ, 11 (1950),
        417-424. The author argues that Elizabeth Cooper's The
        Muses Library (1737) had greater influence on Thomas
        Chatterton's work than on Macpherson's Ossianic poetry
        or Percy's Reliques.

1429   Brown, Beatrice C. Elizabeth Chudleigh, Duchess of
        Kingston. New York: Viking, 1927. A biography.

1430   Brown, Beatrice C. The Letters and Diplomatic Instructions
        of Queen Anne. London: Cassell, 1935. A brief introduc-
        tion discusses her reign and her qualities as a ruler.
        The papers are printed with notes. There is a bibliogra-
        phy and the index is detailed.

1431   Brunskill, F. R. "The Ancestry of Dr. Johnson's Wife."
        London Quarterly and Holborn Review, (April 1936), pp.
        228-230. Mrs. Johnson came from a distinguished family
        and deserves respect.

1432   Buchan, Charlotte. Lady Louisa Stuart. Her Memories
        and Portraits. London: Hoddes and Stoughton, 1932.

1433   Butt, John. "The Domestic Manuals of Hannah Wolley" in
        Pope, Dickens, and Others: Essays and Addresses. Edin-
        burgh: Edinburgh University Press, 1969. Her domestic
        manuals, especially her cook books, sold well. The Gen-
        tlewoman's Companion provides a guide from childhood to
        old age on every subject from education to needlework to
        fastidious eating.

1434   Chapin, C. F. "Johnson's Prayer for Kitty Chambers."
        MLN, 76 (1961), 216-218. Passages in Johnson's prayer
        are exact quotations from the Book of Common Prayer and

attest to his thorough knowledge of the prayers.

1435 Chapman, Hester W. _Caroline Matilda, Queen of Denmark, 1751-1775_. London: Cape, 1971. A popular account of the melodramatic life of the Danish queen who was also an English princess and sister of George III.

1436 Charles, B. G. "A Dr. Johnson Discovery at National Library." _Western Mail and South Wales News_, 1 August 1938, p. 9. Announces the discovery of a letter from Johnson to "Miss Owen at Penrhos, near Shrewsbury," prints the letter, and gives some information about Margaret Owen.

1437 Clifford, James L. "Lucy Porter to Dr. Johnson: Her Only Known Letter." _TLS_, 28 August 1937, p. 620. The letter to her step-father is printed. Lucy asks for a silver half-pint cup for her warm beer.

1438 Cockburn, Mrs. (owner). "Lady Chatham's Letter." _Notes and Queries for Somerset and Dorset_, 23 (1940), 159-161.

1439 Conolly, Leonard W. "The Censor's Wife at the Theatre: The Diary of Anna Margaretta Larpent, 1790-1800." _Huntington Library Quarterly_, 35 (1971), 49-64. Anna Larpent read and criticized plays and even acted as censor for her husband during his career as Examiner of Plays. Her diaries comment frankly on plays, actors, sets, music, and audiences. An appendix of actors, actresses, singers, dancers mentioned and plays seen follows generous excerpts.

1440 Cooke, Arthur L. "Addison's Aristocratic Wife." _PMLA_, 72 (1957), 373-389. Charlotte Myddelton, Countess of Warwick, does not deserve her reputation as an haughty, unpleasant woman. Rather, a sensitive reading of the biographical evidence shows her to be a modest, retiring, frugal woman and a good housekeeper.

1441 Crankshaw, Edward. _Maria Theresa_. London: Longmans, 1969; New York: Viking, 1970. A detailed account of her life concentrates on her role in European political struggles and includes a portrait of the cultural milieu.

1442 Crosland, Margaret. _Louise of Stolberg, Countess of Albany_. Edinburgh: Oliver and Boyd, 1962. A biography of Charles Edward Stuart's wife.

1443   Cross, A. G. "A Royal Blue-Stocking: Catherine the
        Great's Early Reputation in England as an Authoress"
        in Gorski Vijenac: A Garland of Essays Offered to Pro-
        fessor Mary Hill, R. Auty, L. R. Lewitter, and A. P.
        Vlasto, eds. Cambridge: Modern Humanities Research
        Association, 1970. Although there was little awareness
        in England of Russian literature before the 1821 publi-
        cation of John Bowring's Specimens of the Russian Poets,
        Catherine the Great, during the latter part of her reign,
        enjoyed a small reputation in England as a writer of
        essays, tales, and plays.

1444   Dale, Donald. "Mrs. Pepys." TLS, 31 August 1940, p.
        423. Elizabeth Pepys was probably born at Somerset.

1445   D'Auvergne, A. The Dear Emma. The Story of Emma, Lady
        Hamilton, her husband and her lovers. London: Harrap,
        1936. A biography focuses on her relations with William
        Hamilton, Greville, and Nelson.

1446   Dart, Thurston. "Miss Mary Burwell's Instruction Book
        for the Lute." The Galpin Society Journal, 11 (1958),
        3-62. The sixteen chapter instruction book was copied
        by Mary Burwell from a manuscript given to her by her
        lute-master between 1668 and 1671. Corrections and
        examples in tablature are in a different hand. The book
        describes the history of the instrument and teaches grace-
        ful lute playing.

1447   Dearnley, Moira. "Christopher Smart, Seed of the Welch
        Woman." Anglo-Welsh Review, 18 (1970), 171-177. Smart
        refers satirically to his mother a number of times in
        his published work and Taffy's Gwinnifred in Smart's ep-
        ilogue to The Conscious Lovers may be Winifred Griffiths
        Smart.

1448   de la Torre, Lillian. Elizabeth is Missing; or, Truth
        Triumphant: an Eighteenth Century Mystery, being a true
        relation of her mysterious disappearance. New York:
        Knopf, 1945; London: Joseph, 1947. An account of the
        sensational case of Elizabeth Canning. Bibliography.

1449   Delpech, Jeanine. Life and Times of the Duchess of
        Portsmouth, trans. Ann Lindsay. London: Elek Books,
        1953. A popular biography by a French author describes
        the life of one of Charles II's mistresses.

1450 Dewes, Simon (pseud. John St. Clair Muriel). Mrs. Delaney. London: Rich and Cowan, 1940. Mary Granville,
Mrs. Delaney, was an admired paragon of feminine virtue
to an impressive list of contemporaries.

1451 Digby, George W. "Lady Julia Caverley: Embroideress."
Connoisseur, 145 (1960), 82-88 and 169-177. Lady Julia
did two important embroideries, one of ten large wall-
panels and another, a six-fold screen. The panels are
based on traditional European designs but have original
elements displaying other influences. The screen shows
scenes from Virgil's Eclogues and Georgics and is most
remarkable for its sense of distance and adaptation of
Cleyn's illustrations of Ogilby's Virgil.

1452 Donnelly, Lucy Martin. "The Celebrated Mrs. Macaulay."
William and Mary Quarterly, 6 (1949), 173-207. An appre-
ciative reassessment of the author of the Whig History
of England from the Accession of James I to that of the
Brunswick Line as a crusader for liberty.

1453 Esdaile, K. A. "Cousin to Pepys and Dryden: A Note on
the Works of Mrs. Elizabeth Creed of Tichmarsh." Bur-
lington Magazine, 77 (1940), 24-27. Elizabeth Creed
retired to Barnwell All Saints after her husband's death
and gave free classes in needlework, drawing and painting. She doctored the local sick and decorated near-by
churches with her work.

1454 Ferguson, J. D. "Robert Burns and Maria Riddell." MP,
28 (1930), 169-184. Circumstances surrounding Burns'
quarrel with her are explained. Burns was not responsible for the lampoon Esopus to Maria.

1455 Fineman, D. A. "The Case of the Lady 'Killed' by Pope."
Modern Language Quarterly, 12 (1951), 137-149. The woman
referred to is apparently Victoria, Lady Vandeput.

1456 Fitzgerald, Brian, (ed.). The Correspondence of Emily,
Duchess of Leinster, 1731-1814. Dublin: Stationers
Office, 1949. The letters of Lady Emilia Mary Lennox,
third daughter of Charles, second Duke of Richmond, and
Sarah, daughter of William, Earl Cadogan.

1457 Fitzgerald, Brian. Lady Louisa Conolly, 1743-1821: An
Anglo-Irish Biography. London: Staples Press, 1950.

239

1458   Fitzhugh, Robert T. "Burns' Highland Mary." _PMLA_, 52
        (1937), 829-834. New manuscript evidence allows the
        author to describe the relationship between Burns and
        Mary Campbell.

1459   Foster, Dorothy. "Sir George Etherege: Collections."
        _N&Q_, 158 (1927), 456-459. The author describes the
        Chancery trial resulting from Mary Etherege's making a
        mortgage loan on some Westminster land.

1460   Forster, E. M. "Eccentric Englishwomen: vii, Luckie
        Buchan." _Spectator_, 158 (1937), 986-987. Elspath Simp-
        son founded a religion promising "translation" (immor-
        tality without death) to the faithful who fasted forty
        days.

1461   G., E. "Archbishop Tillotson to Lady Russell." _More
        Books_, 20 (1945), 442. She appealed to him for a favor.

1462   Gilmore, Margaret. _The Great Lady: A Biography of Bar-
        bara Villiers, Mistress of Charles II_. London: Lory,
        1944. A detailed biography.

1463   Gower, Sir George, and Iris Palmer. _Hary-O. The Letters
        of Lady Harriet Cavendish, 1796-1809_. London: Murray,
        1940.

1464   Green, David. _Queen Anne._ London: Collins, 1970. A
        scholarly life of Queen Anne which concentrates on her
        personal life. Green especially emphasizes Anne's
        friendship with Sarah, Duchess of Marlborough.

1465   Guttmacher, Manfred S. "Catherine Macauley and Patience
        Wright: Patronesses of the American Revolution." _Johns
        Hopkins Alumni Magazine_, 24 (1936), 308-326.

1466   Halsband, Robert. "_Virtue in Danger_: The Case of Gri-
        selda Murray." _History Today_, 17 (1967), 693-700. Re-
        lates the historical basis for an attack on Griselda
        Murray by a servant as publicized in a broadside ballad,
        _Virtue in Danger: Or Arthur Gray's last Farewell to the
        World_ and the subsequent trial.

1467   Hamblin, F. J. "A Minister's Wife of the Eighteenth Cen-
        tury." _Transactions of the Unitarian Historical Society_,
        10 (1954), 185-192. The Rev. Samuel Bury's _An Account of
        the Life and Death of Mrs. Elizabeth Bury_ with an elegy

by Isaac Watts includes Bury's discussion of her "useful" life, an abridgement of her diary, and selections from her letters.

1468   Hamilton, Lady Elizabeth. William's Mary: A Biography of Mary II. London: Hamilton; New York: Taplinger, 1972. A scholarly biography which reveals Mary's devotion to William and to Holland and which concentrates on her family affairs and her staunch Protestantism.

1469   Hartcup, Adeline. Angelica: The Portrait of an Eighteenth Century Artist. London: Heinemann, 1954. This biography of the renowned painter concentrates on her life and personality rather than on her art.

1470   Heal, Ambrose. "Hannah Glasse and Her 'Art of Cookery.'" N&Q, 174 (1938), 401-403. Presents the problems in identifying the author of The Art of Cookery Made Plain and Easy.

1471   Herbert, Lord. The Pembroke Papers: Letters and Diaries of Henry, Tenth Earl of Pembroke and his Circle. London: Cape, 1942. Includes the letters of Lady Elizabeth Pembroke.

1472   Hesselgrave, Ruth A. Lady Miller and the Batheaston Literary Circle. New Haven: Yale University Press, 1927. Anna Riggs Miller instituted breakfast poetry contests as a way of patronizing the arts and assuring her social position. She collected the poems written for these competitions and published them in Poetical Amusements at a Villa near Bath. Anna Seward contributed poems.

1473   Hilles, Frederick W. "Sir Joshua and the Empress Catherine" in Eighteenth Century Studies in Honor of Donald Hyde, W. H. Bond, ed. New York: Grolier Club, 1970. New evidence from documents in Russia shows that Reynolds considered his relations with Catherine to have been the climax of her very successful career. These documents further reveal that, in her relations with Sir Joshua, the Empress acted with consistent magnanimity and grace.

1474   Hillhouse, James T. "Teresa Blount and 'Alexis.'" MLN, 40 (1925), 88-91. Teresa and Martha Blount's letters are of interest because they are society gossips and illustrate the lives of two of Pope's friends. They wrote to Henry Moore, not James Moore-Smythe and, therefore, cannot explain Pope's antipathy toward Moore-Smythe.

1475   Hornbeak, Katherine. "Swift's Letter to a Very Young
        Lady on her Marriage." _Huntington Library Quarterly_,
        7 (1943/44), 183-186. Establishes the identity of the
        very young lady as Deborah Staunton, married to John
        Rochfort on 19 January 1722, O.S.

1476   Hughes, Helen S. "A Romantic Correspondence of the Year
        1729." _MP_, 37 (1939), 187-200. Publication of several
        letters exchanged between the Countess of Hertford and
        Grace Cole.

1477   Iremonger, Lucille, _Love and the Princess_. London: Fa-
        ber & Faber, 1958. A popular account of the lives of
        King George III's six daughters whose lives were affected
        by their father's madness and by his Royal Marriages Act.
        Iremonger concentrates particularly on Princess Sophia.

1478   Isdell-Carpenter, Andrew. "On a Manuscript of Poems
        Catalogued as by Mary Barber in the Library of Trinity
        College, Dublin." _Hermathena_, 109 (1969), 54-64. Mary
        Barber is probably not the author and addressee of the
        poems in the Trinity College library manuscript, "Poems
        on Several Occasions 1714." Many of the 120 poems show
        strong Whig sentiments.

1479   Jerrell, Mackie L. "Mrs. Constantia Crawley (Crowley?)
        Grierson." _N&Q_, 210 (1965), 19-20. Constantia Grier-
        son was a midwife and part of "The Grubstreet Cavalcade"
        and should not be confused with Constantia Phillips.

1480   Jesse, John H. _Notes by Lady Louisa Stuart on George
        Selwyn and His Contemporaries_. New York: Oxford Uni-
        versity Press, 1928. Lady Louisa commented on Jesse's
        four volume correspondence with Selwyn.

1481   Johnson, James William. "'My dearest sonne'" Letters
        from the Countess of Rochester to the Earl of Lichfield."
        University of Rochester Library Bulletin, 28 (1974), 25-
        32. Letters reveal the financial and psychological power
        the countess exercised over her son.

1482   Johnson, R. Brimley. _The Letters of Lady Louisa Stuart_.
        London: John Lane, 1906. There is an introductory sketch.

1483   Jones, Rufus M. _The Life of George Fox, Seeker and Friend_.
        London: Allen and Unwin, 1930. Margaret Fell is nearly

as important to the formation and growth of the Society
of Friends as George Fox.

1484   Jordan, Ruth. Sophie Dorothea. London: Constable,
        1971. A popular account of the unhappy life of George
        of Hanover's wife. The author concentrates on Sophie
        Dorothea's love affair with Count Philip Konigsmark
        and on court life in the late seventeenth century.

1485   Kirchberger, C. "Elizabeth Burnet, 1661-1709." Church
        Quarterly Review, 148 (1949), 17-51.

1486   Kirk, Rudolph. "Jane Bell. Printer at the East End of
        Christ-Church." Essays in Dramatic Literature. The
        Parrott Presentation Volume, Craig Hardin, ed. Prince-
        ton: Princeton University Press, 1935, pp. 443-454. She
        took over Moses Bell's shop and in ten years printed over
        thirty books and pamphlets including cook books, religious
        tracts, and such plays as Friar Bacon and Friar Bungay and
        King Lear.

1487   Kroll, Maria. Sophie, Electress of Hanover; a Personal
        Portrait. London: Gollancz, 1973. An account of Sophie's
        personal life and character which is drawn chiefly from
        her own writings and which deals with politics and mat-
        ters of state only when they touched Sophie directly.

1488   Lansdowne, Marquis of. Johnson and Queeney: Letters
        from Dr. Johnson to Queeney Thrale, from the Bowood
        Papers. London: Cassell, 1932. Letters from Johnson
        to Hester Maria Thrale, Mrs. Thrale's eldest daughter.

1489   le Fanu, W. R. Betsy Sheridan's Journal: Letters from
        Sheridan's Sister, 1784-86 and 1786-90. London: Eyre
        and Spottiswoode, 1960. Letters from Elizabeth Sheridan
        in England to her sister Alicia Le Fanu in Dublin.

1490   Legouis, Pierre. André Marvell, Poète, Puritain, Pa-
        triote. Paris:Henri Didier, 1928. In a few pages, the
        author summarizes the speculations about Mary Palmer's
        "marriage" and motives.

1491   Leslie, Anita. Mrs. Fitzherbert. New York: Scribner's,
        1960. This biography is based on her private papers and
        the author's father's collection.

1492   Leslie, Shane. Mrs. Fitzherbert. A Life chiefly from
        Unpublished Sources. London: Burns,Oates, 1939. A

biography with generous quotations from letters and papers with appendices printing the Prince of Wales' proposal, wills, and a discussion of her adopted daughter. The book argues that she was woman of great integrity.

1493   Leslie, Shane. The Letters of Mrs. Fitzherbert and Connected Papers. London: Burns Oates, 1940. Letters and papers by and about Mrs. Fitzherbert are prefaced by a biography. Notes are provided for the documents.

1494   Lewis, W. S. (ed.). Horace Walpole's Correspondence. New Haven: Yale University Press, 1937- . Various volumes include the correspondence of Walpole with women.

1495   Lindsey, John (pseud. John St. Claire Muriel). The Lovely Quaker. London: Rich and Cowan, 1939. George III probably married Hannah Lightfoot, a lovely Quaker whom he met in 1749 when he was eleven years old. Her children by the king were paid to be silent and she was sent away and eventually expelled from her church.

1496   Lynch, Kathleen M. "Henrietta, Duchess of Marlborough." PMLA, 52 (1937), 1072-1093. Congreve's contemporaries and biographers have treated Henrietta unjustly. Generous quotations from letters explain her unhappy family relationships and her appeal to Congreve.

1497   Lyons, N. J. L. "William Shenstone, Mary Graves, and Mrs. Delany." N&Q, 217 (1972), 379-380. Correspondence between the two women traces Shenstone's brief courtship of Mary Graves.

1498   Macartney, Carlile A. Maria Theresa and the House of Austria. London: English University Press, 1969. A brief scholarly introduction to Maria Theresa's life and times. There is a list of books, "For Further Reading."

1499   Mallam, Duncan. "The Dating of Lady Luxborough's Letters to William Shenstone." PQ, 19 (1940), 139-145. Establishes the dates of the letters of Henrietta Knight, Lady Luxborough, to William Shenstone, between 1741 and 1756 with the exception of about a score of letters.

1500   Mallard, Ian. "The Hymns of Katherine Sutton." Baptist Quarterly, 20 (1963), 23-33. Hanserd Knollys encouraged such hymn writers as Katherine Sutton, whose book he recommended specifically for its record of Christian experience. Selections indicate that her hymns are fervent if unpoetic.

1501   Main, C. F. "The German Princess; or, Mary Carleton in Fact and Fiction." Harvard Library Bulletin, 10 (1956), 166-185. She inspired a great deal of curiosity and many pamphlets. Arranges her pamphlets in order.

1502   McClelland, John. Letters of Sarah Byng Osborn, 1721-1773, from the Collection of the Hon. Mrs. McDonnel. London: H. Milford, 1930. Her letters reveal a woman very much involved in her domestic affairs, managing family and servants, and perceptive about the changes in government and society. Includes introductory notes to letters and a biographical sketch.

1503   McCue, Lillian B. "Elizabeth Canning in Print." Elizabethan Studies and other Essays in Honor of George F. Reynolds. Boulder: University of Colorado Studies in the Humanities, 1945, ii, pp. 223-232. A sixty-five item bibliography with introduction shows that Elizabeth Canning's case occasioned pamphlets at every stage of her trials and is still the subject of numerous books by mystery buffs.

1504   McGill, William J. Maria Theresa. New York: Twayne, 1972. A long biography focuses on the question of her authority as a monarch, on the question of whether or not she was actual ruler of her lands, and was she, therefore, directly responsible for the achievements and failures of the monarchy.

1505   Mitchell, W. Fraser. "Bishop Berkeley's Family. An Eighteenth-Century High Church Conversation Piece." Theology, 36 (1938), 288-298. Eliza Berkeley was a pious, strict woman whose Poems by the late George-Monck Berkeley, Esq., LL.B., F.S.S.A. includes autobiographical material along with her son's poems and her memories of her son.

1506   Mitchener, Margaret. No Crown for the Queen. Louise de Stolberg. London: Cape, 1937. A biography of Louise de Stolberg, wife of Bonny Prince Charlie, based largely on letters and papers.

1507   Moyne, Ernest J. The Journal of Margaret Hazlitt: Recollections of England, Ireland, and America.

Lawrence: University of Kansas Press, 1967. Written between 1835 and 1838 by the daughter of the Reverend William Hazlitt, the journal includes eighteenth century experiences in England and America. Margaret Hazlitt's descriptions provide a comparative guide to the social milieu of the three countries and changing customs.

1508 Mullett, Charles F. The Letters of Dr. George Cheyne to the Countess of Huntingdon. San Marino: Huntington Library, 1940. Letters with an introduction.

1509 Nichol, John W. "Dame Mary Etheredge." MLN, 64 (1949), 419-422. New biographical information on Mary Arnold Etherege concludes she was "a rich old widow."

1510 Niemeyer, Carol. "Henry Killigrew and the Duke of Buckingham." RES, 12 (1936), 326-328. Letter from the Countess Dowager of Roscommon to Mrs. Frances Fresheville provides information about the quarrel between Killigrew and Buckingham.

1511 Notestein, Wallace. Four Worthies: John Chamberlain, Anne Clifford, John Taylor, Oliver Haywood. London: Cape, 1956; New Haven: Yale University Press, 1957. Anne, Countess of Dorset, fought her husband and the King to retain her Westmoreland property. She endured the loss of the land and her husband's unpredictable behavior with patience. As Countess of Pembroke, she restored castles and read good books.

1512 Oman, Carole. (Pseud. for Carola Mary Oman Lenanton). Mary of Modena. London: Hodder and Stoughton, 1962. A sympathetic popular biography of Mary of Modena, Duchess of York, who was James II's wife and Queen. There are notes and a detailed index.

1513 Osgood, Charles G. "Lady Phillipina Knight and her Boswell." Princeton University Library Chronicle, 4 (1943), 37-49.

1514 O'Sullivan, Seumas (Pseud. James Starkey). "Fanny Maccartney" in Essays and Recollections. Dublin and Cork: Talbot Press, 1944, pp. 48-54. Sections of Greville's Maxims, Characters, and Reflections were written by his wife, Fanny.

1515 Parsons, Coleman. "Francis and Mary Colman--Biographical Glimpses, 1691-1767." N&Q, 192 (1947), 288-293 and 310-314. Clarifies biographical details.

1516   Paston, George (Pseud. Emily Morse Symonds). Mrs. De-
        lany--Mary Granville. A Memoir, 1700-1788. London:
        Grant Richards, 1900. An abridged version of the au-
        thor's earlier three volume Autobiography and Corres-
        pondence (1861).

1517   Pedicord, Harry W. "Mr. and Mrs. Garrick: Some Unpub-
        lished Correspondence." PMLA, 60 (1945), 775-783. Des-
        cribed are six letters in the manuscript collection of
        the Historical Society of Pennsylvania, including one
        by Mrs. Garrick to Hannah More, written at age 93.

1518   Phillipson, Wulfstan. "Homage to Mrs. Fitzherbert."
        Downside Review, 58 (1940), 17-28. Mrs. Fitzherbert's
        stormy life is admirably portrayed in Shane Leslie's
        biography as quotations from the letters bear out Les-
        lie's hypotheses.

1519   Pinto, V. de Sola. "Rochester, Dryden, and the Duchess
        of Portsmouth." RES, 16 (1940), 177-178. Argues that
        the Duchess of Portsmouth rather than Rochester was the
        instigator of the infamous "Rose Alley ambuscade."

1520   Porter, Kenneth. "Burns and Peggy Chalmers." MLN, 63
        (1948), 487-489. Information from Mrs. McMicking on
        Burns and Chalmers was collected by Henry Lee.

1521   Pottle, Frederick. Boswell and the Girl from Botany
        Bay. London: Heinemann, 1938. Boswell befriended a
        young criminal, Mary Broad, who was deported to Botany
        Bay but escaped to England.

1522   Quennell, Peter. Caroline of England, An Augustan Por-
        trait. New York: Viking, 1940. A detailed popular
        biography of the wife of George II places special em-
        phasis on the literary culture and personalities of the
        age.

1523   Reid, Loren D. "Sheridan's Speech on Mrs. Fitzherbert."
        Quarterly Journal of Speech, 33 (1947), 15-22. Sheri-
        dan's speech on behalf of Mrs. Fitzherbert before Parlia-
        ment was designed to protect her reputation while saving
        England from internal strife. This meant that he needed
        to both affirm and deny her marriage to the Prince of
        Wales. Sheridan succeeded by appealing to Parliament's
        gallant instincts.

1524   Riddehough, Geoffrey B. "Priscilla Wakefield." Dal-
        housie Review, 37 (1938), 341-347. A rather conserva-
        tive feminist, she wrote extensively on proper conduct
        and education and proposed reforms such as certain occu-
        pations being reserved exclusively for women, thereby
        acting in the interests of propriety and economics.

1525   Roberts, Philip. "Swift, Queen Anne, and The Windsor
        Prophecy." PQ, 49 (1970), 254-258. A copy of the
        diary of Sir David Hamilton, physician to Queen Anne,
        provides evidence that Swift's attack on the Duchess
        of Somerset in his The Windsor Prophecy was seen by the
        Queen only a few days before the deanery of Wells fell
        vacant and that it was the Queen's anger over this poem
        that led to Swift's not being appointed to the English
        deanery.

1526   Roider, Karl A., Jr. (ed.). Maria Theresa. Englewood
        Cliffs, New Jersey: Prentice Hall, 1973. A composite
        picture of Maria Theresa drawn from her own writings,
        writings of her contemporaries, and the studies of modern
        historians. There is a detailed biographical note.

1527   Rosenberg, Albert. "The Sarah Stout Murder Case: An
        Early Example of the Doctor as an Expert Witness." Journal
        of the History of Medicine and Allied Sciences, 12 (1957),
        61-70. The trial was to determine if her death was a
        suicide or a murder; it was deemed to be the latter.

1528   Ross, Isabel. Margaret Fell, Mother of Quakerism. Lon-
        don: Longmans, Green, 1949. Shortly after hearing
        George Fox, she opened her home to Quakers and became
        an important and respected influence on the developing
        Society of Friends. During her imprisonment, she wrote
        a number of books on church doctrine including a defense
        of women speaking in church.

1529   Sampson, Harriet. Introduction to The Life of Mrs. Go-
        dolphin, by John Evelyn. London: Oxford University
        Press, 1939. The introduction discusses her contemporary
        reputation, her piety, her attendance at court, and her
        participation in the "cult of friendship."

1530   Sandner, Oscar, comp. Angelika Kauffmann und ihre Zeit-
        genossen. Bregenz, Austria: Vorarlberger Landesmuseum,
        1968. Prints with commentary and introduction. Includes
        locations and work by her contemporaries.

1531 Sands, Mollie. "Mrs. Tofts, 1685?-1756." Theatre Notebook, 20 (1966), 100-113. A biographical sketch dis-
cussing her theatrical career, reputation, and years
in Venice.

1532 Savidge, Alan. The Foundation and Early Years of Queen
Anne's Bounty. London: S.P.C.K., 1955. A history of
Queen Anne's Acts of Royal Bounty by which the "Revenues
of the First Fruits and Tenths," taken from the Church
by Henry VIII, were restored for church use.

1533 Sclater, W. L. "Letters Addressed by Eliza Draper to
the Strange Family, 1776-1778." N&Q, 186 (1944), 201-
204, 220-224; N&Q, 187 (1944), 7-13, 27-33, and 48-
54. Provides biographical information and publishes
correspondence.

1534 Scott, Florence R. "The Marriages of Sir Robert Howard."
MLN, 55 (1940), 410-415. Identifies Howard's four wives
and the dates of the marriages.

1535 Scott, Florence R. "The Third Wife of Sir Robert
Howard." N&Q, 192 (1947), 314-316. Provides information
concerning the identity of Sir Robert Howard's mistress.

1536 Sherbo, Arthur. "Anecdotes by Mrs. LeNoir." Durham
University Journal, 57 (1965), 166-169. Her letters con-
tain valuable information about her father, Christopher
Smart, and about Johnson, Goldsmith, Wilkes, Richardson
and others. Three letters in the Chapter Library of
Durham Cathedral are quoted extensively.

1537 Shure, David S. Hester Bateman, Queen of English Silversmiths. London: W. H. Allen; Garden City, New York:
Doubleday, 1959. She mastered the demanding craft of
fine silver work and practiced the trade into her eigh-
ties. Eighty-seven plates of work by her and her children and apprentices demonstrate her extraordinary skill.

1538 Sichel, Walter. Emma, Lady Hamilton. New York: Dodd,
Mead, & Company, 1907. A detailed biography arguing
that she was treated unjustly.

1539 Sitwell, Osbert, and Margaret Barton. Brighton. London:
Farber and Farber, 1935; Boston: Houghton, Mifflin, 1935.
Chapter VIII describes Mrs. Fitzherbert's life, framing
it with a description of her appearance in mourning in

1782 and with her death in Brighton. Mrs. Fitzherbert
was connected with Brighton throughout her life.

1540   Stuart, Dorothy M. Dearest Bess: The Life and Times
        of Lady Elizabeth Foster, afterwards Duchess of Devon-
        shire, from her Unpublished Journals and Correspondence.
        London: Methuen, 1955. A popular biography of Lady
        Foster, 1757-1824.

1541   Stuart, Marie W. "Countess Charming." Cornhill Maga-
        zine, 156 (1937), 64-73. Romantic life of Susanna Kennedy.

1542   Swedenberg, H. T., Jr. "Letters of Edward Young to
        Mrs. Judith Reynolds." Huntington Library Quarterly,
        2 (1938), 89-100. Letters in the Huntington Library
        reveal a correction to the date of Elizabeth Lee Young's
        death. Previously believed to be January 1741, it, in
        fact, occurred before 21 May 1740.

1543   Sykes, Norman. "Historical Revisions. xl. Queen Caro-
        line and the Church." History, 11 (1927), 333-339. The
        Queen was largely unsuccessful in advancing Latitudin-
        arian divines.

1544   Tayler, Henrietta. Lady Nithsdale and Her Family. Lon-
        don: Lindsay Drummond, 1939. Winifrede Herbert, Lady
        Nithsdale, lived a life of adventure and hardship. Her
        letters and other papers portray the energetic, coura-
        geous woman who contrived her husband's escape from the
        Tower in 1715 and lived in great poverty in James' court.

1545   Thomas, Gertrude. Richer than Spices. New York: Knopf,
        1965. A popular account of the ways in which Charles
        II's marriage to Catherine of Braganza brought changes
        in the social and cultural life of England and America.

1546   Thomson, Ronald W. "Anne Steele, 1716-1778." Baptist
        Quarterly, 21 (1966), 368-371. A biographical overview.

1547   Tipton, I. C., and E. J. Furlong. "Mrs. George Berke-
        ley and Her Washing Machine." Hermathena, 101 (1965),
        38-47. She kept a record of moral reflections, "things
        to be done," and daily schedules in the back of a note-
        book containing a draft of Treatise concerning the Prin-
        ciples of Human Knowledge. The author discusses her
        children, house in Oxford, family in Ireland, and her
        "washing machine," all referred to in quoted selections.

250

1548   Tisdall, Evelyn E. P. _The Wanton Queen. The Story of Britain's Strangest Queen_. London: Stanley Paul, 1939. A biography of George IV's Queen Caroline.

1549   Tours, Hugh. Introduction to _The Life and Letters of Emma Hamilton_. London: Gollancz, 1963.

1550   Toynbee, Margaret, and Gyles Isham. "Joan Carlile (1606?-1679)-An Identification." _Burlington Magazine_, 96 (1954), 275-277. She is mentioned in Sanderson's _Graphice_ (1658). Recently discovered correspondence and a painting at Lamport Hall, Northamptonshire give new information about her life and works.

1551   Toynbee, Paget. "Gray and 'Lady Bath' in 1769." _TLS_, 17 July 1930, p. 592. There was no "Lady Bath" (as Gray refers to the mistress of Bath House, in Piccadilly) at the time the poet wrote his letter from London to the Rev. James Brown (20 April 1769).

1552   Toynbee, Paget. "'Mrs. E.' in Gray's Letters." _TLS_, 12 February 1931, p. 116. The "Mrs. E." of Gray's letter to Norton Nicholls, written from Cambridge on 14 September 1770, is Mrs. John Erskine, known to Gray as Nicholl's "cousin Fanny."

1553   Tupper, Fred S. "Mary Palmer, alias Mrs. Andrew Marvell." _PMLA_, 53 (1938), 367-392. Mary Palmer was Marvell's landlady for the last several years of his life. After his death, she claimed to be his wife as part of a scheme with the merchant Farrington to collect a loan.

1554   Vieth, David M. "A 'Lost' Lampoon by Katherine Sedley?" _Manuscripts_, 6 (1954), 160-165. James Osborn's collection at Yale contains two manuscripts of a lampoon roughly matching Lady Chaworth's description of a satire probably written by Sedley in answer to Carr Scroope's. The manuscript sheds light on court intrigue and Cary Frazier's life.

1555   Vining, Elizabeth G. _Flora MacDonald. Her Life in the Highlands and America_. London: Geoffrey Bles, 1967.

1556   Vulliamy, C. E. _Aspasia. The Life and Letters of Mary Granville, Mrs. Delany_. London: Geoffrey Bles, 1935. This biography alternates narrative with quotations from letters. Mrs. Delany's letters contain witty observations and explain why she is a "representative English gentle-woman."

1557   Walsh, Elizabeth. "'Mrs. Mary Beale, paintress.'" Con-noisseur, 131 (1953), 3-8. Mary Beale was the first Englishwoman to earn her living as an artist and com-peted successfully with Kneller and Lely. Letters and notebooks describe her career. She experimented on make-shift canvases and was commissioned to do portraits "after Lely," causing difficulties in identifying her work.

1558   Ward, Charles E. "Andrew Marvell's Widow." TLS, 14 May 1938, p. 336. The discovery of the Chancery suit, Mary Marvell v. John Farrington, throws light on the problem of Marvell's alleged marriage and suggests that the poet died on 10 August 1678.

1559   Wellington, Barnett R. The Mystery of Elizabeth Canning. New York: Peck, 1940.

1560   Wells, John Edwin. "Manuscripts of Thomson's Poems to Amanda and Elegy on Aikman." PQ, 15 (1936), 405-408. A collation of an autograph copy of "Accept, loved Nymph, thus tribute due," and an autograph copy of the elegy on Aikman. Amanda is Elizabeth Young.

1561   Weston, John C. "The Text of Maria Riddell's Sketch of Burns." SSL, 5 (1958), 194-197. Notes toward a defin-itive edition of the sketch.

1562   White, H. O. "William Collins and Miss Bundy." RES, 6 (1930), 437-442. Clarifies that the relationship of Collins to Bundy was of a landlady to a tenant in Lon-don.

1563   Whiting, George W. "Mrs. M-- and M.M." N&Q, 202 (1957), 446-447. Author of "Progress of Poetry" in the London Magazine, February and March 1759, is Mrs. Madan. An-other poet, M. M., remains unidentified.

1564   Wilkins, William H. Mrs. Fitzherbert and George IV. Lon-don: Longmans Green, 1905. 2 vols. This detailed biogra-phy establishes the marriage of George IV and Mrs. Fitz-herbert, examines their relationship and personalities, and discusses the public pressures affecting their de-cisions and actions.

1565 Wilkinson, John T. Introduction to <u>Richard Baxter</u> <u>and</u>
<u>Margaret Charlton</u>: <u>A Puritan Love-Story</u>. <u>Being</u> <u>the</u>
<u>Breviate</u> <u>of</u> <u>the</u> <u>Life</u> <u>of Margaret Baxter</u>, <u>1681</u>. London:
Allen and Unwin, 1928.

1566 Williams, J. Anthony. "Katherine Gawen, Papist." <u>Month</u>.
n.s., 29 (1963), 169-175.

1567 Woodward, L. D. <u>Une Anglaise</u> <u>amie</u> <u>de</u> <u>la</u> <u>revolution</u>
<u>francaise</u>, <u>Helene-Maria</u> <u>Williams</u> <u>et</u> <u>un</u> <u>ami</u>. Paris:
Champion, 1930.

1568 Young, Ruth. <u>Father</u> <u>and</u> <u>Daughter</u>, <u>Jonathan</u> <u>and</u> <u>Maria</u>
<u>Spilsbury</u>, <u>1737-1812</u>, <u>1777-1820</u>. London: Epworth, 1952.

INDICES

257

Chalmers, Peggy, 1520.
Chambers, Kitty, 1434.
Chandler, Mary, 801-803.
Chapone, Hester, 804-806.
Charke, Charlotte, 331, 807-813.
Chatham, Lady, 1438.
Cholmondeley, Mary Woffington, 1371, 1410.
Chudleigh, Elizabeth, 1429.
Chudleigh, Mary, 255.
Churchill, Henrietta, 1496.
Churchill, Sarah, 814-833.
Cibber, Susannah, 262, 324.
Clement, Dorothy, 1423.
Clifford, Anne, 1511.
Clive, Catherine, 356, 834-839.
Cockburn, Catharine Trotter, 840-845.
Cole, Grace, 1476.
Coleman, Mary, 1515.
Conolly, Louisa, 1457.
Cooper, Elizabeth, 1428.
Cowley, Hannah, 846-848.
Creed, Elizabeth, 1453.

Davys, Mary, 163, 399, 660, 849-851.
Dawson, Nancy, 250, 251.
Delaney, Mary Granville, 607, 1450, 1497, 1556.
De Stolberg, Louise, 1442, 1506.
Douglas, Catherine Hyde, 852-855.
Draper, Eliza, 1533.

Edgeworth, Maria, 856-915.
Elstob, Elizabeth, 916-921.
Erskine, Fanny, 1552.
Etherege, Mary, 1459, 1509.

Fell, Margaret, 1483, 1528.
Fenton, Lavinia, 236.
Fielding, Sarah, 922-929.
Finch, Anne, 930-939.
Fitzherbert, Maria, 1491, 1492, 1493, 1518, 1523, 1539, 1564.
Foster, Elizabeth, 1540.

Gardner, Sarah, 276, 277.
Gawen, Katherine, 1566.
Glasse, Hannah, 1470.
Godolphin, Mrs., 1529.
Green, Anne, 560.

258

Grierson, Constantia, 1479.
Griffith, Elizabeth, 1055.
Gwynn, Nell, 346, 940-963.

Hamilton, Emma, 1445, 1538, 1549.
Hawkins, Laetitia, 964, 965.
Hays, Mary, 966-971.
Haywood, Eliza, 972-989.
Hazlitt, Margaret, 1507.
Henrietta Maria, 990-998.
Herbert, Harriet, 278.
Hesketh, Lady, 1417.
Hutchinson, Lucy, 999-1002.

Inchbald, Elizabeth, 1003-1016.

Johnson, Esther, 1017-1040.
Johnson, Elizabeth, 1431.
Jordan, Dorothy, 339, 1041-1049.

Kauffmann, Angelica, 1469, 1530.
Kelly, Isabella, 376.
Kennedy, Susanna, 1541.
Knight, Cornelia, 1050-1052.
Knight, Henrietta, 1499.
Knight, Phillipina, 1513.

Larpent, Anna Margarita, 854.
Leinster, Emily, Duchess of, 1456.
Le Noir, Mrs., 1536.
Lennox, Charlotte, 1053-1071.
Lennox, Sarah, 1072-1074.
Lightfoot, Hannah, 1495.
Linley, Elizabeth, 1425.

Macauley, Catherine, 1452, 1465.
MacCartney, Fanny, 1514.
MacDonald, Flora, 1555.
Manley, Delariviere, 254, 1075-1097.
Marvell, Mary Palmer, 1553, 1558.
Montagu, Elizabeth, 1098-1115.
Montagu, Lady Mary Wortley, 1116-1155.
More, Hannah, 1156-1184.
Murray, Griselda, 1466.

Nithsdale, Winifrede Herbert, 1544.
Nossiter, Maria, 284, 333.

260

Toft, Mary, 1349-1351.
Tofts, Catherine, 1531.

Vesey, Elizabeth, 1409.
Vandeput, Victoria, 1455.
Villiers, Barbara, 1462.

Wakefield, Priscilla, 1524.
Waldegrave, the ladies, 1423.
Ward, Sarah, 253.
Weamys, Anne, 1186.
Wesley, Susanna, 1352-1357.
West, Jane, 1358-1360.
Williams, Helene-Marie, 1567.
Woffington, Peg, 339, 1361-1371.
Wolley, Hannah, 1433.
Wollstonecraft, Mary, 1372-1405.

Yearsley, Ann, 1406-1408.
Young, Elizabeth, 1343, 1542, 1560.

AUTHOR INDEX

Abbott, John L., 1.
Adams, M. Ray, 966, 967, 1277.
Adams, Percy G., 529.
Adams, Robert M., 1337.
Adburgham, Allison, 2, 505.
Addleshaw, S., 1292.
Adelstein, Michael E., 688.
Aden, John, 529.
Adlard, John, 940.
Aikin-Sneath, Betsy, 1156.
Albion, Gordon, 990.
Aldridge, Alfred Owen, 3, 4, 1157.
Alleman, Gellert, 5, 234.
Allen, B. Sprague, 968, 1372.
Allentuck, Marcia, 1203.
Allison, James, 1204.
Alspach, Russell K., 683, 1193.
Altick, Richard D,, 6.
Altieri, Joanne, 856.
Anderson, Howard, and Ehrenpreis, Daghlian, 7, 208.
Anderson, Paul B., 506, 507, 508, 777, 930, 1075, 1076, 1077,
    1078, 1079, 1080, 1081.
Arkell, Ruby, 1411.
Armstrong, Martin, 1412.
Armytage, W. H. G., 858.
Arnaud, Pierre, 1247.
Ashdown, Margaret, 916.
Ashley, L. R. N., 807.
Ashley, R. N., 684.
Ashley-Montagu, M. F., 1413.
Ashmun, Margaret, 1293.
Aspinall, A., 1041.
Aspinall-Oglander, Cecil, 1414.
Athell, Lawrence, 1415.
Autrey, Carrie C., 1385.
Avery, Emmett, 8, 237.

B., G. F., 941.
B., J., 917.
B., W. C., 238.
Backscheider, Paula, 224.
Badstuber, Alfred, 574.
Baine,Rodney, 433.
Baker, C. H. C., 9, 1116.
Baker, Donald, 509.
Baker, Herschel, 597.

263

Balderston, Katherine C., 1205.
Balleine, George, 1338.
Barnett, George, 357.
Barrett, Alberta G., 598.
Barrington, E., 1278.
Barry, Iris, 1199.
Batten, Charles L., 599.
Bax, Clifford, 942.
Bay, J. Christian, 10.
Bayley, A. R., and Jaggard, 239.
Bayne-Powell, Rosamond, 11, 12, 13.
Beard, Mary R., 14.
Beatty, Joseph, 1416.
Beaty, Frederick, 1248.
Belloc, Hilaire, 1206.
Benkovitz, Miriam J., 693, 694.
Bennett, C. H., 1158, 1406.
Bennett, Gilbert, 240, 1082.
Bennett, R. E., 600.
Bentley, G. E., 1417.
Berkeley, David, 241.
Bernard, Kenneth, 358.
Bernbaum, Ernest, 601, 602, 603, 1418.
Bessborough, Vere B. Ponsonby, 9th Earl of, 1419, 1420.
Bevan, Bryan, 1421, 1422.
Bickley, Francis, 760.
Biddulph, Violet, 852, 1423.
Black, Frank, 1424.
Black, George, 15.
Blakeney, T.S., 695, 696.
Blanchard, Rae, 16.
Bland, D. S., 1249.
Blashfield, Evangeline, 604.
Blease, Walter L., 17.
Blewett, David, 434.
Block, Tuvia, 452.
Bloom, Edward A., and Lillian, 697.
Blumenthal, Walter H., 18.
Blunt, Reginald, 1098.
Bode, Robert, 242.
Bogardus, Janet, 19.
Boker, Uwe, 605.
Bond, Richmond P., 510.
Bond, W. L., 1185.
Bor, Margot, and Clelland, 1425.
Borkat, Roberta, 243.
Boswell, Eleanore, 244.

Bouchot, Henri, 20.
Boulton, James T., 1099.
Bowen, Marjorie, 1426.
Bowers, Fredson, 245.
Bowyer, John Wilson, 778, 779, 780.
Boyce, Benjamin, 259.
Boys, Richard C., 781.
Bracey, Robert, 698, 1159.
Bradbrook, Frank, 246, 804, 1160, 1373.
Bradbrook, M. C., 1427.
Bradbury, Malcolm, 424.
Bradley, Rose, 21.
Brailsford, Dennis, 22.
Brailsford, Mabel, 1352.
Braudy, Leo, 425.
Braund, E., 999.
Brissenden, R. F., 23, 360.
Bronson, Bertrand, 1428.
Brooke, Iris, 24, 25, 26.
Brooke, Iris, and Laver, 26.
Brooking, Cecil, 247.
Brooks, Cleanth, 530.
Brooks, Douglas, 361.
Brooks, Elmer, 531.
Brower, Reuben, 931.
Brown, Beatrice C., 814, 1429, 1430.
Brown, John R., 27.
Brown, Lloyd, 435.
Brown, Richard, 815.
Bruce, Donald, 248, 606.
Brunskill, F. R., 1431.
Brustein, Robert, 28, 249.
Buchan, Mrs. John, 1432.
Buck, Howard, 491.
Buckley, Mary, 859.
Bugenot, A. S., 699.
Burgess, C. F., 853.
Burke, Terrence, 782.
Burnim, Kalman, 250, 251, 1207.
Burwash, Ida, 252.
Bushnell, George, 253.
Busse, John, 1100.
Butler, Harriet,.and Butler, 860.
Butler, Iris, 816.
Butler, Marilyn, 861, 862.
Butler, Ruth F., 863.
Butt, John, 1433.

Buxton, John, 532, 932, 933.
Bye, A. E., 29.
Byrd, Jess, 783.

C., C. S., 943, 1313.
C., R. W., 700.
Camden, Charles Carroll, 30.
Cameron, W. J., 607, 608.
Campbell, Hilbert, 1342, 1343.
Campbell, Kathleen, 817.
Canby, Henry, 462.
Carhart, Margaret, 575.
Carre, Henri, 991.
Carter, Herbert, 254.
Case, Arthur, 801.
Cecil, Lord David, 701, 702.
Champion, Larry, 533.
Chancellor, Frank, 818.
Chapin, C. F., 1434.
Chapman, Hester, 1435.
Chapman, R. W., 1208, 1209, 1210, 1211, 1212.
Charles, B. G., 1436.
Chew, Samuel, 1308, 1309.
Child, Philip, 1161.
Clancey, Richard, 463.
Clark, Alice, 31.
Clark, W. S., 1314.
Clarke, Isabel, 864.
Clifford, James L., 703, 1213, 1214, 1215, 1216, 1217, 1218, 1294,
    1437.
Climenson, Emily, 1101.
Clinton, Katherine, 32.
Cockburn, Mrs., 1438.
Cohen, Ralph, 534.
Cohen, Richard, 464.
Cohen, Selma Jean, 33, 944.
Cole, F. J., 34.
Coleman, Antony, 255.
Coley, W. B., 865.
Collins, Charles, 256.
Collins, Sarah, 918.
Colville, Olivia, 819.
Colvin, Christina E., 576, 866, 867, 868, 869, 870, 871, 872.
Colvin, Christina E. with Butler, 872.
Conolly, Leonard, 854, 1439.
Cooke, Arthur, 1440.
Coolidge, Archibald, 1250.
Coolidge, Theresa, 704.

Dooley, Roger, 571.
Doty, Gresdna, 261.
Doughty, Oswald, 802, 803.
Doughty, W. L., 1353.
Douglas, David, 919.
Douglas, Emily, 47.
Doyle, Charles, 48.
Drew, Elizabeth, 49, 1117.
Duchovnay, Gerald, 610.
Duff, Dolores, 1083.
Dufrenoy, Marie, 1118.
Dugdale, E. T. S., 706.
Dunbar, Janet, 1365.
Duncan, Carol, 50.
Duncan-Jones, E. E., 466.
Durant, Clark, 1374.
Durant, David, 1252.
Dussinger, John A., 467, 468.

Earengey, Florence, 51.
Eaton, Walter, 1317.
Eaves, T. D., 707.
Eddison, Robert, 262.
Eddy, Donald, 1055.
Edgerton, Giles, 52.
Edmunds, J. M., 263.
Edwards, Averyl, 708.
Edwards, Duane, 874.
Edwards, Irene, 53.
Ehrenpreis, Anne Henry, 709, 1325, 1326, 1327, 1375.
Ehrenpreis, Irvin, 7, 54, 55, 1020, 1021.
Ehrenpreis, Irvin, and Halsband, 54, 55.
Elmen, Paul, 1194.
Elwood, Anne, 209.
Elwood, John R., 972, 973, 974, 975, 1084.
Engel, Gloriane, 264.
England, A. B., 1022.
Epes, Sr. Alice Regina, 364.
Epstein, Lynne, 1253, 1254.
Erickson, James P., 976.
Erikson, J. P., 710.
Esdaile, Arundell, 1219.
Esmond, Rosalee, 56.
Eva, John, 1004.
Evans, Lord, 875.
Ewald, W. B., 511.
Ewert, Leonore, 755, 1103.
Ewing, Majl, 1220.

Fairchild, Hoxie, 536.
Fauchery, Pierre, 365.
Faure, Jacqueline, 784.
Faurot, Ruth, 498.
Fausset, Hugh, 934.
Fea, Allan, 946.
Feil, J. P., 454.
Ferguson, J. D., 537, 1454.
ffrench, Yvonne, 1318.
Figes, Eva, 57.
Fineman, D. A., 1455.
Firth, C. H., 761.
Firth, J. R., 711.
Fischer, John I., 1023.
Fitzgerald, Brian, 1456, 1457.
Fitzgerald, Percy, 835.
Fitzhugh, Robert T., 1458.
Flanagan, Thomas, 876.
Fleming, Alison, 841.
Fletcher, Edward G., 977, 1221.
Fletcher, Ifan, 58.
Flexner, Eleanor, 1376.
Folkenflik, Robert, 469.
Forbes, Thomas, 59, 60.
Forster, E. M., 1164, 1460.
Foster, Dorothy, 1459.
Foster, James, 1328.
Foster, Joan, 436.
Fothergill, Brian, 265, 1042.
Fothergill, Robert, 210.
Foxon, David, 61.
Franke, Wolfgang, 1119.
Franks, A. H., 62.
Freeman, Carol C., 470.
Friend, Beverly, 366.
Fries, Maureen and Daunis, 63.
Frushell, Richard C., 835, 836, 837, 838, 839.
Fry, Carol, 1329.
Fry, Roger, 64.
Fulford, Roger, 1050.
Fullard, Joyce, 538, 539.
Fullard, Joyce, and Schueller, 438.
Fussell, G. E., and Fussell, 65.
Fyvie, John, 66, 266, 267, 1056, 1104.

G., E., 1461.
Gagen, Jean, 67, 268, 269, 611, 762, 763, 1085.
Gale, Fred, 270.
Gantz, Kenneth, 685.

Gardiner, Dorothy, 68.
Gates, William, 712.
George, Dorothy M., 69, 70, 71.
George, Margaret, 1377.
Gerin, Winifred, 713.
German, Howard, 714.
Gibbons, G. S., 588.
Gibbs, Lewis, 1120.
Gilbert, Dorothy, and Pope, 540.
Gilboy, E. W., 72.
Gilder, Rosamond, 271, 272, 612.
Gilmore, Margaret, 1462.
Gilmour, J., 1222.
Glock, Waldo, 715.
Gold, Maxwell, 1024.
Golden, Morris, 471.
Goodman, Theodore, 877, 878.
Goodwin, Gordon, 947.
Gore-Brown, Robert, 273.
Gorowara, K., 274.
Gosch, Marcella, 1005.
Gosse, Edmund, 842, 843.
Goulding, R. W., 766.
Gower, Sir George, and Palmer, 1463.
Graham, C. B., 613.
Graham, John, 1330.
Graham, W. H., 716.
Graham, Walter, 512, 513, 514, 1086.
Grant, Douglas, 764, 765.
Gray, Charles, 275.
Green, David, 822, 823, 1464.
Greenberg, Janelle, 73.
Greene, Godfrey, 276.
Gregory, Allene, 367.
Gregory, Alyse, 1025.
Greven, Philip, 74.
Grey, Jill, 923.
Grey, Rowland, 879, 880, 881.
Grice, F., and Clarke, 277.
Grow, L. M., 1289.
Grundy, Isobel, 1121, 1122, 1123.
Guffey, George, 614.
Gule, Janet, 75.
Guttmacher, Manfred, 1465.

Hagstrum, Jean, 541.
Hahn, Emily, 615, 616, 717.

Haller, William, and Haller, 76.
Halsband, Robert, 7, 55, 77, 278, 1124, 1125, 1126, 1127, 1128,
    1129, 1130, 1131, 1132, 1133, 1134, 1135, 1136, 1137, 1138,
    1139, 1140, 1141, 1466.
Hamblen, Abigail, 617.
Hamblin, F. F., 1467.
Hamelius, Paul, 618.
Hamil, F., 78.
Hamilton, Adrian, 79.
Hamilton, Catherine, 211.
Hamilton, Elizabeth, 1468.
Hamm, Roswell, 592.
Hamnet, Ian, 1006.
Hampshire, G., 756.
Hanbury, William, 1366.
Hand, George, 1026.
Hanford, James, 1295.
Hardie, Martin, 80.
Hare, Robert, 1378, 1379.
Hargest, W. G., 279.
Hargreaves, H. A., 619, 620, 621, 622, 623.
Hargreaves-Mawdsley, W. N., 81.
Harland, Marion, 1165.
Harmon, Rebecca, 1354.
Harmson, Tyrus, 1105.
Harper, G. M., 1380.
Harris, Brice, 542, 624.
Harris, Harvey, 718.
Harrison, G. Elsie, 1355.
Hartcup, Adeline, 1469.
Harth, Philip, 82.
Hartley, Lodwick, 499.
Hartmann, Cyril, 673, 992.
Hartog, Curt, 437.
Havens, Raymond D., 1255.
Haviland, Thomas, 83.
Hawkins, Harriet, 280.
Hawthorne, Mark, 882, 883.
Hayden, Lucy, 1381.
Hayden, Mary, 84.
Hayes, Elizabeth, 1057.
Haynes, Henrietta, 993.
Hayward, Arthur, 85.
Hazelton, George, 948.
Heal, Ambrose, 1470.
Hearsay, Marguerite, 1027.
Hecht, J. Jean, 86.

271

Hegeman, Daniel, 1106.
Heinrich, Joachim, 515.
Heltzel, Virgil, 281.
Hemlow, Joyce, 225, 226, 719, 720, 721, 722, 723, 724, 725, 726, 727, 805, 884, 1166.
Hennig, John, 885.
Herbert, Lord, 1471.
Hesselgrave, Ruth A., 728, 1296, 1472.
Hicks, Phyllis, 729.
Highfill, Philip, Burnim, and Langhams, 87, 282.
Hilbish, Florence, 1331.
Hill, Christopher, 472.
Hill, Constance N., 886.
Hill, Georgina, 88.
Hill, Rowland, 625.
Hill, Vicki, 89.
Hilles, Frederick W., 1473.
Hillhouse, James T., 1474.
Hine, Ellen, 90.
Hiscock, W. G., 1195.
Hobman, D. A., 1000.
Hodges, James, 227, 516, 517, 979, 980.
Hodgson, Norma, 283.
Hogan, Charles, 284.
Hogan, Floriana, 626.
Holdsworth, William, 91.
Hole, Christina, 92, 93.
Holman, D. L., 1058.
Hook, Lucyle, 285, 286, 593, 594, 677, 678, 679, 844, 1087.
Hopkins, Mary, 1167.
Hornbeak, Katherine, 212, 228, 473, 1107, 1475.
Horner, Joyce, 368.
Houlahan, Michael, 500.
Houston, Janetta, 887.
Howard, George, 94.
Howarth, R. C., 287, 680.
Howells, William Dean, 369.
Howson, G., 438.
Hoyt, Charles, 370.
Huchon, Rene, 1108.
Hufstader, Alice, 213.
Hughes, Helen S., 935, 981, 1142, 1282, 1283, 1344, 1345, 1346, 1347, 1348, 1476.
Hughes, Leo, 288.
Humiliata, Sister M., 214.
Humphrey, George, 1256.
Humphreys, A. R., 95.
Hunt, Hugh, 289.

Hurst, Michael, 888.
Hyde, Mary, 1223.

Ilchester, Mary, and Stavordale, 1073.
Inglis-Jones, Elizabeth, 889.
Ingpen, Ada, 215.
Insch, A. G., 577.
Ireland, Norma, 96.
Iremonger, Lucille, 1477.
Irving, William, 916.
Isdell-Carpenter, Andrew, 1478.
Isles, Duncan, 1059, 1060.
Ivker, Barry, 371, 427.
Izard, Forrest, 290.

Jackson, Robert, 97, 1028, 1029.
Jacobs, Elijah, 1143.
James, H. R., 1382.
Janes, Regina, 566, 1383.
Jarrell, Mackie, 1479.
Jarrett, Derek, 98.
Jason, 785.
Jeffares, A. Norman, 890, 891.
Jeffrey, Sydney, 1384.
Jerrold, Clare, 1043.
Jerrold, Walter, and Jerrold, 99, 1200.
Jesse, John, 1480.
Johnson, Edgar, 217.
Johnson, J., 100.
Johnson, James William, 1481.
Johnson, Jeffrey, 455.
Johnson, R. Brimley, 101, 218, 372, 730, 731, 924, 1168, 1482.
Jones, C. E., 1109.
Jones, Mary G., 1169, 1170.
Jones, Rufus, 1483.
Jones, W. Powell, 1110, 1111.
Jordan, Robert, 628.
Jordan, Ruth, 1484.
Jost, Francois, 373.
Joughin, G. Louis, 1007, 1008, 1009.

Kamm, Josephine, 102, 732.
Kauf, Robert, 1144.
Kaufman, Anthony, 291, 292.
Kaufman, Michaiel, 103.
Kauver, Elaine, 1061.
Kay, Donald, 518.

273

Keast, William, 1224.
Keebler, Lee, 1257.
Kelsell, Malcolm, 925.
Kelso, Ruth, 104.
Kennedy, Sr. Eileen, 892.
Kent, John P., 982.
Kent, Muriel, 1297.
Keogh, J. G., 543.
Kerman, Sandra L., 105.
Kestner, Joseph S., 439.
Kettle,Arnold, 440.
King, William, 824.
King-Hall, Magdalen, 1074.
Kirchberger, C., 1485.
Kirk, Rudolph, 1486.
Kirkpatrick, T. Percy C., 1030.
Kline, Richard, 493, 1088.
Klinger, George, 293.
Knapp, Lewis M., 494, 495.
Knapp, O. G., 1225.
Knox, E. V., 1171.
Koster, Patricia, 1089, 1090.
Krier, William J., 441.
Kroll, Maria, 1487.
Kronenberger, Louis, 825.
Kropf, C. R., 442.
Kulishek, Clarence, 544.
Kurtz, Benjamin, and Autry, 1385.
Kynaston, Agnes, 1062.

L., F. F., 1367.
Laborde, G. M., 629.
Laithwaite, P., 1298.
Lambertson, Chester, 578.
Langhans, Edward A., 630.
Lanier, Henry, 294.
Lansdowne, Marquis, 1488.
Larned, J. N., 229.
Larson, Martin, 295.
Laski, M., 733.
Lawless, Emily, 893.
Lawrence, W. J., 1044, 1045, 1046, 1368.
Leavis, Q. D., 374.
Le Fanu, William, 1489.
Legouis, Piere, 443, 1490.
Leja, Alfred, 631.
Leslie, Anita, 1491.
Leslie, Shane, 1492, 1493.

Marshall, Dorothy, 113, 114, 115.
Marshall, Julian, 949.
Martia, Dominic, 299.
Masefield, Muriel, 383, 736, 737.
Mason, John, 230.
Mathews, Ernest, 635.
Mathey, Jacques, 119.
Matthews, Arnold, 1189.
Matthews, William, 219.
Maud, R. N., 547.
Maxfield, Ezra, 787.
Maynadier, G. H., 1063.
Mayo, Robert D., 384, 520, 1001, 1259.
McAllester, Susan, 116.
McBurney, William H., 378, 572, 589, 850.
McClelland, John, 1502.
McCoy, Raymond, 117.
McCue, Lillian, 1503.
McDowell, M. M., 118.
McElderry, B. R., 1112.
McGavren, Margaret, 1387.
McGill, William, 1504.
McIntosh, Carey, 476.
McKee, William, 1011.
McKillop, Alan D., 475, 476, 477, 478, 788, 1258, 1332.
McManmon, John, 548.
McMaster, Juliet, 444.
McPharlin, Paul, 300, 808, 809.
McWhorter, Oleta, 895.
Mead, Kate, 120.
Meakin, Annette, 1174.
Melander, Martin, 1358.
Melville, Lewis, 121, 122, 301, 302, 950, 1145.
Mendenhall, John C., 738, 1280.
Menon, K. P., 549.
Menzies-Wilson, Jacobine, and Lloyd, 1187.
Merritt, Percival, 1229.
Metcalf, C., 303.
Mews, Hazel, 385.
Meyer, Arlin, 636.
Meyer, Gerald, 123, 767.
Meynell, Alice, 580.
Michael, Friedrich, 896.
Mignon, Elizabeth, 304, 637.
Milford, R. T., 521, 1091.
Miller, Henry K., 124, 1146, 1147.
Millhauser, Milton, 897.

Minogue, Valerie, 125.
Mintz, Samuel, 768.
Mise, Raymond, 386.
Mish, Charles C., 983.
Mitchell, W. Fraser, 1505.
Michener, Margaret, 1506.
Mitrani, Charles, 479.
Mizener, Arthur, 638.
Moers, Ellen, 387.
Moler, Kenneth L., 739, 898, 1359.
Molloy, J. Fitzgerald, 826.
Moncada, Ernest, 951.
Monk, Samuel Holt, 1300.
Montague, Edwin, and Martz, 740.
Mood, Robert, 899.
Moore, C. A., 126.
Moore, Catherine E., 585.
Moore, J. R., 305.
More, Paul E., 639.
Moreux, Francoise, 1012.
Morgan, Charlotte, 388.
Morley, Edith J., 741.
Morris, Clara, 1319.
Morris, David B., 306.
Morrison, Marjorie L., 742.
Morrissey, Leroy and Morrissey, 428.
Morrissey, Leroy, 307.
Morrissey, Slepian, and Morrissey, 428.
Morrow, Thomas, 127.
Mortier, Roland, 429.
Mourey, Gabriel, 128.
Moyne, Ernest, 1507.
Moynihan, Robert, 480.
Mukherjee, Sujit, 308.
Mullett, Charles F., 1508.
Mulliken, Elizabeth Y., 743.
Mundy, P. D., 640, 641.
Munsterberg, Hugo, 129.
Murphy, Michael, 920.
Murray, Adrian, 130.
Murray, E. G., 1260.
Murray, Patrick, 900.
Murry, J. Middleton, 936.
Myers, Robert, 1301.
Myers, Sylvia, 131.

Napier, Elizabeth, 481.
Needham, Arnold, 926.

Needham, Gwendolyn B., 686, 1092, 1093.
Neill, D. G., 789.
Nettels, Elsa, 1261.
Neuberg, Victor, 132.
Newby, Percy, 901.
Newcomer, James, 902, 903, 904, 905.
Newell, A. G., 389, 1175.
Newton, John A., 1356.
Nichol, John W., 1509.
Nicholes, Eleanor, 1388, 1389.
Nickles, Mary, 309.
Nicolson, Marjorie Hope, 133.
Niemeyer, Carl, 1510.
Nitchie, Elizabeth, 1390.
Nixon, Edna, 1391.
Norman, William, 642.
Norton, J. E., 567, 790, 846.
Notestein, Wallace, 134, 1511.
Novak, Maximillian E., 310.
Noyes, Catherine, 135.
Noyes, Gertrude, 231.
Noyes, Robert G., 311, 681, 687.

Oake, Roger B., 136.
O'Dowd, M. C., 137.
O'Faolain, Julia, and Martines, 138.
Officer, G. H., 1339.
Oliver, Jane, 996.
Oman, Carola, 674, 994, 1512.
Onderwyzer, Gaby E., 1290, 1291.
Oppel, Horst, 1148.
Ormsbee, Thomas, 139.
Orr, Lyndon, 952.
Osborn, James M. 550.
Osgood, Charles, 1513.
O'Sullivan, Seumas, 1514.
Overman, A. A., 744.

Park, Bruce, 1013.
Park, William, 390, 456.
Parnell, Paul E., 312.
Parreaux, Andre, 1149.
Parrish, Ann, 927.
Parry, Edward, 1190.
Parsons, Coleman, 1515.
Paston, George, 1516.
Paterson, Alice, 906.
Patterson, Emily, 745.

Paulson, Kristoffer, 551.
Paulson, Ronald, 1031.
Peake, Charles, 921.
Pearce, 313.
Pearson, Hesketh, 1302, 1303.
Pearson, Norman, 1176.
Peavy, Charles D., 810.
Pedicord, Harry, 1517.
Peltz, Catharine, 552.
Penning, C. P. J., 1150.
Percival, A. C., 140.
Perigault-Duhet, P. M., 1392.
Perry, Henry Ten Eyck, 769, 770.
Peterson, Spiro, 445.
Petherick, Maurice, 141.
Petitjean, A. M., 1032.
Phillips, George L., 1113.
Phillips, Margaret, and Tomkinson, 142.
Phillipson, Wulfston, 1518.
Pierce, R. B., 143, 391.
Pierpont, Robert, 953.
Pieszczek, Rudolf, 581.
Pilon, Edmond, 1151.
Pinchbeck, Ivy, and Hewitt, 144.
Pinchbeck, Ivy, 144, 145.
Pinto, J. De Sola, 1519.
Pitou, Von Spire, 314.
Plant, Marjorie, 146, 147.
Plarr, Victor, 582.
Platt, Harrison, 643.
Platz, Norbert, 771.
Pollard, Graham, 522.
Pollard, M., 907, 908.
Pollin, Burton R., 970, 1333.
Pons, E., 1033.
Ponsonby, Lord, 1201.
Porter, Kenneth, 1520.
Posner, Donald, 148.
Poston, Carol, 1393.
Pottle, Frederick A., 1230, 1293, 1521.
Pounds, Edward, 1262.
Povey, Kenneth, 1188.
Prasad, Kashi, 772.
Pratt, Dallas, 827.
Preedy, George, 1394.
Price, F. G. H., 954.
Price, Jonathan, 1064.
Prideaux, W. F., 955.

Priestley, Mary, 984.
Proper, C. B. A., 392.
Purvis, A., 644.
Putney, Rufus, 496, 502, 503.

Quaintance, Richard, 553.
Quennell, Peter, 746, 1231, 1522.
Quinlan, Maurice, 232.

Rabkin, Norman, 482.
Radzinowicz, Mary Ann N., 149.
Raeburn, Eleanor, 315.
Ramsaran, J. A., 645.
Ransom, Harry, 1152.
Rawson, C. J., 150, 483.
Raynal, Margaret, 928.
Redman, B., 151.
Rees, Christine, 152.
Reich, Emil, 153.
Reid, Loren, 1523.
Reid, Stuart, 828.
Renwick, W. S., 554.
Revard, Stella, 154.
Rewa, Michael, 1304.
Reynolds, Myra, 155, 937.
Rhodes, R. C., 847.
Rice, J. A., 1034.
Richetti, John, 393, 1284.
Riddehough, Geoffrey, 1524.
Riedenauer, Annemarie, 938.
Riely, Elizabeth, 829.
Riely, John C., 1052, 1232, 1233, 1234, 1235.
Riely, John C., and Ribeiro, 1235.
Riese, Teut., 909.
Roberts, E. V., 457.
Roberts, William, 1196, 1197.
Robins, Edward, 316.
Rodgers, Betsy, 156, 586.
Rodgers, Katherine M., 555, 1035.
Rodway, Allen, 317.
Rogal, Samuel J., 157, 1357.
Rogers, Francis, 318, 319.
Roider, Darl, 1526.
Ronald, Margaret, 1263.
Roper, Derek, 1395.
Rosbottom, Ronald C., 158, 394.
Rose, E. J., 556.
Rosen, Marvin, 159.

Rosenbalm, John, 320.
Rosenberg, Albert, 830, 1527.
Rosenfeld, Sybil, 321.
Ross, Alan, 910.
Ross, Ian, 1114.
Ross, Isabel, 1528.
Rousseau, G. S., 497, 1305, 1349.
Roussel, Roy, 484.
Rowan, D. F., 322.
Rowbotham, W. B., 160.
Rubenstein, Jill, 748.
Rubin, Barbara, 323.
Rudolf, Jo Ellen, 395.
Ruff, William, 1264.
Ruhe, Edward, 757.
Ruksheena, K. S., 1396.
Russell, Norman, 1310.

S., M., 646.
Sabiston, Elizabeth, 396.
Sachse, William L., 161.
Sackville-West, Victoria, 647, 648.
Sadleir, Michael, 1265.
Sale, William M., 397, 485.
Salomon, Louis, 557.
Sambrook, A. J., 430, 749.
Sampson, Harriet, 1529.
Sandner, Oscar, 1530.
Sands, Mollie, 1531.
Sarchet, Helene C., 398.
Savidge, Alan, 1532.
Sawyer, Paul, 324.
Schermerhorn, Karen, 325.
Schlater, W. L., 1533.
Schleiner, Winfried, 162.
Schneider, Ben R., 326.
Schulte, Edvige, 649.
Schulz, Dieter, 163, 399, 400, 985.
Scott, Clayton, 650.
Scott, Florence R., 1534, 1535.
Scott, W. S., 1370.
Scott, Walter, 164.
Scudder, Harold, 1306.
Seeber, Edward, 651, 652.
Segre, Carlo, 956.
Sejourne, Philippe, 401, 1065.
Seligman, S. A., 1350.
Sena, John, 758, 939.

Senior, Dorothy, 165.
Sergeant, Philip, W., 166, 1048, 1094.
Seton-Anderson, James, 1371.
Seward, Patricia, 653.
Sewell, Brocard, 675.
Sewell, Ernestine, 167.
Shaaber, M. A., 595.
Shafer, Yvonne, 327.
Shapiro, Karl, and Baum, 654.
Sharma, O. P., 402.
Shaver, Chester, 1177.
Shea, Peter, 655.
Sheffey, Ruthe T., 656, 657.
Shelmerdine, Joan, 997.
Sherbo, Arthur, 1536.
Sherburn, George, 791, 855.
Shinagel, Michael, 431, 446, 447.
Shugrue, Michael, 573, 590.
Shure, David, 1537.
Sichel, Walter, 1538.
Siegel, Paul, 658.
Simon, Brian, 911.
Simon, Irene, 558.
Simpson, Harold, and Braun, 328.
Simpson, Joan, 659.
Sinclair, Upton, 403.
Singleton, Robert, 168.
Sitwell, Osbert, and Barton, 1539.
Skrine, Francis, 965.
Slade, Bertha, 912.
Slomen, Judith, 1066.
Small, Miriam, 1067, 1068.
Smith, Eric, 169.
Smith, Florence M., 568, 569.
Smith, G. C. Moore, 1191.
Smith, John H., 329, 330, 523.
Smith, Nelson C., 1267.
Smith, Warren, 170.
Snodgrass, A. E., 1178.
Snyder, Henry L, 831, 1095.
Solomon, Stanley J., 404, 913.
Souers, Philip W., 1198.
Soulbury, Viscount, 171.
Southam, B. C., 486.
Spacks, Patricia Meyer, 172, 173, 174, 175, 176, 405, 1237.
Sparke, Archibald, 1179.
Sparrow, W. S., 177.

Speaight, George, 331, 811.
Speakman, James, 406, 750.
Spector, Robert, 1180.
Spencer, Anna, 178.
Spencer, Hazelton, 682.
Stanford, Ann, 559.
Stanglmaier, Karl, 591.
Starr, George A., 448, 524.
Stathas, Thalia, 792, 793.
Stauffer, Donald, 179, 220, 221.
Staves, Susan, 1069, 1334.
Stearns, Bertha M., 525, 526.
Stebbins, Lucy, 180.
Stecher, Henry, 1285.
Steen, Marguerita, 1281.
Steeves, Edna, 407.
Stefanson, Donald, 851.
Stenton, Mary, 181.
Stephens, Kate, 570.
Stephenson, Peter, 660.
Stevenson, Lionel, 408.
Stewart, J. Douglas, 182.
Stimpson, Dorothy, 773.
Stokes, Sylvia, 183.
Stoler, John, 1268.
Stoll, Elmer, 332.
Stone, George W., 333.
Strachey, G. L., 1014.
Stratman, CArl, 794.
Strozier, Robert, 795.
Stuart, Dorothy, 1540.
Stuart, Marie, 1541.
Summers, Montague, 596, 661, 662, 663.
Sunstein, Emily, 1397, 1398.
Sutherland, James, 560, 796.
Sutherland, John, 561.
Suwannabha, Sumitra, 334, 664, 986.
Swale, Ellis, 1321.
Swedenberg, H. T., 1542.
Swigart, Ford, 1270.
Sykes, Norman, 1543.
Sykes, W. J., 1153.
Sypher, Wylie, 665, 1269.

Takada, Mineo, 1238.
Tasch, Peter, 335.

Tayler, Henrietta, 1544.
Taylor, G.R. Stirling, 1399.
Taylor, Gordan, 409.
Taylor, I. A., 998.
Taylor, John T., 410.
Ten Hoor, Henry, 797.
Thaler, Alwin, 336.
Thomas, Donald, 458, 1271.
Thomas, Gertrude, 1545.
Thomas, K. Bryn, 1351.
Thompson, C. J. S., 184.
Thompson, L. F., 1272.
Thomson, Ronald W., 1546.
Thorpe, James, 1239.
Tieje, Arthur, 411.
Tierney, James E., 337.
Tillotson, Geoffrey, 1154.
Tinker, Chauncey B., 222, 1181, 1407.
Tipton, I. C., and Furlong, 1547.
Tisdall, E. E. P., 338, 1548.
Tobler, Klara, 1015.
Todd, William B., 848, 957.
Todd-Naylor, Ursula, 1070.
Tomalin, Claire, 1400.
Tomkievicz, Shirley, 1401.
Tompkins, J. M. S., 185, 412, 1016, 1182, 1273, 1360, 1408.
Tourrellot, Arthur, 751.
Tours, Hugh, 1549.
Towers, A. R., 413, 459.
Toynbee, Margaret, and Isham, 1550.
Toynbee, Paget, 1551, 1552.
Trevelyn, George M., 186.
Troubridge, St. Vincent, 339.
Trumbull, H. Clay, 1183.
Tucker, Joseph E., 666.
Tucker, William J., 223.
Tufts, Eleanor, 187.
Tupper, Fred S., 1553.
Turberville, Arthur, 774, 1322.
Turner, Margaret, 667.
Turner, Rufus, 1335.
Tyne, James L., 1036.
Tyson, Mose, and Guppy, 1240.

Ulmer, Gregory, 487.
Upham, A. H., 188.
Uphaus, Robert W., 1037, 1038.

Wheatley, Katherine, 345.
Wheeler, Ethel R., 198.
Whibley, Charles, 775.
Whicher, George F., 988, 989.
Whinney, Margaret, 199.
White, Cynthia, 527.
White, Eugene, 753.
White, H. O., 1562.
White, Robert B., 528, 798.
White, W. D., 200.
Whiting, George W., 1336, 1563.
Wieten, A. A. S., 1276.
Wilding, Michael, 432.
Wiles, Roy M., 201, 418.
Wiley, Autrey N., 346.
Wilkins, William H. 1564.
Wilkinson, Andrew, 450.
Wilkinson, D. R. M., 233, 347.
Wilkinson, John, 1565.
Williams, A. L., 1155.
Williams, Aubrey, 348, 562.
Williams, Gordon, 349.
Williams, Harold, 1039, 1040.
Williams, Hugh. 959.
Williams, Ioan, 419.
Williams, J. Anthony, 1566.
Williams, Neville, 202.
Williamson, George, 203, 204.
Williford, Miriam, 205.
Wilson, John Harold, 350, 351, 352, 353, 354, 355, 563, 564, 960,
    961, 962, 963.
Wilson, Mona, 759, 799, 806, 1071, 1311.
Wingrave, Wyatt, 813.
Winton, Calhoun, 1096.
Witmer, Anne, and Freehafer, 671.
Wolff, Cynthia G., 206, 461, 489.
Wonchope, A. J., 754.
Wood, Frederick, 800.
Woodcock, A. J., 754.
Woods, Charles B., 356, 1049.
Woodward, L. D., 1567.
Woolf, Virginia, 207, 420, 504, 776, 1192, 1202.
Woolley, James, 1307.
Woolsey, Dorothy, 1405.
Wright, Eugene P., 1340, 1341.
Wright, H. Bunker, 565, 833, 1286.
Wurzback, Natascha, 421.

Yeazell, Ruth, 422.
Young, Ruth, 1568.
Yung, K. K., 1244.

Zanick, M., 1245.
Zbinden, E. O., 1097.
Zigerall, James, 490.
Zimmerman, Everett, 451.
Zinn, Zea, 423.